D1592717

Coaching as a Leadership Style

The economic and political environment of the business of healthcare is undergoing rapid change. The future will demand a more team-oriented approach, emphasizing group cooperation and execution, than has historically existed in most systems. The challenge for current and future leaders will be managing the social/political dynamics of change at both the individual and group level, while overcoming attitudes favoring autonomy and independence over coordination and compliance. Success will require a sophisticated set of leadership skills that will resonate with the values, needs, and personality of healthcare professionals – especially physicians.

This book asserts that leadership and coaching go hand-in-hand. The author introduces a unique and practical coaching framework that will guide the reader through the four stages of a successful coaching experience, whether it consists of a single conversation or a series of conversations. To implement the framework, the reader will learn a set of competencies based on several evidence-based models for effectively interacting with others and facilitating change. Additionally, the author reviews the tenets and components of transformational leadership and demonstrates how the use of the models, methods, and tools for coaching assist one in becoming the transformational leader required in today's healthcare organization.

Robert F. Hicks, PhD, is a Clinical Professor of Organizational Behavior at the University of Texas at Dallas and founding director of the Organizational Behavior and Executive Coaching program in the Naveen Jindal School of Management. Dr. Hicks is a licensed Psychologist and holds an appointment as Faculty Associate in the Department of Psychiatry at UT Southwestern Medical Center. His program at UT Dallas provides on-site MS/MBA degree programs with a concentration in healthcare organization leadership for academic medical centers and healthcare systems. He has three decades of experience teaching leadership and coaching skills to physicians and senior executives of both healthcare systems and Fortune 500 companies.

Coaching as a Leadership Style

The Art and Science of Coaching Conversations for Healthcare Professionals

Robert F. Hicks, PhD

Routledge
Taylor & Francis Group

NEW YORK AND LONDON

First published 2014
by Routledge
711 Third Avenue, New York, NY 10017

Simultaneously published in the UK
by Routledge
2 Park Square, Milton Park, Abingdon, Oxon OX14 4RN

Routledge is an imprint of the Taylor & Francis Group, an informa business

Library of Congress Cataloging-in-Publication Data

Hicks, Robert, 1947–
Leadership coaching in health care: how to flourish as a leader in today's
    healthcare environment / Robert F. Hicks, PhD.
        pages cm
    Includes bibliographical references and index.
 1. Health services administration.   2. Health services administrators—
Training of.   3. Leadership—Study and teaching.   4. Health care teams—
Management.   I. Title.
    RA971.H53 2013
    362.1—dc23
    2012049324

ISBN: 978-0-415-52805-4 (hbk)
ISBN: 978-0-415-52806-1 (pbk)
ISBN: 978-0-203-11866-5 (ebk)

Typeset in Berling
by Apex CoVantage, LLC

Printed and bound by CPI Group (UK) Ltd, Croydon, CR0 4YY

To my wife, Kathy, and my children, Jennifer and Brian
They have taught me what's truly important in life.

Contents

Acknowledgements

To write a book, the contents of which is as much the result of one's experience as it is the theories and models upon which it is based, involves the influence of many people, who over the years have helped shape the ideas written about in this book. I especially wish to express my gratitude to my colleagues at the University of Texas at Dallas and UT Southwestern Medical Center for their thoughts, feedback, and support. In addition, I have often said that I have learned as much, or more, from those whom I have coached than they have from me; therefore, I thank all of you who I have had the honor of helping. You know who you are.

Introduction

Is this a business book or a textbook? Actually, it is a little of both. Its dual purpose is to provide a practical, how-to approach for conducting coaching conversations and explain the science behind those conversations. It also ties the coaching methodology to transformational leadership practices. The operating hypothesis is that effective leadership requires many of the same methods and competencies as effective coaching.

This book is written for those people whose professional roles require them to use a *coach-like* approach in helping individuals:

1. find a resolution to social or political problem situations
2. improve personal or professional effectiveness; and
3. tap into unused or undeveloped potential so as to increase their professional talents.

This book is not a treatise on leadership, nor is it a review of different models of coaching. The coaching competencies set forth are principally derived from evidence-based theories and practices; however, their use, as prescribed by the Four-square Coaching approach developed by the author originates from his experience in coaching professionals and executives in a multitude of industries.

Finally, you are able to use this book as it suits your needs. If you are the type of person that wants to understand the science underlying the practices that you employ, you can find it here. On the other hand, if you are primarily interested in skill development the examples and "how to" sections will suit your purpose. Either way, the more often you think in terms of the Four-square Coaching Framework, and practice the competencies needed to implement it, the quicker it will become second nature. Fortunately, many of the required competencies can be developed in your day-today interactions, even if you are not coaching. There is a lot of mate-rial to absorb. Be patient and think of this as a reference to use over time rather than a "one and done" read. Although this book utilizes the healthcare context for its examples, any leader or coach practitioner will profit from the use of the Four-square Coaching Framework and its related competencies.

Chapter Descriptions

1. THE MYSTIQUE OF LEADERSHIP

Chapter one summarizes the current trends in healthcare and their implications for leading in an industry that is undergoing tumultuous change. Transformational leadership is introduced as the approach best suited for leading during times of change and for leading the types of professionals (especially physicians) that comprise the majority of employees in healthcare organizations. The four components that define transformational leadership—Idealized Influence, Inspirational Motivation, Intellectual Stimulation, and Individualized Consideration—are defined. The concept of the Elite Professional is introduced, and its characteristics described, along with the challenges of helping this type of personality adapt to the new realities of healthcare delivery. A case is made for coaching as a means to help Elite Professionals make the transition to a team-based, task-interdependent work environment, and for coaching as a skillset that will help operationalize the components of transformational leadership.

2. THE NATURE OF HELPING CONVERSATIONS

Chapter two focuses on why people want or need a helping conversation. The nature of the helping conversation is explained by comparing commonly held myths to what research has shown to be actually true. The idea of wearing different "hats" during a helping conversation as a metaphor for the activities of teaching, mentoring, and coaching is introduced and explained. Each activity is discussed, with special emphasis given to the distinction between mentoring and coaching. The working definition of coaching, as used in this book, is provided. In addition, a linkage is made between coaching and the Individualized Consideration component of transformational leadership.

3. THE STRUCTURE OF COACHING

Chapter three explains the structural framework for the coaching process described in this book. This chapter defines two essential processes for successful coaching conversations: Support and Challenge. Support and Challenge are applied to the elements of Thought and Action to create a two-by-two structure the author has labeled the Four-square Coaching Framework. This structure has four components: Support-for-Thought, Challenge-for-Thought, Challenge-for-Action, and Support-for-Action. Each component is defined as to its purpose and objectives; however, the majority of this chapter concentrates on Support-for-Thought and, specifically, the techniques for building rapport as a requirement for facilitating open communication, and for demonstrating the Individualized Consideration component of transformational leadership.

4. SUPPORT-FOR-THOUGHT: ADULT-TO-ADULT COMMUNICATION

Chapter four is the second of three chapters devoted to Support-for-Thought. This chapter addresses the role of ego states in conversations and describes the characteristics that define the Parent, Child, and Adult ego states. The differences between Adult-to-Adult communication and Parent-Child communication are discussed and illustrated. This chapter emphasizes the importance of Adult-to-Adult communication as a means of providing Support-for-Thought. The rules and guidelines for communicating from the Adult ego state are specified and related to the Idealized Influence component of transformational leadership.

5. SUPPORT-FOR-THOUGHT: INTELLIGENT LISTENING

Chapter five teaches the final stage-related activity of Support-for-Thought: Intelligent Listening. Listening is a requisite coaching skill, and inquiry is its companion. The "magical" nature of questions is illustrated by discussing the variety of ways that questions can be used in a coaching conversation. Intelligent listening is explained and demonstrated as a method of inquiry to clarify a person's narrative. This chapter teaches the specific linguistic techniques for identifying and recovering important information that will enrich a person's narrative as well as clarify his thinking for better problem solving. Intelligent listening, with its use of inquiry, is a critical competency for providing Intellectual Stimulation as a transformational leader.

6. BECOMING A SOLUTION-FOCUSED LEADER

Chapter six discusses the benefits of a solution-focused approach to coaching rather than the traditional problem-solving model used by most professionals, especially those in the field of medicine, who rely on the use of diagnostic practices and procedures in their professional specialties. In this chapter, the differences between problem talk and solution talk during the coaching conversation are illustrated, and the reader learns how to distinguish between the two types of talk. The solution-focused principles upon which the Four-square Coaching Framework is based are explained. Furthermore, adopting a solution-focused approach to leadership is advocated as a means of positively impacting all four components of transformational leadership.

7. CHALLENGE-FOR-THOUGHT: DESIGNING THE FUTURE

Chapter seven introduces the Challenge-for-Thought stage of the Four-square Coaching Framework and explains the helping role that challenge plays during a coaching conversation. Guidelines for challenging without confronting are provided. The primary objective of this chapter, however, is to teach the stage-related activities of Challenge-for-Thought. Specifically, readers are taught how to help the person being coached clarify their thinking so that they know specifically what they want in terms of their goals and outcomes. To that end, this chapter teaches the techniques for developing discrepancy in pursuit of defining a desired future state and the criteria that must be met to construct a well-formed outcome. The competencies required for Challenge-for-Thought are related to the leaders role in developing a clear and compelling vision as part of the Inspirational Motivation component of transformational leadership.

8. CHALLENGE-FOR-ACTION: A PATH TO DOING

Chapter eight is the first of two chapters devoted to the Challenge-for-Action stage of the Four-square Coaching Framework. This chapter introduces the concept of depth versus movement in a coaching conversation. The goal of the Challenge-for-Action stage is to promote movement by constructively challenging the person to specify what she is going to do and how she is going to achieve the outcomes identified during the Challenge-for-Thought stage. Readers learn how to create a psychologically safe way to experiment with new behavior. The heuristic approach to action planning is explained, and guidelines for creating successful action experiments are presented along with tactics for helping a person overcome inertia. The ideas discussed in this chapter are related to action-oriented leadership and leading organizational change.

9. CHALLENGE-FOR-ACTION: GO SLOW TO GO FAST

Chapter nine continues with the principles and practices that are most likely to generate movement toward one's change goals and desired future state. Readers learn how to use an individual's current and past successes to formulate a strength-based approach to moving forward. In addition, the notion that small steps lead to big changes is introduced, and its rationale explained in detail. In order to operational-ize this principle, the technique of scaling is presented as a means of establishing achievable next steps and evaluating progress toward one's goal. The reader is pro-vided a step-by-step formula for using the scaling technique as well as a listing of its uses. The principle of doing little things each day to achieve one's desired outcome is also applied to the concept of "mundane" leadership.

10. SUPPORT-FOR-ACTION: READINESS FOR CHANGE

Chapter ten begins discussion of the fourth stage of the Four-square Coaching Framework: Support-for-Action. The purpose of Support for Action is to assess and build readiness for change and action-taking in support of the person's goals and well-formed outcomes. This chapter presents a model for assessing a person's readi-ness for change. Two types of resistance to change are discussed along with their causes and methods for overcoming them. The coaching skills used to overcome resistance are shown to be relevant for organizational change efforts.

11. SUPPORT-FOR-ACTION: IMPORTANCE AND CONFIDENCE

Chapter eleven focuses on the motivational factors of readiness for change: Impor-tance and Confidence. The subject of motivation is discussed in depth and the con-ditions necessary for the development of intrinsic motivation to support action, and overcome ambivalence about change, are described. The technique of Change Talk is introduced to amplify and reinforce the motivational elements of Importance and Confidence. The reader will learn specific methods for eliciting and respond-ing to Change Talk during the coaching conversation. The stage-related activities presented in this chapter are shown to be relevant for transformational leaders who must stimulate the requisite motivation throughout their organization to support actions toward their vision of the future and desired change goals.

12. A COACHING ROADMAP: PUTTING IT ALL TOGETHER

Chapter twelve reviews and summarizes the key concepts, models, and compe-tencies explained in this book. This chapter reviews the Four-square Coaching Framework, emphasizing the concept of fluidity. The reader is reminded that the Four-square Coaching Framework represents a dynamic process that occurs within the confines of a coaching conversation. Example coaching conversations are presented to illustrate how to use the framework as a coaching "map." The competencies necessary to do "Four-square Coaching" are reviewed. Finally, the relationship between the competencies and stage-related activities of the Four-square Coaching Framework and the components of transformational leadership are summarized.

Chapter 1

The Mystique of Leadership

The French poet, novelist, and critic Remy de Gourmont (1858–1915) said a definition is a sack of flour compressed into a thimble. Perhaps that is why different definitions of leadership have been presented in countless essays and discussions; there is just not enough room in one definition to cover all facets of the subject. Is leadership a role? Is leadership a position? Is leadership a collection of attributes? Is leadership the exercise of influence? Is leadership a process? Is leadership a set of traits? Is leadership the art of inducing compliance? Is leadership a power relationship? Is leadership a form of persuasion? Is leadership a means of motivating? The answer to all of these questions is yes. How to define leadership can generate endless discussions, but according to Bass (2008, p. 25), "the definition of leadership should depend on the purposes to be served." For the purposes of this book, leadership is transformational.

The ground-breaking work of James MacGregor Burns (1978) conceptualized leadership as either transactional or transformational. Transactional leaders operate through the principle of social exchange; exchanging rewards for services or desired behavior. Transformational leaders go further, seeking to satisfy higher needs and engaging the full person through the leadership process. The transactional/transformational classification has been used to study leaders in many sectors; both types of leadership serve a purpose, but transformational leadership was determined to be important in every sector and every setting (Avolio & Yammarino, 2002). Let's take a closer look at the differences between the two and what these two types of leadership mean for healthcare leaders.

Transactional leadership is based upon the attainment of material and personal reward being contingent on demonstrating the performance and behavior set forth by the leader. Transactional leaders recognize what subordinates want from their work and try to see that they get it if their performance warrants it; if not, they provide contingent negative feedback. Transactional leadership contains the themes common to many taxonomies of leadership (Bass, 2008):

1. The leader helps set and clarify the missions and goals of the individual members and groups.
2. The leader directs others to pursue the mission and goals.
3. The leader helps provide the structure, methods, and tactics for achieving the stated goals.
4. The leader helps resolve conflicting views about means and ends.
5. The leader evaluates the individual's or group's contribution to the effort and rewards and disciplines accordingly.

Transformational leadership can be thought of as an expansion of transactional leadership. Although transactional leadership is necessary, it is not sufficient to create the conditions needed for success in today's challenging environments. Research on transformational leadership suggests that it is a form of leadership especially suited to fostering organizational change (Yukl, 2008), which will be sorely needed in the evolving healthcare environment. Transformational leadership is a way of interacting that stimulates others, both intellectually and motivationally. Transformational leadership has been shown to motivate others to higher levels of performance; often more than they originally believed to be possible. Furthermore, it builds strong follower commitment and loyalty while increasing satisfaction with leadership. Bass and Riggio (2006) state that transformational leaders achieve superior results by employing one or more of four core components of transformational leadership: (a) Idealized Influence; (b) Inspirational Motivation; (c) Intellectual Stimulation; and (d) Individualized Consideration.

Idealized Influence means that leaders behave in ways that allow them to be seen as role models and, by doing so, are admired and respected. When Idealized Influence is present, followers identify with the leader and want to emulate him or her. Trust is also built because the followers believe that the leader will do the right thing. High standards of moral and ethical conduct are demonstrated.

Inspirational Motivation means that leaders behave in ways that motivate and inspire others. They do this by getting followers involved in envisioning attractive future states, and providing meaning and challenge to their work. When Inspirational Motivation is present, followers see a leader who is optimistic, acts with purpose, and has the communication skills to make the vision understandable and engaging. The leader demonstrates and builds confidence in the ability of people to accomplish what needs to be done.

Intellectual Stimulation means that leaders challenge followers to think about problems in new ways. They question assumptions, reframe problems and promote solution-focused thinking. When Intellectual Stimulation is present, followers are encouraged to try new approaches, take risks, think creatively, and contribute their ideas. There is no public criticism of mistakes by individual members of the team so that a climate of exploration and experimentation can exist.

Individualized Consideration means that leaders pay attention to follower needs for achievement and growth by acting as a coach or mentor. They value people for the individuals that they are, and are sensitive to their differing personalities, needs, concerns, and goals. When Individualized Consideration is present, followers and colleagues are developed to successively greater levels of effectiveness through new learning opportunities and a supportive climate. In the process of demonstrating Individualized Consideration, individual self-efficacy is increased and self-esteem enhanced.

It is the premise of this book that mastering the competencies (i.e., knowledge, skills, abilities, behaviors, and attitudes) required to carry out a successful coaching conversation using the Four-square Coaching Framework presented herein will not only allow the reader to demonstrate Individualized Consideration, but will positively affect their ability to display and execute the remaining core components that comprise transformational leadership. In an industry that is undergoing a fundamental restructuring, a style of leadership that is transformational in nature is essential. A "coach-like" approach will be beneficial to healthcare leaders as they attempt to gain cooperation and commitment in a demanding healthcare environment populated with challenging professionals.

MEDICINE IS A PRESTIGIOUS PROFESSION

As a profession, medicine holds a distinctive place in society. Lundberg points out: "From antiquity, humans have required certain services from individuals who, in order to provide that service, must gain the most intimate knowledge of the person's mind, body, and even soul" (2004, para. 1). Health professionals in general, and physicians specifically, provide such a service and in so doing have garnered the respect and admiration of society at large—as evidenced by the venerable model of the wise and trusted physician. Adding to the medical mystique is the fact that physicians and other healthcare professionals are possessors of a body of knowledge that is exclusive to them. Their education is extensive, and their training is intensive. Competition to enter the field is fierce. As a result, the profession of medicine has been elevated to special status among the myriad of professions, and those who practice it in its many forms share in that status.

Medical professionals are also part of a unique population in which success in the field is attained through individual accomplishment in a very competitive environment. Accordingly, while people who are attracted to the healthcare professions come with a wide range of attributes, they are generally typified by a personality that is driven by what David McClelland (1976) would describe as a strong need for individual achievement. The intersection of a prestigious profession with the high-achieving personality produces what can be called the *Elite Professional*. Elite

Professionals can be found in the arts, sciences, law, academia, and similar professions that require more brains, more education, more talent, and more motivation to succeed. If leading in the healthcare environment is, as the saying goes, like herding cats, then Elite Professionals are the ultimate cat. Healthcare organizations are overflowing with Elite Professionals and to lead—and coach—them successfully you must understand them.

THE ELITE PROFESSIONAL

The Elite Professional is driven. He or she has a deep desire to perform at the highest level, often accompanied by an exaggerated fear of not succeeding. Their self-worth is directly tied to ambition and competence. Many of the attitudes and behaviors displayed by the Elite Professional are a byproduct of this high-achievement focus.

The Case of Dr. Alexander *(Hicks & McCracken, 2009)*

Dr. Alexander is an extremely competent neurosurgeon. He has aspirations of becoming chief of neurosurgery in a top-tier academic medical center. As you might expect, he is highly intelligent, analytical, and capable of cutting to the core of a problem quickly and accurately. He is current on the latest research and produces a steady stream of research and papers, which he eagerly presents at the top neurological conferences around the country—and the world. Consequently, he is highly regarded in his field, and this makes him a candidate for a leadership position in the opinion of many at his institution.

As is typical of Elite Professionals, Dr. Alexander desires to be the best and is extremely competitive. Competing to have more papers accepted than his colleagues, receiving awards that signify his "number one" standing, obtaining positions of status at an earlier age than his peers, are all important to him because these accolades provide a means by which he is able to gage his competence. Whether it's winning an argument with a peer, or competing for research funding, he gives it his all and is not a graceful loser. Interestingly, he is rather shy in purely social situations.

Dr. Alexander thrives on challenge. For him, a job is a series of trials and tests of his competence. However, he is also somewhat risk-averse and wants to avoid failure at all costs. Any challenge he undertakes must have a realistic chance of success from his perspective. For that reason, much to the chagrin of the Executive Vice President for Academic Affairs (EVP), Dr. Alexander is hesitant to accept leadership roles in situations where he is not the expert. He believes that he needs to know everything in order to lead, or he might fail. His aversion to failure is an obstacle for the EVP because he is trying to groom Dr. Alexander to become the future departmental chair. Placing him in charge of various teams and groups in which he is not the expert, but still must lead, is part of the developmental strategy.

In spite of his accomplishments, Dr. Alexander is always looking to grow professionally. To that end, he wants feedback. Sometimes, the feedback he seeks is inherent in the work itself. For example, when he removes a brain tumor or clips an aneurysm, he knows immediately how he has done. In other situations feedback must come from other people, but not just anybody. He is very selective in his acceptance of feedback. The feedback must come from a respected source or it will be discounted. Also, it must be actionable; feedback for its own sake is not his goal.

Dr. Alexander is perceived as being hypercritical when judging the work of others. He rarely gives positive feedback and is perceived as a "glass is half-empty" type of guy. Younger physicians find that no news is good news because he never seems to have anything positive to say. He believes that people shouldn't have to be told when they're doing well, only when something needs to be improved. While he is disparaged behind his back, what most people don't realize is that he is harder on himself than others.

Dr. Alexander often finds himself frustrated when working in a team where he is not in charge because it interferes with his ability to do what needs to be done as he sees it. He values his autonomy and has an aversion to anything that restricts his independence. This leads to a low tolerance for bureaucracy. He wants to work free of constraints with control over the parameters he deems necessary for success. Dr. Alexander also resists delegating anything important. After all, he knows best and doesn't want to lose control over the outcome.

The case of Dr. Alexander illustrates the high-achieving traits and behaviors of the Elite Professional.

- *Ambitious and competitive:* Competition is a means by which the Elite Professional can gauge his or her own level of competence. Competition doesn't always involve others; one can just as easily be in competition with oneself to get better.
- *Motivated by a meaningful challenge:* Their aversion to failure, however, means that any challenge, while a stretch, must be perceived as realistic in their eyes.
- *Wants actionable feedback:* Feedback, in order to be accepted, must meet two criteria: (a) it must come from a respected source; and (b) it must be actionable.
- *Provides little feedback to others:* There is a belief that others should be self-motivated, and feedback is not needed unless something is wrong. Thus, on those occasions when feedback is provided it tends to more critical than positive.
- *Values autonomy and control:* Freedom is needed to accomplish objectives and goals as they see fit. Control is needed so that things are accomplished in ways approved of by them. Delegation is a challenge because it means a loss of control.

When these characteristics are combined with the milieu of prestige and exclusivity that is attached to a specific profession, it attracts people whose levels of education, skill, and penchant for influence are substantially above that of the general population. Their unique blend of talent and status gives them a special standing in their organization and undue influence regarding their work environment. Not understanding the consequences of this standing has led many leaders to encounter serious problems, and even failures, in leading Elite Professionals. Healthcare leaders would do well to remember certain realities regarding this "breed of cat." DeLong, Gabarro, and Lees (2007) spell out the unique realities that accompany their presence at work.

1. Elite Professionals often have many options outside the organization. This increases their already independent nature and gives them a form of immunity from the organization and its leadership.
2. Elite Professionals can be difficult to replace. Because they have distinctive skills, talents, experience, and influence, their loss hurts an organization. Finding someone to replace them is often a long-term and expensive project.
3. Elite Professionals, especially those in healthcare organizations, play an influential role in choosing their leader. Consequently, they tend to believe that the leader works for them, rather than it is they who are working for the leader.
4. Elite Professionals have their own followers and constituencies within the organization. They are often influenced more by those people and groups than their own leadership.
5. Elite Professionals have strong loyalties to their professional discipline and colleagues in the field. The praise, criticism, and direction they receive from those professional groups and colleagues frequently have more impact on their behavior than what their organizational leader might do or say.
6. Elite Professionals, by nature, do not think of themselves as followers. They see themselves as special, as leaders in their own right, and want to be treated as such. They are quick to challenge those that try to "manage" them in the traditional sense of the word.
7. Elite Professionals have a sense that, because of their special value, they are entitled to special benefits and privileges that other persons in the organization do not have. They will constantly negotiate in order to obtain from their leadership that, which they believe, they are rightfully due.

The Case of Dr. Raymond Bernard

Dr. Bernard is the former Chair of Obstetrics and Gynecology at a major academic medical center. He held that position for sixteen of the twenty-five years he has been at the institution. Although no longer the chair, he still wields a great deal of influence. This is due in part because he is nationally recognized in his field. Dr. Bernard is the former president of the academy for his specialty, the editor of a leading journal, and the author of a textbook that is considered a classic in the field. The acclaim he receives from outside the institution feeds his already inflated ego.

His influence also comes from his relationship to the senior faculty of the department—most of whom he hired. He was liked as the chair because he gave them a lot of autonomy, although some would say he just stayed out of their way and let them do what they wanted. He has the ear of the faculty and believes that what he has done has been right for the department and the institution. Because of his reputation, the admiration of senior faculty, and his well-spoken manner, he also has sway over new recruits. In short, he still views himself as a leader in the department.

Under his leadership, however, the department stagnated, and Dr. Bernard was replaced as chair a few years ago. Since then, he has been a thorn in the side for the new leader of OB/GYN. The department needed new revenue streams, new faculty, and new ways of doing things, but Dr. Bernard doesn't see the need for change. He resists the efforts of the new chair to recruit or change practices within the department. In meetings, he commonly says, "This will never work"; "We've tried this before"; "The community is filled with this specialty so we won't be able to build a practice in this area"; and one of his favorites, "The university won't support it"; and to make matters worse his colleagues listen to him.

When the current chair tries to reduce his compensation so that it is more in line with his current duties, he runs to senior levels in the organization and says, "I'm entitled to maintain my compensation because of the work I've done, my reputation, and my longevity." He is also fond of reminding leadership that he has other opportunities awaiting him if he is not treated in the manner which he is due. If he were to leave it would send a negative message to current faculty and potential recruits. Besides, even if the current chair wanted to remove him without his consent, it would be difficult because of his tenured position and the university structure.

Dr. Bernard and Dr. Alexander, between them, illustrate the defining aspects of the Elite Professional. While many professions have their share of Elite Professionals, comparatively, healthcare is significantly overrepresented in this category. Not all physicians or other healthcare professionals will fit the entire pattern for the Elite Professional, but most will embody some of the characteristics, and a significant number will fit the stereotype. Leaders in healthcare who are charged with steering their organizations through the massive change that is currently underway in this industry will find that success in this new world will require attitudes and behaviors that are often at odds with the fundamental make-up of Elite Professionals. It will be their job to help them make the transition.

FROM "ME" TO "WE"

As Bob Dylan penned, "The Times They Are A-Changin'." To say that medicine is in the midst of a revolution is stating the obvious. While many factors have contributed to its current state, there are two fundamental themes that predominate. First, medicine's complexity has exceeded individual capabilities; and second, delivering healthcare to an aging population presents new challenges. Early in the twentieth century, hospital work was mostly custodial. "Medicine made little or no difference" (Thomas, 1995). Atul Gawande (2011), in his *Harvard Medical School*

Commencement Address, stated that now there are more than six thousand drugs and four thousand medical and surgical procedures available to today's physicians and healthcare providers. The difference between now and then is symbolic of the change in the medical landscape for the practicing physician.

As medicine has advanced, so has the complexity of the healthcare environment. Today insurance companies, government regulations, malpractice litigation cause such difficulties for the practitioner that, as Gawande points outs, many doctors of former generations say they wouldn't choose the profession today. Gawande believes, however, that these conditions are not the cause for the frustration experienced by today's physician but "are symptoms of a deeper condition—which is the reality that medicine's complexity has exceeded our individual capabilities as doctors." Thus, in the last half of the twentieth century there was a shift towards specialization. The primary care physician was its casualty and a silo approach to healthcare delivery was the result.

In addition to the transformation in the practice of medicine, the economic and political environment of healthcare as a business is also undergoing rapid change. Healthcare, as a system, is economically unsustainable as it exists today. "By 2020, nearly 20 cents of every dollar spent in the U.S. will be spent on health care" (Jacob, 2012, p. 4). Waste, duplication, poor communication, all contribute to the size and scope of increasing costs. In an environment where health costs are growing faster than employee wages and the economy at large, the historically fractured approach to delivery has shifted towards integration. While coordinated healthcare organizations, such as the Mayo Clinic, have existed for some time they have been the exception rather than the rule. This is changing for two reasons: (a) decreasing provider incomes; and (b) health reform.

There is no doubt that provider incomes are going to decrease. For example, payers are moving away from fee for service to bundled payments. A single check will be written for a full episode of care. Physicians in small practices will not be able to afford to stay in business without joining larger organizations where more cost-effective care can be delivered through better organization, a reduction in duplication and waste, and the effective use of information technology to increase efficiency and coordination.

Regardless of what eventually happens to The Patient Protection and Affordable Care Act of 2010, the economics of the specialist-dominated U.S. health care system will drive the change towards integration. Two such experiments are Accountable Care Organizations (ACOs) and the Patient-Centered Medical Home (PCMH). While there is no single formula or definition for ACOs, the development of partnerships between hospitals and physicians to coordinate and deliver efficient care is the notion underlying the ACO concept (Miller, 2009). It is believed that providers who are jointly held accountable and whose incentives are aligned will achieve measureable quality improvements and reductions in the rate of spending growth. Although the existence of organizations that currently utilize Integrated

Delivery Systems (IDSs) will facilitate the formation of ACOs, there will still be plenty of hurdles driven by the challenge of assimilating a diverse group of providers (i.e., primary care physicians, specialists, and a hospital) with the ability to administer payments, determine benchmarks, measure performance indicators, and distribute shared savings.

The PCMH is a complementary model to the ACO. Both models promote the utilization of enhanced resources to achieve the goal of improved care, but the PCMH approach emphasizes strengthening and empowering primary care providers (Fisher et al., 2010). In this model, the primary care doctor is like the quarterback of the delivery team and has responsibility for the coordination of care across the delivery continuum. This approach, however, could proves to be difficult if the providers do not have resources or established relationships with other providers to undertake the tasks required for such coordination. Furthermore, "the PCMH model does not offer explicit incentives for providers to work collaboratively to reduce costs and improve quality" (American Hospital Associate, 2010, p. 4). Whether the PCMH concept will work on its own or become incorporated as the primary care base for an ACO remains to be seen. However, what is known is that regardless of the model, the transition to accountable and integrated healthcare is underway and will require a change in the attitudes and behaviors of healthcare providers generally, and healthcare professionals specifically.

FITTING SQUARE PEGS INTO ROUND HOLES

Due to the complexity and economics of healthcare, the future of medicine will demand a more team-oriented approach emphasizing group precision and execution. However, success under these conditions of task interdependence is generally at odds with the values, needs, and personality of Elite Professionals. Physicians, for example, are described by Gawande as cowboys—independent, self-sufficient, and strong individual performers. Overcoming physician attitudes favoring autonomy and individual accountability over coordination will pose a major challenge to healthcare leaders as they attempt to build an organizational culture of teamwork and compliance. One of the biggest trials will be managing the social/political dynamics of change at both the individual and group level. Success will require an approach to leadership and individual interactions that may be at odds with the style of most healthcare leaders, given that most have risen from the ranks of Elite Professionals.

A DIFFERENT TYPE OF LEADER

Elite Professionals do not think of themselves as followers, but as leaders in their own right. They *allow* themselves to be led; leadership is a role they *voluntarily* confer upon others and is not automatically accepted as a position of formal authority.

Consequently, a purely transactional approach to leadership is insufficient. Gaining cooperation from fellow Elite Professionals in the healthcare environment will be more a matter of personal persuasion than formal authority. As explained earlier in this chapter, the pattern of interactive behaviors that will be most effective are those that stem from transformational leadership because it has been proven to be a recipe for success in generating commitment, loyalty, and cooperation.

Healthcare leaders will need to gain two types of cooperative behavior from their colleagues: (a) rule-following behavior; and (b) sacrificing for a larger gain. Physicians, for instance, will have to accept the fact that they are a member of a healthcare delivery *system*. They will no longer have the degree of autonomy they have historically enjoyed and will have to comply with rules and regulations that come with integration. The second type of cooperative behavior, sacrificing for a larger gain, means that healthcare professionals will need to engage in behaviors that benefit the group and its goals as a whole, sometimes at the expense of individual preferences and practices. For example, the orthopedic surgeon whose patients with total knee replacements spend five days in the hospital, although the norm is three days, will be asked to modify his or her practices if they conflict with the standards needed for a profitable organization.

COACHING AS A LEADERSHIP STYLE

Elite Professionals don't want to be managed, but they *do* want guidance. Their drive for personal excellence and success at work means that actionable feedback for professional improvement, developmental discussions, and mentor relationships are highly valued, especially by those in the early stages of their careers. Young professionals often focus on the technical side of their job at the expense of the behavioral elements. Therefore, help from leaders and more experienced colleagues is often needed to deal with the social and political problems that inevitably arise in team-based, task-interdependent environments.

Leadership and coaching go hand-in-hand. A good coach must be able to relate to people in a way that will help them solve problems and pursue their goals. A healthcare leader that has a "coach-like" approach will demonstrate a collegial style of interaction that will develop relationships that lend themselves to persuasion and influence—the means by which Elite Professionals are led. As the coaching approach advocated in this book is explained, and the competencies associated with its implementation are illustrated and understood, it will become apparent that attitudes and behaviors associated with coaching can assist any leader in becoming more transformational.

Chapter 2

The Nature of Helping Conversations

We all need help. No one makes it through life without assistance and support from others. Providing help to another is both an honor and an obligation, especially for those holding positions of leadership. To understand how to conduct helping conversations, it is important to understand why people want or need help in the first place.

PROBLEM SITUATIONS

Healthcare professionals are educated and trained to be problem solvers. Why, then, do people who solve problems on a daily basis need help? The answer is that the types of problems with which people struggle are not those for which their education and training prepares them. Consider the case of Dr. Bernard presented in chapter one. Suppose, for example, that you have to deal with his disruptive behavior without alienating him. How would you go about it? This is the type of problem people want help with because there is no "schoolbook" solution.

The problems for which people seek help come from crises, troubles, doubts, difficulties, frustrations, or concerns. These problems have no clear-cut solutions because they are complex and messy. They are the product of living and working in a people-driven setting, and they often cause emotional turmoil. They are problems that stem from the trials and tribulations of professional life in a complicated environment. In fact, they are not problems; they are problem *situations*. Problem situations "arise in our interactions with ourselves, with others, and with the social settings, organizations, and institutions of life" (Egan, 2010, p. 5). A healthcare leader's skillset must include a method for helping people work through, or cope with, the problem situations they face in the complicated world of healthcare.

DEVELOPMENTAL OPPORTUNITIES

People want or need help because they are not as effective as they would like to be. Sometimes it is because they are getting in their own way. In other words, the attitudes and behaviors that have historically worked for them are now impeding their effectiveness. The case of Dr. Alexander is a good example; his perfectionistic tendencies drive him to produce outstanding work, but they also prevent him from letting go of projects and trusting others. His drive for individual excellence has helped him achieve an outstanding reputation, but it now stands in the way of doing the things that will help him become a good leader. This situation is common for many Elite Professionals. They often have to learn that what got them to their present level of success won't necessarily maintain it, or help them go further.

People want help tapping into unused potential, or in finding opportunities to better utilize their talents so as to be more personally or professionally effective and satisfied on the job. Perhaps they feel locked into dead-end roles, or they are frustrated because they lack challenge at work, or because they have a set of values and ideals that drive them to want to do something more constructive and personally fulfilling with their lives. They may also want help to develop skills and abilities that are weak or non-existent. Whatever it is, it is not necessarily a question of what is going wrong, but of what could be better. These conversations are not about problem situations; they are about developmental opportunities. Helping conversations that explore developmental opportunities are fundamental to a coaching style of leadership.

THE TRUTH ABOUT HELPING CONVERSATIONS

What do we know about helping conversations that make them beneficial to the recipient? What can we extract from research about these conversations that will separate myth from truth?

Myth: Helping Others Means Having the Answers and Providing Them with Solutions

People who enter the field of medicine often have a strong need to set things right. It is a part of their nature, as well as the model of helping they are taught. Manning describes that model as prescriptive, "imposing outside, external remedy for human needs and ailments" (Manning, 1991, p. 67). So when healthcare leaders see something wrong they want to fix it. This urge to "help" someone by providing a solution and correcting what is wrong often becomes automatic, almost reflexive. In fact, this phenomenon has a name: the *Righting Reflex* (Rollnick, Miller, & Butler, 2008). The Righting Reflex is the instinctive inclination to offer advice, information, tips, and so forth, to correct what is "wrong" or to "help" by offering advice based upon what you would do. Healthcare leaders have more than their share of this affliction as illustrated by the following example.

Dr. Jacobs is a medical director in a physician-owned group that provides emergency medicine services to local hospitals. Her colleagues view her as a "know it all" who constantly intervenes to provide answers to their problems immediately upon hearing about their situation. By her way of thinking, she is saving them time because she has the experience and knows what to do, and in all fairness, her answers are often correct. She cannot understand why they get upset when she is offering what is clearly a workable solution to their difficulty. She is proud of her ability to get to the heart of a problem and provide a solution.

When a younger physician was chatting with her one day, the new doctor mentioned having problems with his medical director. The Righting Reflex took hold, and Dr. Jacobs could not stop herself from answering a question the younger physician did not ask: "What should I do?" Thinking she was helping, Dr. Jacobs overwhelmed the young physician with prescriptive advice. Consequently, the young physician felt foolish for having mentioned it in the first place, and seemed to shut down and resist Dr. Jacobs's "help." When asked why she thought the physician didn't accept her help, Dr. Jacobs was confident that it was because of the insecurity of the young physician, certainly not anything she had done.

Truth: *Helpful outcomes are the result of a person gaining insight and being challenged to think about what they want and how to get it rather than the leader fixing something or solving the problem for them.*

Dr. Jacobs failed to realize a paradoxical truth: even though people want and ask for help, it is a natural tendency to resist being told what to do. Outcomes are better when people are helped to help themselves. Facilitating self-determined and self-directed change and problem-solving, rather than giving prescriptive solutions leads to better results, outcomes, and accomplishments. The person will be more committed to the process, and will more likely capitalize on what they learn from the conversation.

The requirements for the leader are to keep the conversation focused on what the person wants, help them gain insight, challenge their thinking, urge them to take action, hold them responsible for changing their situation, and—when appropriate—offer advice and provide information so they can proceed from a more educated perspective. This does not mean being passive or unresponsive, but it is different from taking responsibility for their problems and fixing them.

The challenge for the leader is to resist the *Righting Reflex* and find the proper balance in managing the conversation. Unsuccessful discussions are often the result of over managing the conversation, just as a non-directive, laissez-faire approach is also rarely sufficient and productive. It takes awareness and practice to be able to facilitate helping conversations toward solutions and insight without just listening on the one end of the continuum and prescribing on the other.

Myth: Helping Conversations Need to Be Formal Appointments

The luxury of having 30 to 90 minutes of uninterrupted time to focus on another person's agenda can be extremely beneficial. When followed by additional sessions on a regular basis, they allow for an orderly exploration of subjects and issues important to dealing with problem situations or enhancing developmental opportunities. It can be argued that they even build in an element of accountability due to the anticipated follow-up sessions. The author refers to helping conversations that are in the form of formal appointments as *sit-down coaching*. However, sit-down coaching is not always practical given the time pressures and hectic nature of the healthcare environment.

> Truth: *Most Helping Conversations Are Informal and Unplanned.*

As a young boy, I spent a lot of time at my grandparents' home. One of my favorite activities was watching my grandmother fix popcorn. She would pour the kernels into a deep pan with hot oil, and I would anxiously wait for each kernel to pop—not knowing which kernel would pop and when. Helping conversations are often like watching popcorn pop; you never know when they are going to occur because they are impromptu and unexpected. These *popcorn coaching* opportunities are not to be wasted because they allow you to take advantage of spontaneous, teachable moments to advance a helping agenda.

Given the hectic nature of work, it is difficult, if not impossible, to engage in sit-down coaching on a regular basis. However, there are popcorn coaching opportunities available if a leader is on the lookout for them. A popcorn coaching opportunity might be a 10-minute conversation by the proverbial water cooler, or it might be an opportunity that unexpectedly materializes within the context of a task-related discussion on a different matter.

Example:

Dr. Neely, the Chair of Radiation Oncology, was having coffee with his Chief of Radiation, Dr. Newsom, a colleague he had known for several years. Throughout their time together they enjoyed many conversations on a range of topics and Dr. Newsom had frequently asked Dr. Neely for his opinions and advice. Over time, Dr. Neely had noticed that, while

> very intelligent, Dr. Newsom had difficulty understanding and operating within the political environment of the academic medical center.
>
> During the conversation, Dr. Newsom mentioned that he understood the Dean was hosting an informal social event at his home. Although he was invited, he didn't think he would attend because he "hated the idea of hanging around a bunch of professors making small talk." It was obvious to Dr. Neely that he hadn't considered the political implications of not attending, nor the political opportunities available if he did attend. Dr. Neely thought that perhaps Dr. Newsom might want to reconsider his decision if he thought about it from a political, rather than a task, point of view. Rather than giving him advice Dr. Neely asked a series of questions: "Why do you think the dean is holding this event in the first place? What message might it send to the dean if you don't go? How might you take advantage of this event to further some of your own goals?" Needless to say, Dr. Newsom hadn't thought of these questions and, upon reflection, began to see this seemingly inconsequential event in a different light.

Dr. Neely was coaching, but it wasn't planned. It was a popcorn coaching opportunity. Taking advantage of popcorn coaching opportunities is dependent upon your mindset. To quote Louis Pasteur, "Chance favors only the prepared mind." When your mind is prepared to look for and respond to helping opportunities, you will find that there are many more opportunities than what might be apparent. Most people have experienced this phenomenon when buying a new car. Upon discovering that you are interested in a certain make and model of car, you suddenly begin to notice the car everywhere; your readiness to perceive has changed. Popcorn coaching opportunities are all around you. You have but to be mindful to take advantage of them.

Myth: Your Expertise Is What They Are Looking For

Without question, people respect and seek the counsel of leaders or colleagues who have special skills or knowledge, i.e. Expert power. *Expert power* exists when a person has the knowledge, skills, or experience that another person needs (Stroh, Northcraft, & Neale, 2002). Providing your expertise works well in situations where the problem under discussion has one solution, and it is simply a matter of educating the other person as to what that solution is. Most helping conversations, however, will be about problem or issues where there is no one correct answer.

> Truth: *It Is You—Not Your Expertise—That Is the Most Powerful Tool in Most Helping Conversations.*

A study undertaken by the National Institute for Careers Education and Counseling (Hirsh, Jackson, & Kidd, 2001) asked people, in both the public and private sectors, to comment on when they had a helpful conversation, and what happened in the conversation that made it work. The study gathered information from 250 participants. Analysis of the results indicated that the single most important factor in predicting the successful outcome of a helping conversation was the *behavioral characteristics of the person doing the helping*. This is contrary to the belief that it is one's expertise that is most helpful. In the medical profession, there tends to be a great deal of emphasis on technical knowledge and skills to the detriment of an understanding of how interpersonal factors affect the success equation. Helpful conversations occur because there is a quality interaction between the two parties.

Interpersonal effectiveness has always been a part of successful leadership. Developing the attributes and behaviors for engaging in helpful conversations will automatically contribute to your abilities as a leader because there are so many overlapping competencies. The ingredients that make for good relationships as a leader also make for good helping conversations. For example, putting people at ease so that they feel relaxed and comfortable in your presence is essential to the helping process—and to effective leadership. It's not that difficult; a lot of it is common sense. For instance, treat the person with respect, treat them as an equal, be humble, and show *interest*.

The most powerful part of you that can be brought to a helping conversation is an interest in the other person. If you look up synonyms for the word *interest*, you will find words such as *attention, curiosity, concentration, attentiveness*, and *concern*. The common theme among these words is an external focus; you are attending to the other person. Focusing on their frame of reference, suspending judgment, and avoiding other internal mental activities that interfere with your genuine attention puts you in a better position to assist the other person, whether you are taking advantage of a five-minute popcorn coaching opportunity or engaging in a thirty-minute sit-down coaching conversation.

In summary, helping conversations do not have to be formal appointments. Most often they are informal and unplanned popcorn coaching conversations. It is not incumbent upon you to have all the answers and provide solutions. Resist the *Righting Reflex*; learn to be a thinking partner to help them gain insight and think through what they want and how they can take responsibility for solving their problems and achieving their objectives. Finally, remember that the most important thing you can bring to the conversation is *you*. Your genuine interest and your skillful interpersonal behavior during a conversation serves as a catalyst that accelerates productive outcomes.

THREE HELPING HATS

Helping conversations will require you to engage in three fundamental activities: Teaching, Mentoring, and Coaching. These activities can be thought of as *helping hats* because, like a hat that can be put on or taken off, one can move in and out of these activities, depending on what's required in the conversation (Hicks &

McCracken, 2010b). Each activity is used for a specific purpose and differs in its level of sophistication and the skillset needed to carry out that purpose.

Teaching

Teaching is the activity of instructing or imparting knowledge or skill (Smith, 1969). In many ways it is the easiest helping hat to wear. Consider the following situation:

The Chief Nursing Officer for a small hospital system attended a series of leadership classes as part of her hospital's professional development program. During one of the classes, she received feedback from a 360-leadership questionnaire which showed that her peers and subordinates rated her low in listening skills. She, and the Vice President of Human Resources (VPHR) were holding a discussion on another topic when she casually mentioned that she had recently received some feedback that concerned her. The VPHR asked if she wanted to spend a few minutes talking about the feedback, and she said, "Yes, I knew we were meeting today and wanted to get your advice." The VPHR asked what she would like to know. She proceeded to tell her about the low ratings with regard to her listening skills and asked if there were some hints that she could give her to help in this area. The VPHR put on her teaching hat and outlined the steps for effective listening. She also gave her some "how to" hints, and then demonstrated those about which she was unclear.

This example illustrates the teaching hat. When asked to help, many people often default to teaching; it is relatively easy to do, it allows people to "show off" what they know, and—for a short time—a teacher-student power differential is created. However, if all you wear is your teaching hat, you severely limit your ability to help others.

Mentoring

Mentoring is similar to teaching, but with one crucial difference: you are providing *advice and opinion* based upon knowledge and wisdom that can only be gained through your personal or professional experience. The advice you give during mentoring can't be learned from someone else or in a class somewhere. In this sense, mentoring is more personal than teaching. It is about sharing a part of you with someone else for the purpose of imparting a "higher" learning or wisdom.

Mentor is an ancient word. In Homer's *Odyssey*, Athena, the Greek goddess of wisdom, disguises herself as Mentor, an elderly and respected man in Odysseus's kingdom, Ithaca. As Mentor, Athena counsels Telemachus, Odysseus's son, in his efforts to make his way in a dangerous world. His father has been absent, fighting the war at Troy. His mother is protecting her household, and her virtue, from the avaricious ambitions of suitors who seek her hand in order to gain control of the kingdom. Telemachus needs to learn to become shrewd enough to survive, and to learn the virtues of a prince since someday he will have to provide for the prosperity and happiness of his people. Mentor provides a guiding hand and is a source of wisdom to Telemachus thereby accelerating his growth and development.

Mentoring is what we do when a colleague approaches us with a problem or issue they need help with and we act as a trusted friend or advisor. Typically, we share our professional or personal wisdom by giving advice based on what experience has taught us. Sometimes mentoring is exactly what the doctor ordered. Consider the following conversation between Dr. Rhymer, Chairman and CEO of an employed physician group of an urban, four-hospital health system, and a senior cardiology colleague who has come to him to ask about the recently posted Chief of Cardiology position at the system's heart hospital.

Cardiologist: *I was thinking about applying for the chief's position, but I really wasn't sure what the situation is over there or what they're looking for and I have some concerns. Do you think it's something I should do?*

Dr. Rhymer: *I'll be glad to help, but first tell me more about your concerns.*

Cardiologist: *Well, probably foremost is whether I can get along with the leadership over there.*

Dr. Rhymer: *I see. Well, in my opinion the most immediate challenge will be coming to terms with Dr. Hanson, Chief of Cardiac Surgery. He's been in that role for a long time, and you might know that he's very opinionated. He really doesn't listen to anyone else's ideas and can be difficult at times. He'll be retiring next year though, so you'll only have to work with him—or around him—for a few months. Would that be a problem for you?*

Cardiologist: I don't think so. I've been in meetings with him and, while I certainly agree with your observations, I can get along with him. However, if I were to get this position what would be the best way to work with him?

Dr. Rhymer: *I've known Dr. Hanson for a long time. I've found that if you keep him informed and solicit his ideas you can keep him on your side. The important thing for him is to be given the respect he believes he deserves. If you can put up with his quirks, I think you can learn a lot from him while he's here. Does that make sense?*

Cardiologist: *Definitely. What else do you think I should know about the situation?*

Dr. Rhymer: *Let's see . . . you'd be working with the cardiologists on the service line development. I've found them to be quite supportive, though, so that shouldn't prove too difficult. The Cath labs are in good shape, but the EP labs need a technology upgrade, and probably relocation to a different floor.*

Cardiologist: *Do you think I can handle it?*

Dr. Rhymer: *I think so. You've got the necessary experience, and you seem to have an interest in medical leadership. It's a logical next step for you. I've found over the course of my career that once you "leap in" to a role like this it's not nearly as bad as it might seem from afar. If I were you, I'd go ahead and apply.*

This is an example of a typical mentoring conversation. Dr. Rhymer immediately understood that what his colleague wanted was the benefit of his advice and professional experience. He put on his mentoring hat, gave advice, and offered opinions based on his professional observations and beliefs about what the job entails. Unlike teaching, which is essentially a mild lecture with room for questions, a good mentoring conversation will be an interchange of ideas and questions even though the person doing the mentoring will be giving his or her advice. A good mentor won't just start throwing advice in the direction of the other person but will take the time to understand the person's desires, needs, and concerns so that the advice is well-targeted. The Harvard Mentoring Project summed up the mentoring process in a *New York Times* (2003) advertisement by providing the following step-by-step guide to mentoring:

Step One: Listen.
Step Two: Share what you know.
Step Three: Repeat Step One.

Coaching

Coaching extends what mentoring begins. In transitioning from mentoring to coaching, one moves from being the "sage on the stage to guide on the side" (King, 1993, p. 30). When you put on your coaching hat, you are tacitly acknowledging that you believe that it is best if they solve their own problem, with your help. As a matter of fact, you may not possess the wisdom that will solve their problem, improve their situation, or define their goals and how to achieve them, but you do know how to help them learn for themselves, uncover their strengths, think through their problems, state what they want and define the actions that will help them achieve it.

Whereas statements are the language of teaching and mentoring, questions are the language of coaching. Consider the conversation later that afternoon, when another colleague approaches Dr. Rhymer to talk about the same job; however, in this instance Dr. Rhymer has put on his coaching hat.

Cardiologist: *I've been thinking about the chief of cardiology job at the heart hospital, but I'm not sure. I'd like more of a leadership role, but maybe it would be better just to remain in my practice and continue what I'm doing.*
Dr. Rhymer: *So what would be the downside of doing that?*
Cardiologist: *I might not get another chance at a medical leadership role, certainly not one here in town.*
Dr. Rhymer: *What else is a possible downside?*

Cardiologist: *Actually, I'm concerned about having to work with the chief of cardiac surgery. We both know Hanson can be difficult. I'm not sure I can handle the conflict.*

Dr. Rhymer: *So, although you say that you want more of a leadership role, you also say that there are some real liabilities to taking on the chief's job. Suppose you did take on the job and were able to handle it, what would be the upside for you?*

Cardiologist: *Well, the job could be really interesting, and it would give me an opportunity to lead the expansion of our cardiology service line, which is something the community really needs. I would find that challenging.*

Dr. Rhymer: *What else would you find worthwhile?*

Cardiologist: *It would also give me an opportunity to learn more about hospital operations. I don't have much opportunity to observe them as a practicing cardiologist.*

Dr. Rhymer: *Based on what I've heard so far, you're interested in a leadership role, and in becoming more involved in service line development and hospital operations, but you have been in a situation where you've been successful in handling conflict with another physician with whom you've had to work closely?*

Cardiologist: *Well . . . yes, as a matter of fact. Several years ago when I became chief resident, three months into my tenure they appointed an interim residency director who had an impossible personality.*

Dr. Rhymer: *How did you handle it?*

Cardiologist: *Day-to-day. Mainly, I was able to win the support of the other residents and the chairman of internal medicine. They really supported me, and that gave me the leverage I needed.*

Dr. Rhymer: *So based on your experience, what does that tell you about your ability to handle any potential conflicts with Hanson?*

Cardiologist: *I guess I can deal with him; especially since I hear he has only a few months left on the job.*

Dr. Rhymer: *OK, so based on what you're telling me, how sure are you that you really want to pass this up and remain doing what you're doing?*

Cardiologist: *(Pause) . . . Now that I think about it, I don't think I should pass it up.*

Dr. Rhymer: *Because. . .?*

Cardiologist: *Because I know it would take me in the direction I want to go, and I could deal with Hanson just like I did the interim residency director. All things considered, it sounds doable for me.*

This is an example of a coaching conversation. Dr. Rhymer quickly picked up that what his colleague needed was not advice, but rather assistance in self-discovering what was right for him and what action he ought to take. Rhymer's professional experience and knowledge of the chief of cardiology's job was not required when he put on his coaching hat. A good coach doesn't have to know anything about the specifics of the issue; in fact, it probably helps if they don't because it prevents slipping into the role of mentor/adviser.

COACHING DEFINED

Coaching can be defined as *the process of facilitating self-determined and self-directed problem solving or change within the context of a helping conversation.* Coaching is akin to leading a person through a process of self-discovery. From this, it follows that coaching must be an *inquiry-based* method in the spirit of Socrates. Socrates insisted that he was not a teacher or mentor. He claimed, rather, to be a "midwife"—someone who did not transmit knowledge to his companions but, through critical, self-examining dialogue, helped them labor successfully to find the answers they sought (Plato, *Theaetetus*, 150b-d).

Coaching is a hat that needs to be worn more often by healthcare leaders because it is a process that works well with Elite Professionals. However, it is a skillset that is somewhat at odds with teaching and mentoring. Teaching and mentoring are prescriptive, and generally come naturally to healthcare professionals, who are used to prescribing, telling, informing, and directing. Teaching and mentoring are necessary but insufficient methods for helping people meet the challenges of a complex social/political healthcare environment. Furthermore, without the ability to coach, it will be impossible to demonstrate one of the core components of transformational leadership: Individualized Consideration.

COACHING AS A LEADERSHIP STYLE

In Bass and Riggio's (2006) transformational leadership model, the individually considerate leader personalizes relationships with colleagues and followers. One way in which transformational leaders personalize their relationships is to know people as individuals; their desires, needs, and concerns. In the process, they pay attention to each person's needs for achievement and growth. New learning opportunities are created to help followers reach successively higher levels of development. Through informal conversations, which encourages two-way communication, and by listening effectively, transformational leaders become familiar with how people are doing and when help is needed with problem situations. As a result, they are seen as accessible and approachable for coaching and mentoring. For the transformational leader, showing Individualized Consideration through helping conversations is not a passive process, but one that is proactively practiced.

Chapter 3

The Structure of Coaching

"I THINK YOU SHOULD BE MORE EXPLICIT HERE IN STEP TWO."
Copyright ScienceCartoonsPlus.com

Coaching is an interaction between two activities: support and challenge. To support means to encourage, comfort, strengthen, validate, and reinforce. To challenge means to confront, question, test, and dare. Support and challenge must work together in a balanced way. If support is provided without challenge, people will feel good, but they do not change. Conversations will be enjoyable but will have no clear outcomes. People's thinking and perceptions are accepted, but they will have no opportunity to see things differently. The person doing the coaching is a cheerleader rather than a facilitator of change. If people are challenged without support, they may be compelled to change, but are bulldozed in the process. Goals are developed, but they may be overambitious. Thinking is challenged, but in a way that leads to intellectual sparring or defensiveness. The person doing the coaching is a driver rather than a facilitator. Support and challenge are what you do when you are coaching, but what do you support and what do you challenge? Consider the following situation.

> *Dr. Francis is an excellent emergency room physician with years of experience. In many ways, her peers and certainly the younger professionals she works with, both nurses and physicians, see her as a role model. Her chair has noticed her standing in the department and has encouraged her to take on more formal leadership responsibilities. While flattered, Dr. Francis is uncertain. On the surface, it seems like a pretty good idea. She feels that she has the necessary experience and skills to be a good leader, but she doesn't know if this is what she really wants. She is concerned that taking more of a leadership path would reduce the time she is able to devote to her clinical work; therefore, she feels stuck and can't seem to find the motivation to move forward. She wonders if she has not thought it through enough, but then believes she is overthinking the situation. Sometimes she thinks that maybe she should just start taking on more leadership responsibility and see what happens. However, even if she decides to act she is not sure what to do first.*

Dr. Francis is doing a lot of thinking, but lacks clarity about her priorities. She wants to act, but is not sure what to do. In order for Dr. Francis to find resolution she must decide what is important to her and what actions she will take based on those priorities. Dr. Francis is not unlike any other person you may coach, in that the content of the coaching conversation will revolve around thoughts and actions. Thoughts and actions are to a coach what clay is to a potter. The coaching process, then, can be thought of as applying the activities of support and challenge to the elements of thought and action (Pemberton, 2006).

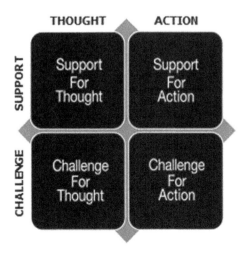

This Four-square Coaching Framework provides a structure for coaching. Each square represents a stage, or phase, of the coaching process. The leader who understands and uses this structure along with the competencies that make it work will be able to act as a catalyst for individual change and problem-solving within an environment of support, guidance, and encouragement. The goal of each stage is briefly explained below and a simple example provided to show how a coaching conversation may move through the various stages. The remainder of the book will be devoted to understanding and using the Four-square Coaching Framework to help people change, resolve problem situations, or attain their developmental objectives – while simultaneously enhancing one's transformational leadership capabilities.

SUPPORT-FOR-THOUGHT

A helping conversation, and especially coaching, is a relationship-driven experience. A successful coaching conversation requires a relationship that consists of mutual respect, and clear and open communication. The stage-related activities of Support-for-Thought are intended to:

1. Establish professional rapport;
2. Convey mutual respect and collegiality;
3. Clarify the person's narrative and build a platform of understanding.

Detailed instructions on how to implement Support-for-Thought are provided later in this chapter and chapters four and five.

CHALLENGE-FOR-THOUGHT

Challenging a person's thinking is a crucial part of any coaching conversation. Challenging the person to describe, in detail, a desired future and then establishing a specific outcome that sets the stage for designing the actions to make it happen is the primary purpose of this stage. The stage-related activities of Challenge-for-Thought are intended to:

1. Clarify what the person wants going forward (and how that's different than what exists currently);
2. Construct an outcome that specifies the indicators of success and ensures that the person has control over the actions and circumstances to be successful.

Challenge-for-Thought is explained in detail in chapters six and seven.

CHALLENGE-FOR-ACTION

Change does not occur without action. Translating solutions into actions is the goal of the Challenge-for-Action phase of the Four-square Coaching Framework. The stage-related activities of Challenge-for-Action are intended to:

1. Identify what the person can *do* to get what is wanted;
2. Specify how they are going to do it, and when and where they will start;
3. Ensure the actions are viable given the constraints and conditions currently present in the person's life.

Challenge-for-Action is explained in detail in chapters eight and nine.

SUPPORT-FOR-ACTION

Before a person will take action, there must be a willingness and commitment to do so. In other words, there must be a readiness to act; a readiness for change. The purpose of Support-for-Action is to evaluate and reinforce that readiness. The stage-related activities of Support-for-Action are intended to:

1. Evaluate the person's readiness to act or change;
2. Build the individual's intrinsic motivation to follow through with the actions needed to get what is wanted.

Support-for-Action is discussed in detail in chapters ten and eleven.

Helping people resolve their problem situations and translate their developmental goals from wishes to reality is a messy business. It is easy to get lost. The Four-square Coaching Framework is a map that can help you keep track of where you are in a conversation, and where you want to go. The following short, and very simple, example illustrates the use the Four-Square Coaching Framework. This conversation is between a nurse manager and a nurse new to the practice. The nurse manager has noticed that the new employee appears to be somewhat stressed and out of sorts. She approaches her and asks how things are going.

New Nurse: *I've been a little upset and stressed the last few days.*
Nurse Manager: *Yeah, I've noticed. Do you want to talk about it for a few minutes? I've got some time.*
New Nurse: *I don't know if there's anything you can do, but I guess it might help me get it off my chest.*

SUPPORT-FOR-THOUGHT

Nurse Manager: *I'm happy to be a sounding board, what's going on?*
New Nurse: *I love my job but, I really feel stressed because I don't seem to be fitting in with the team and I'm not sure they like me.*
Nurse Manager: *What causes you to think that you're not fitting in with the team?*
New Nurse: *Well, I feel like an outsider.*
Nurse Manager: *How so?*
New Nurse: *They seem distant and unfriendly.*
Nurse Manager: *What do they do that's distant and unfriendly?*
New Nurse: *They go to lunch together and I never get asked. They never ask me how my weekend was or what's going on outside of work. Things like that.*
Nurse Manager: *Yeah, I can see how that would be uncomfortable for you.*

CHALLENGE-FOR-THOUGHT

Nurse Manager: *What would you like to be different going forward?*
New Nurse: *I want to feel as if I have more than just a work relationship with them. We don't have to be best buddies, but it would be nice if there were some socializing. They seem to do that with each other.*
Nurse Manager: *Let me ask you a question; how would you know if you had more than just a work relationship with them and you were experiencing some of the socializing you want?*
New Nurse: *I wouldn't be excluded from some of the things they do outside of work.*
Nurse Manager: *What would be happening instead?*
New Nurse: *I would feel as if I could go to them and say, "Hey, I heard you're going out to lunch, mind if I come along?"*
Nurse Manager: *What else?*
New Nurse: *We'd talk about what was happening outside of work, our kids, that sort of thing.*
Nurse Manager: *That makes sense. If I were in your situation, I would want the same thing. What do you think you can start doing to get the kind of relationship you want?*

CHALLENGE-FOR-ACTION

> **New Nurse**: Oh gee I haven't really thought about that.
>
> **Nurse Manager**: Let me ask it a different way. What would you be doing differently that would let them know that you were interested in "being more social and being a part of the team"?
>
> **New Nurse**: One thing that pops into my head is that I would be initiating more conversations myself with them on a personal level?
>
> **Nurse Manager**: That's a good idea. What else?
>
> **New Nurse**: There's one person—Maria—that has been pretty friendly with me. I think it might be a good idea to take her to lunch, and while I'm there I could get a read from her on what is going on and what I might do to help the situation.
>
> **Nurse Manager**: Perfect! Are you willing to try those things?
>
> **New Nurse**: Sure, it can't hurt.

SUPPORT-FOR-ACTION

> **Nurse Manager**: It sounds as if this is something that is really important to you. What makes it so important to you?
>
> **New Nurse**: Probably because I had a similar situation in the last place that I worked that never changed, and I don't want to go through that again.
>
> **Nurse Manager**: So if it's that important, when are you going to try out what you've suggested [Challenge-for-Action]?
>
> **New Nurse**: I'm going to go talk to Maria now and see if we can go to lunch this week. Heck, I might even see if a couple of others would like to go with us.
>
> **Nurse Manager**: Sounds good. Let me know how it goes.

This conversation followed a very simple path. The nurse manager guided the conversation through each stage in sequence, and ended by returning to the Challenge-for-Action stage to promote immediate action.

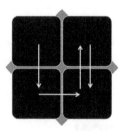

Most coaching conversations are more complex than this simplified example, but the process is the same; each stage serves a different purpose, but all stages must eventually be explored.

Using the Four-square Coaching Framework to guide you during a helping conversation provides a roadmap to follow that makes the coaching process easier for you, and more effective for the person you are helping. However, while the map seems to take you through a predictable sequence, the stages are not meant to be linear steps. Instead, they are purpose-driven activities designed to achieve the intention of that part of the conversation. Depending on whether it is a first conversation or a follow-up conversation you may start in a different stage of the framework, and move around accordingly, but all stages of the Four-square Coaching Framework must be navigated sooner or later. Finally, while simple, it does require that you develop competencies specific to each stage of the framework.

SUPPORT-FOR-THOUGHT

It's a busy day in the clinic. Your next patient is a 55+ male with the presenting complaint of joint pain in his knees. You sit down with him and ask what the problem is. He begins to describe his symptoms, and it immediately becomes clear to you that he is experiencing arthritis symptoms. In fact, you don't even need to hear his complete story once you have a description of the problem. After all, you're on a tight schedule and time is valuable. So you authoritatively provide your initial diagnosis, and prescribe a conservative treatment plan to see how he will initially respond. Now it's off to the next patient . . . and the next. . . .

A couple of hours later you are recording some notes in your office when you receive a phone call from a colleague. He says "Do you have a minute, I've got a problem and could use your help?" You say, "Sure, come on by." Immediately you are back in your problem-solving mindset and ready to provide answers; why else would he ask for your help? Your colleague arrives, and after a couple of minutes of small talk you ask, "How can I help?" He begins his narrative of the problem. It's hard to concentrate as you look at your incomplete notes but within a minute or two you have formed your opinion. As with the patient situation above, you jump into the conversation, confidently give your opinion, and tell him why you think it's the solution he's looking for—another problem solved. Now it's back to the notes.

This may be a helpful conversation, but it is not a coaching conversation. It is, however, typical of what often happens due to time and task pressures; not to mention that to most healthcare professionals, especially physicians, helping people means giving them opinions and solutions. However, coaching is different; coaching is facilitating self-directed thinking and problem solving. This is not to say that sharing your ideas and advice is never a good thing, sometimes your opinion is just what the doctor ordered—but don't rush into it. People must have the space, and conditions, to talk to you about what they want and how to achieve it at their own pace and in a way that is most helpful to them. For those conditions to exist, you must be able to build rapport.

BUILDING PROFESSIONAL RAPPORT

Beginning with the work of Carl Rogers (1951), the importance of relational factors in facilitating successful change efforts was established. While technical expertise on the part of the helper (e.g., choice and timing of interventions) has always been thought of as an essential discriminant between those who were effective and those who were ineffective in facilitating change, the notion that good relationships can expedite one's technical interventions is now accepted practice (Farber & Lane, 2001). Coaching is the ultimate in relationship-driven change efforts, and for that reason, the establishment and maintenance of rapport is essential.

The establishment of rapport creates the conditions that engender the kind of trust and mutual respect required for direct and honest communication. When rapport is present, a connection exists with the other person that signals comfort and acceptance. When coaching, it is up to you to lead the way in establishing professional rapport through an attitude of positive regard, the display of empathy, and genuine attention.

POSITIVE REGARD

Dr. Werner, Chair of Urology, is a colleague with whom you have worked for several years, although you wouldn't describe your relationship as close. In fact, Dr. Werner doesn't seem to have close relationships at work, and it's not surprising given the arrogance that he displays with his colleagues and staff. If he is not talking about his latest research paper, he's challenging others on what they know (which of course is not as much as he does). It's not that you dislike him. He is a very good urologist, but he can also be very irritating. So it comes as a surprise when one day he approaches you and asks for a few minutes of your time because he could use your help. Upon sitting down with him, he proceeds to tell you of problems he's having with senior hospital leaders because they find his administrative skills lacking as chair of the department, and are pushing him to "get his act together" if he is going to continue as chair.

What are you thinking now? Perhaps, it is, "Good, it's about time he gets taken down a few notches" or "Maybe now he'll realize he is not as good as he thinks he is." While these thoughts may be normal, and even justified, they will not help you to carry on a helping conversation with Dr. Werner. Without the proper attitude on your part, there is little chance that you will be able to establish the necessary rapport to support such a conversation. Rapport begins with having a positive attitude toward the person you are helping—an attitude of *positive regard.*

Positive regard is an attitude of acceptance of the person as they are, without judgment so that respect and support are possible (Farber & Doolin, 2011). It entails finding some aspect of a person to which you can positively relate so that you can demonstrate the genuine caring and consideration that is a part of rapport. This does not mean that you have to be "friends" with the person, approve of everything he says or does, nor share his values—or even pretend that you do. It does mean that you must set aside feeling-based judgments so that they don't interfere with your ability to relate to the other person. You can respect his model-of-the-world, but you don't have to live in it; you can allow the person to be different from you and it is okay because you can still find value in him as a person. Positive regard is present when:

- You are able to relate to someone in some positive way.
- You are nonjudgmental.
- You accept someone as a person, even with flaws.
- You value the person's uniqueness.
- You want the best for the person.
- You want to help the person.
- You can feel compassion for the person, given their situation.

Positive regard is easy with people you like, and for whom you care. It becomes more difficult to maintain with people such as Dr. Werner, about whom you may have mixed feelings. Nevertheless, it is essential that you are able to find and maintain positive regard for the purpose of creating the kind of professional rapport required for constructive helping conversations. However, achieving positive regard is difficult without empathy.

EMPATHY

Empathy is a word that everyone uses, but few understand. A good example of empathy can be found in a story related by Alfred Benjamin in his book *The Helping Interview* (1981); it is paraphrased below.

> In a small village, in Israel, there was a donkey. It had long and silky ears, large and shiny eyes, and all of the children loved it very much. Every day the parents would bring their children to pet it or ride it, or just give it treats. Indeed, it was the most popular animal in the village, but one day the donkey went missing. The people looked everywhere, but it was nowhere to be found. Needless to say, all of the children and their parents were very

> *upset. The people in the village were so distressed that they gathered together to decide what to do next.*
>
> *In that same village lived an old man, the father of one of the earliest settlers. He was so old that he had become somewhat senile, and, sometimes, people even made fun of the old man behind his back. While the people were gathered together wondering what to do, in walked the old man leading the donkey. The jubilation was great, and their astonishment was even greater. "How is it," they asked him, "that you of all people have found the donkey? What did you do?" "It was simple," he said. "I just asked myself, 'If you were the donkey where would you go off to?'" So I went there and found him and brought him back.*

When the old man assumed the donkey's perspective, he was showing empathy as Carl Rogers defined it: "an accurate, empathic understanding of the client's world as seen from the inside" (1961, p. 284) Demonstrating empathy means to understand the *private logic* of others. Empathy is often confused with sympathy, but sympathy means having the same feelings and concerns as another, whereas empathy is a cognitive shift from our perspective to another person's perspective—but without getting caught up in it. It is the ability to see through the other person's eyes and to understand his or her frame-of-reference. The challenge for most people is suspending their perspectives, opinions, and judgments long enough to willingly understand another person's thoughts, feelings, and struggles from his or her point of view.

It is not easy to suspend our point-of-view, especially when something important is at stake. However, seeing things from another person's perspective gives us access to a different type of information that is often very useful. In their national bestseller, *Getting to Yes*, Roger Fisher and William Ury (1991) wrote that negotiating a win-win outcome with another party involves focusing on the other party's interests. In the opinion of Fisher and Ury, viewing the situation from the point-of-view of those with whom you are negotiating to better understand the desires and concerns which underlie the other person's negotiating position is a prerequisite to being able to find a mutually agreeable solution. This empathic response requires a temporary shift in perspective on the part of the negotiator. If a negotiator can do it to achieve a better outcome, what prevents a leader from showing empathy to create a more supportive conversation? Nothing—except a lack of desire and a big ego.

Big egos are found in all professions; however, in the world of healthcare, big egos abound. When one's ego is in the way, the world revolves around only one point-of-view - yours. This is known as egocentrism (Windschitl, Rose, Stalkfleet, & Smith, 2008). The egocentric thinker is absolutely convinced that her understanding of things is the absolute truth. This myopic view of the world causes the egocentric thinker to ignore the viewpoints of others, without any attempt to understand them. To quote Robert Schuller, "Big egos have little ears" (Kremers, 2006, p.4)

Rapport requires that you "put your ego in a refrigerator" so that you may understand the other person's world from his perspective. Once another person knows that you understand, he is more inclined to communicate his thoughts openly and honestly. As his communication becomes more open and his ideas and beliefs exposed, vulnerability is increased, and trust grows. Without trust, helping another becomes virtually impossible. Empathy promotes intellectual exploration and assists people to think more productively (Greenberg, Elliott, Watson, & Bohart, 2001); empathy supports thought.

GENUINE ATTENTION

Shortly after Ronald Reagan's second term, this author had the opportunity to hear the president speak about issues of the day at a small gathering in Northern California. After his talk, I approached him and said, "Thank you, Mr. President, for what you have done for our country—and the world." We shook hands, and I told him that I had two small children that would grow up in a safer world in large part because of him. I don't remember much else about the conversation, but one thing stands out in my memory to this day: he made me feel like I was the only person in the room. For that short period, I had his full and undivided attention. A friend of mine related a similar experience with president Bill Clinton. He said that when he talked to you, he made you feel special because of his ability to focus only on you and what you were saying. In both instances, we experienced the value of genuine attention.

Attention is validating. It lets the other person know that he or she is important. Arguably, the most valuable thing you can offer someone—from a helping standpoint—is your genuine attention because it signals that you are putting them first. There are three kinds of attention: Behavioral Attention, Mental Attention, and Verbal Attention. When you provide all three during a helping conversation you are exhibiting the necessary *genuine attention* to provide support for thought.

Behavioral Attention

  "I speak two languages, Body and English."—Mae West

A significant amount of our communication is nonverbal (Mehrabian, 2007). Nonverbal communication refers to the "music" of the conversation, rather than the substance or words of the conversation. It is the feelings and attitudes communicated by nonverbal cues, such as facial expressions and tone-of-voice. Reading these nonverbal cues is a common human practice. For example, when you care about someone, you are generally very attentive to the mood her body language seems to be communicating. If it appears as though a friend is carrying the weight of the world on her shoulders, you may ask, "Is everything alright? You look kind of down today." The same monitoring of body language and nonverbal cues occurs in a helping conversation, but it is the other person that is monitoring *your* body language and nonverbal cues for messages that signal attention—or the lack of it.

Recently, a colleague related an interesting story about how he communicates his degree of interest in carrying on a conversation with another person. He stated that he has an open-door policy, but sometimes it is more open than other times. When someone stops by to ask if he has a couple of minutes to help with a problem, and he is sincerely interested in helping the person, he will turn away from his computer, face the person squarely, adopt an open posture—often leaning somewhat towards the other person—and make appropriate eye contact (all very good indicators of behavioral attention). However, when he feels obligated to listen, but doesn't really want to, he will continue to face his computer and only turn his head toward the person while simultaneously asking what he can do for the person. Needless to say, in the latter example, people quickly get the message that this is not a good time for an extended conversation, and will keep their communication short and sweet. He does not need to tell the person directly because his body language communicates it for him. This illustrates that the manner in which we behaviorally attend to a person will either encourage or discourage discussion.

Visually attending to the other person (i.e., providing eye contact) is an essential part of behavioral attention. An appropriate amount of eye contact (not staring) communicates interest in the other person. The example below illustrates what can happen when visual attention is lacking.

> A young technician was in conversation with his clinic manager when the clinic manager opened her iPad and began checking her e-mail. Although she periodically looked up, her attention was clearly on the iPad rather than the technician. She might have been listening intently, but he wouldn't have known it from appearances. The young technician later said that he not only felt disconnected during the conversation, but disrespected, as well.

Behavioral attention encourages the speaker by providing signals that reinforce the message "I'm interested in what you are saying." Signals, such as a nod of the head, smiling, and adding a "Hmm" or "Uh-uh" once in a while, reassures the other person that you are focused on her. However to demonstrate a genuine interest in the other person, behavioral attention must be accompanied by mental and verbal attention.

Mental Attention

"The quality of your attention determines the quality of other people's thinking (Kline, 2008)."

Attention is mental energy focused in a specific direction. When you are fully engaged in a task, activity, or conversation, your mental focus is on what you are doing; you are "in the zone." Being in the zone is a common experience. Think of a conversation you have had with someone where you were absolutely fascinated by him, or what he was saying. Were you primarily focused on the dialogue, rather than the thoughts and words in your own head? Was your attention so absorbed by the conversation that your perception narrowed to the point where you were less aware of your surroundings and outside distractions? Was it energizing rather than draining? If your answers to these questions were "Yes," then you were in the zone. Now, imagine how good the other person must have felt about receiving that level of mental attention from you.

You can't fake attention, and yet, some people try. They use their body language to pretend to focus on the other person while their mind is elsewhere. Madelyn Burley-Allen (1982, p. 48) makes this point by asking this question, "Have you ever watched a person fake listening by smiling and head-nodding, when neither the smile nor the head-nodding matched what the other person was saying?" Pretending to show interest, while mentally doing other things, is a world apart from showing genuine interest. M. Scott Peck (2003) says that one cannot truly listen to another person and do anything else at the same time.

Limit Your Distractions—and You Are Your Biggest Distraction!

There are always two conversations going on within any helping discussion. The one we have with the other person, and the one we have with ourselves. A conversation that we have with ourselves is called an internal dialogue, also known as self-talk. When our self-talk dominates, our mental energy is directed inward, thereby reducing our connection to the external world (i.e., the other person). We become the object of our attention. Self-talk is natural. It is the amount and type of self-talk that determines whether it becomes an impediment to Support-for-Thought. The self-talk most detrimental to a helping conversation is judgmental self-talk.

Dr. Rajiv is a 42-year-old internist. He prides himself on his analytical skills, which certainly help his differential diagnostic abilities. He also likes to use his rationality to appraise a situation and to point out flaws inherent in an idea, a plan, or a proposed solution. While he sees himself as analytical, his peers describe him as a nitpicker. They feel he is overly critical and is always challenging their thinking. This is a pattern that carries into his personal life and, as it turns out, has caused problems over the years with both his wife and children.

Dr. Rajiv had functioned as Medical Director for his hospital's telemetry unit for about a year when he came to the author for some "leadership" coaching. When asked why he was coming for help at this time, he said that his boss, the Chief of Medical Services, was critical of his inability to develop some of the younger physicians in the group and was questioning his leadership skills. He was asked to describe some of the developmental conversations, and what he was thinking during those conversations. As one might expect, he wasn't listening to what was being said. Instead, he was judging what people were telling him, rather than attempting to understand them.

Once your self-talk is dominated by judgment, it takes you out of the zone. As your judgments become the center of attention, your attention is hijacked by your judgmental self-talk. In essence, you become your own distraction. Contrast that with what happens when you attempt to understand the other person's perspective, but without judgment. It forces your mental attention on what the other person is saying and signals your interest in the other person as a person; Support-for-Thought is increased. When you are absorbed by the process of better understanding another person, you are in the zone, and empathy is present.

Verbal Attention

Verbal attention is an overt indication that you are listening and attempting to understand the other person. Verbal attention encourages the speaker to continue, but has an additional benefit: it draws out the other person's thoughts and ideas through the techniques of inviting, reflecting, and summarizing.

Inviting can be accomplished with a gentle command or a quick, wide-open question that leaves space for the person to fill in blanks that are important to him or her. For example, invitations like "Tell me more" and "What else?" are quite effective in encouraging the person to expand on what he or she is saying. Inviting serves as a means of drawing additional information from someone. If empathy is the cognitive attempt to understand the other person, inviting is a means for accomplishing it.

Reflecting is a method of acknowledging what the other person is saying, but it also has the added benefit of potentially extracting more information. Reflecting is simply mirroring what the person has said using your own words and phrases. It is more than mere repetition; it is reflecting back to the person a short summary of what you heard but in your own words. The other person will then either confirm to you that you have heard them correctly or correct any misunderstanding. Reflecting also has the effect of encouraging elaboration—the other person will often expand on their previous statements. It is also proof to the other person that you have been paying attention because it is very difficult to accurately reflect what you have heard if you haven't been listening.

Summarizing occurs at strategic points in the conversation. Its purpose is to assemble the themes and ideas that you have heard from the person during the conversation into a succinct outline of her thinking. As much as anything it helps the person hear what she has said to that point in the conversation. For example, suppose a person has referred to several actions she wants to take toward an important goal. Summarizing those actions so she can evaluate their viability supports her thinking and also demonstrates verbal attention.

Inviting, reflecting, and summarizing, when used during the course of a helping conversation, serve two purposes: first, they are the means by which you display verbal attention as part of the equation for showing genuine interest, and second, they have the added value of eliciting more information from the person you are helping. The following example illustrates the use of these three communication techniques to help a new nurse meet the challenge of finishing her documentation within regular work hours.

New Nurse: *I need your help. I'm finding that at the end of the day I have so much documentation to do that I have to stay late to finish up. At first, I thought that this was going to be temporary, but it seems to be an everyday thing now, and I'm starting to get flack at home because I'm always running late.*

Preceptor: *So tell me more about what is causing you to get behind on your documentation.* **[Inviting]**

New Nurse: *I feel that when I start documenting on a patient I'm being interrupted by a physician phoning me back, or a clinic tech asking me about another patient, or the lab calling me; things like that.*

Preceptor: *OK, so what you're saying is that there are a lot of unplanned interruptions that you don't feel that you have control over, and you are getting sidetracked. Am I correct?* **[Reflecting]**

New Nurse: *That's right. Once I get interrupted I have to take care of that issue, and then something else always seems to come up, and my documentation gets put to the side.*

Preceptor: *Well, tell me what you've tried so far to deal with this.* **[Inviting]**

New Nurse: *One thing I've tried is that when I'm in the room with the patient I get on the computer and try to document while I'm there.*

Preceptor: *How has that worked?* **[Inviting]**

New Nurse: *Not so well. At first I thought I could do it, but I get too confused.*

Preceptor: *It sounds to me that trying to multitask when everything is so new to you is a little too much right now.* **[Reflecting]** *What else have you tried?* **[Inviting]**

New Nurse: *I've also tried sitting down and getting caught up when I have a break between different tasks, but that's not made much of a difference either because I never seem to have the time I need.*

Preceptor: *OK, so let me summarize what I've heard so far. One, you've tried to be efficient by attempting to document while you're already with the patient. Two, you've tried cramming it in between other things. Three, you're feeling further behind because nothing seems to work, and it's starting to affect you at home.* **[Summarizing]**

New Nurse: *That's right.*

Preceptor: *I certainly understand what you're going through because I've been there myself when I first started, so let's talk about some things that you may not have tried.*

By being verbally attentive, the preceptor is getting the nurse to open up. Notice that the preceptor didn't immediately come forth with her ideas, but instead, gave the nurse room to talk. Coaching people requires that you give them your attention, but, not your solutions. If you want to give them your advice, opinions, ideas, and solutions, then take off your coaching hat and put on your mentoring or teaching hat. Notice also that it would be next to impossible to be verbally attentive without being mentally attentive. Inviting, reflecting, and summarizing require one's complete attention. Verbal, mental, and behavioral attention are all a part of the rapport-building process.

COACHING AS A LEADERSHIP STYLE

Individualized Consideration, a core component of transformational leadership, is demonstrated through coaching and mentoring conversations. However, demonstrating Individualized Consideration is more than the activity of mentoring or coaching, it is a pattern of behaviors that promotes open communication and personalizes one's relationships in day-to-day interactions. Individualized Consideration is dependent on a leader's overall *interpersonal competence*, which is manifested in understanding of, caring for, and consideration for others.

The relationship between interpersonal competence and effective leadership has been shown to be positively correlated for some time (Boyatzis, 1982). In recent years, studies have shown how emotional intelligence is a determinate of effective leadership (Goleman, 1995, 1998; Cherniss & Goleman, 2001). Whether you prefer to think in terms of emotional intelligence or interpersonal competence, the conclusion is the same: those abilities that help one connect with others, and build and sustain relationships are critical for any leader. The capabilities that contribute to effective leadership are many of the same interpersonal competencies required for effective coaching; particularly, the knowledge, skills, and abilities associated with the Support-for-Thought phase of the Four-square Coaching Framework. In this chapter, the ability to establish rapport through positive regard, the display of empathy, and providing genuine attention on three levels (behaviorally, mentally, and verbally) was presented as critical to this phase of the coaching process. However, the ability to establish rapport is also a characteristic of an effective leader; a transformational leader.

Chapter 4

Support-for-Thought
Adult-to-Adult Communication

Coaching requires a working alliance. Coaching is not something that you do *to* another person; it is something that is done *with* another person. A working alliance is created by using a style of interacting that signals a collegial relationship rather than an asymmetrical relationship based upon differences in position, status, expertise, or influence. Leaders, due to an innate power differential over followers, must be especially diligent in reducing that differential by adopting a style of interaction that fosters a climate of mutual respect and reciprocal influence.

During the late 1950s and early 1960s, psychiatrist Eric Berne developed a theory of interpersonal interaction that he labeled Transactional Analysis. Central to his theory is the concept of *ego states* (Berne, 1964). An ego state is a set of interrelated thoughts, feelings, and behaviors from which we interact with one another. Berne identified three ego states that are a part of the human personality—Parent, Adult, and Child—each with an important function. He recognized that human communication can be described in terms of exchanges that take place between these three ego states (Berne, 1972). Each ego state has a defining set of words, tones, gestures, postures, and facial expressions that are easily recognized.

THE PARENT EGO STATE

As you would expect, the Parent ego state exhibits a communication style stereotypically associated with parental figures. This ego state is the communication method commonly used to express our opinions and judgments in an authoritative manner. Whether forceful or subtle, there is an underlying theme of superiority associated with this ego state. The Parent ego state is characterized by words, tones, gestures, postures, and facial expressions that communicate "I am the authority" and "I know better."

In the following example, extracted from an article in the *Journal of Medical Management* (Hicks & McCracken, 2010a), note the authoritative tone and parental style of the senior colleague in his attempt to "coach" a new staff member. In particular, notice the use of *pressure words*; these are words and phrases that create psychological pressure to do something, or to refrain from doing something (e.g., should, shouldn't, must, mustn't, need to, and have to).

Situation: *A staff member, new to the practice, is finding the office administrator difficult to work with, and is seeking advice from a senior colleague.*

New Staff Member: *I don't think Mary is being very cooperative. I keep asking her to do some things differently on the front desk, and she just refuses to help. I don't know what to do.*

Senior Colleague: *Haven't you tried talking to her about it?*

New Staff Member: *Not really.*

Senior Colleague*: Why not?*

New Staff Member: *I have tried talking to her about other things in the past and every time I do she gets defensive and we end up arguing.*

Senior Colleague: *You just need to be more patient with her. If you're going to be successful in this practice, then you've got to be able to handle situations like this.*

New Staff Member: *Yeah, but she needs to cooperate too.*

Senior Colleague: *I agree, but that's not the point. The point is that you're the senior person, and you should be the one to take the first step and lead the way.*

New Staff Member: *I have and it hasn't worked.*

Senior Colleague: *Then you've just got to be more persistent.*

New Staff Member: *I don't know how, and you're not helping me. [Clearly showing her frustration.]*

Senior Colleague: *I am helping, but you're not listening to what I'm telling you.*

Although well-meaning, the leader exhibited a form of the Parent ego state known as the Critical Parent. At its best, the Critical Parent is a communication style that is useful in situations where there is little margin for error and compliance with an authority figure is required. The undesirable aspect of the Critical Parent ego state is its corrective and judgmental style. A softer version of the Parent ego state is the Nurturing Parent. It, too, is a controlling style of communication focused on telling a person what he or she *should* do "for their own good." Although it is intended to offer support and care, the Nurturing Parent can be a "smothering" style of interaction. It is an approach that assumes the other person is helpless and needs direction.

A particularly negative aspect of the Nurturing Parent is the tendency to rescue others instead of helping them. Rescuing someone can make the rescuer feel powerful, but it creates a dependency relationship and reduces the ability of the rescued person to be accountable and responsible for his own decisions and actions. Positive aspects of the Critical Parent and the Nurturing Parent are visible in a person's ability to extract right from wrong, make decisions, and fix mistakes. However, either version of this ego state is unproductive as a communication style for coaching because the "I know better" attitude permeates the communication. In addition, there is always a certain degree of arrogance associated with this ego state because of the embedded sense of superiority.

The Parent Ego State

| Critical | Judgmental |
| Nurturing | Rescuing |

Sample Words and Messages

Should . . . Don't . . . Must . . . Ought . . . Always . . . Never . . . Now what . . . If I were you . . . Let me help you . . . Because I said so . . . Don't ask questions . . . Don't be ridiculous . . . Be good . . . What will the neighbors say . . . There, there . . . Sweetie . . . Dearie.
You are: Bad . . . Good . . . Stupid . . . Ugly . . . Beautiful . . . Smart . . . Ridiculous . . . Naughty . . . Evil . . . Talented . . . Horrible . . . A blessing . . . A brat . . . An angel . . . Absurd . . . Asinine.
Try . . . Don't be afraid . . . come on now . . . See . . . It doesn't hurt . . . Don't worry . . . I'll take care of you . . . Here's something to make you feel better.

Gestures and Postures

Pointing an accusing or threatening finger. A pat on the back. Consoling touch. Pounding on the table. Rolling eyes upward in disgust. Tapping feet or wringing hands in impatience. Shaking head to imply "no-no!" Arms folded across chest with chin set. Face tilted up. Looking down your nose. Holding and/or rocking someone.

Tone of Voice

Sneering . . . Punitive . . . Condescending . . . Encouraging . . . Supportive . . . Sympathetic.

Facial Expressions

Scowl . . . Encouraging nod . . . Furrowed brow . . . Set jaw . . . Angry . . . Sympathetic or proud eyes . . . Frown . . . Loving . . . Hostile . . . Disapproving.

Parent ego state communication is exhibited by everyone on a daily basis. People have had plenty of opportunities to become skilled at interacting from this ego state because they have experienced it since childhood. Parents speak with the voice of authority, demand to be listened to, and expect an acquiescent, obedient response. When a person communicates from the Parent ego state he or she expects the same thing. Parent ego state interactions abound in the field of healthcare, and physicians are particularly susceptible to this style of communication. In addition, Parent ego state communication is reinforced in physicians by three external influences: (a) patients who look up to them; (b) role models they have as teachers and supervisors; and (c) society's tendency to placed them on a pedestal.

Since doctors interact primarily with patients, their view of the world is often restricted to that narrow perspective. Patients look to them for advice, direction, and sometimes lifesaving interventions. While this is ego boosting in itself, their authority figure role is reinforced by having nurses and assistants following their every directive. Second, during medical training and residency teachers and supervisors continuously model Parent ego state communication. Young physicians quickly learn that they are expected to take charge, speak with the power of their profession, and provide answers for the problems they are charged with solving, and being wrong is not acceptable. Finally, society rewards their efforts by attaching a great deal of prestige to the profession. Television, movies, and print media create an aura of invincibility and power associated with being "a doctor." The roles of doctor as played in various TV series and movies reinforce the "I know it all" thinking pattern. The result of these influences is that, even if it is not their natural style, by the time physicians have completed their professional training they have mastered Parent ego state communication.

THE CHILD EGO STATE

The complement to the Parent ego state is the Child ego state. The Child ego state is not age dependent; adults operate out of the Child ego state a fair amount of time. For example, having fun and kidding around with friends is an expression of the Child ego state. People also convey this ego state when they adapt to, and follow, the directives and rules set by authority figures or society. The Child ego state is characterized by words, tones, gestures, postures, and facial expressions that communicate obedience to the directives, desires, and the wishes of another; an acceptance of, and willingness to follow, social or societal norms; a playful attitude. When the Child ego state is immaturely expressed one sees emotional reactions to events;

a sense of helplessness and victimization; rebelliousness and resistance to authority. There are two themes associated with the Child ego state: a theme of compliance and adaptation, and a theme of emotional spontaneity and fun. These aspects of the Child ego state can be useful and have an important role in our interactions with others. As with the Parent ego state, the Child ego state can be expressed along two continuums: complying/helpless and playful/emotional.

Sample Words and Messages

Gosh . . . Wow . . . Gee whiz . . . Can't . . . Won't . . . Want . . . Wish . . . Mine . . . Aren't I cute . . . Look at me now . . . Did I do all right . . . I'm scared . . . Help me . . . Do it for me . . . Nobody loves me . . . You make me angry . . . It's your fault . . . I didn't do it . . . He's no good . . . Mine is better than yours . . . I'm going to tell . . . You'll be sorry . . . Let's have fun . . . The heck with this job . . . I hope everybody likes me.

Gestures and Postures

Slumped. Dejected. Temper tantrums. Flirting. Joyful or exhilarated posture. Curling up. Squirming. Obscene gestures. Nail biting. Raising hand to speak.

Tone of Voice

Giggling . . . Whining . . . Manipulating . . . Sweet talk . . . Asking permission . . . Swearing . . . Spiteful . . . Teasing . . . Sullen silence . . . Taunting . . . Needling . . . Belly laughing . . . Excitement . . . Talking fast and loud . . . Playfulness.

Facial Expression

Teary eyed . . . Pouting . . . Eyes looking upward at another . . . Downcast eyes . . . Joyfulness . . . Excited . . . Curious . . . Tilted head . . . Flirty . . . Looking innocent and wide-eyed . . . Woe-be-gone . . . Helplessness . . . Admiration.

In the example between the Leader and the new staff member, the new staff member is acting out of a Child ego state by playing the role of the victim and communicating a sense of helplessness. She responds to the advice of the leader with words and phrases that communicate "there's nothing I can do because I've tried everything, and it's not working because it's her fault." In the meantime, the leader is operating from the Parent ego state, takes on the responsibility for providing a solution, and doesn't like it when she won't follow his advice. At the end of the conversation, the staff member lets her emotional frustration show and blames the leader for not helping her (the helpless victim), to which the leader responds with subtle criticism (the critical parent).

PARENT-CHILD INTERACTIONS

When one person in a conversation communicates from the Parent ego state, there is an unstated expectation that the person to whom he or she is speaking will listen and heed their words. Thus, implicit within a Parent ego state communication is the anticipation that it will produce a Child (Compliant) ego state response. The same dynamic occurs when someone reaches out from a Child ego state for help. The expectation is that the other person will tell them what to do or perhaps even solve the problem for them. The Child ego state expects a Parent (Nurturing) ego state response. The codependent nature of these two ego states creates a *complementary* transaction known as a Parent-Child interaction. For better or worse, when a Parent-Child interaction occurs, both parties are carrying out their corresponding roles.

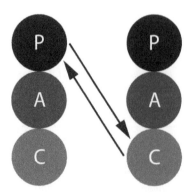

Parent-Child interactions are not without their value in a helping conversation. If you have put on your teaching hat, you will want the other person to pay attention and comply with what you are teaching them. A natural asymmetrical power relationship occurs because of the expert power role assumed by the teacher. In the role of mentor, offering advice and giving your opinions may also involve a Parent-Child interaction. However, Parent-Child interactions must be used judiciously because they are, by nature, power-based and contrary to the collegial relationship needed for helping conversations. A power-based transaction is asymmetrical; there is a person in the "one-up" position, the position of power, and a person who is in the "one-down," or subordinate, position. This ranking has nothing to do with the actual position, status, or formal role of each party. It is created by the dynamics of the Parent-Child exchange. Asymmetrical conversations are counterproductive to the coaching process.

When coaching, it is not your role to diagnose and solve the other person's problem. Your role is to help her think through her situation in such a way that she is able to develop her problem-solving abilities and mature as a professional. In a working alliance, you create a dialogue with the person so that, together, you discover the best means to achieve her desired outcomes. Such an alliance requires symmetrical, or collegially based, interactions where there are opportunities for exploration, reflection, and solution-building. In Transactional Analysis terms, this necessitates engaging in Adult-to-Adult conversations.

THE ADULT EGO STATE

Communicating from the Adult ego state sends a message of parity, reasonableness, and objectivity. When thoughts are expressed, there is neither a judgmental attitude nor a sense of superiority present in the person's demeanor. The communication is relaxed, and the person is attentive, modulated, and speaks with a level tone-of-voice. The attitude and behaviors convey a message of "let's think through this together." Inquiry is a central focus of the Adult ego state.

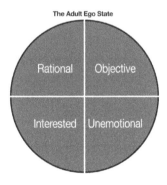

The Adult Ego State

Rational	Objective
Interested	Unemotional

Sample Words and Phrases

How . . . When . . . Who . . . What . . . Where . . . Why . . . Probability . . . Alternative . . . Result . . . Yes . . . No . . . What are the facts . . . This is not proven, but opinion . . . Check it out . . . What has been done to correct it so far . . . Four people have spoken to me about the problem. . . . What are the reasons . . . Have you tried this . . . Mix two parts with one part . . . This is how it works . . . Let's take it apart and look at it . . . Let's look for a solution . . . According to the statistics . . . Change is indicated . . . The meeting is at 2:00 p.m. Friday.

Gestures and Postures

Straight (not stiff) posture. Eye contact that is level. Listening by giving feedback and checking out understanding. Interested. The absence of Parent ego state body language.

Tone of Voice

Clear, without undue emotion . . . Calm . . . Straight . . . Confident . . . Inquiring . . . Providing information.

Facial Expression

Thoughtful . . . Watching attentively . . . Quizzical . . . Active . . . Here and now responsiveness . . . Eyes alert . . . Confident.

Let's reexamine the previous conversation, but with the senior colleague communicating from the Adult ego state. Notice how this approach will elicit different responses from the staff member as compared to the previous Parent-Child exchange.

New Staff Member: *I don't think Mary is being very cooperative. I keep asking her to do some things differently on the front desk, and she just refuses to help. I don't know what to do.*
Senior Colleague: *What have you tried so far?*
New Staff Member: *I've tried giving her the benefit of the doubt.*
Senior Colleague: *In what way have you tried giving her the benefit of the doubt?*
New Staff Member: *I just let it go and figure that she's in a bad mood or very busy and sooner or later she'll come around, but it hasn't worked.*
Senior Colleague: *Have you thought about trying something different with her? Maybe there are some things you can do to help her.*
New Staff Member: *Yes, but she needs to cooperate too.*
Senior Colleague: *I agree, and I've found that sometimes taking the first step works out well. What do you think you can do that might cause her to cooperate a little more than she has?*
New Staff Member: *I've tried a lot of things, but they haven't worked.*
Senior Colleague: *Well, let's talk about what you tried and maybe we can come up with something that might work. What do you think?*
New Staff Member: *That sounds good. Maybe I've missed something.*

The conversation takes on a different tone when the leader communicates from the Adult Ego State. Adult ego state communication attempts to produce a complementary ego state response in the other person. In other words, communicating from your Adult ego state will increase the probability that you will trigger an Adult ego state response in return.

COMMUNICATING FROM THE ADULT EGO STATE

Communicating from the Adult ego state during your coaching conversations will create a working alliance that promotes Support-for-Thought. Admittedly, it is not always easy to do, particularly when the subject matter is emotionally charged or of high professional interest, and about which you have strong opinions. Nevertheless, doing so is an essential condition for successful coaching. There are four guidelines that will help you communicate from the Adult ego state:

- Use owned language.
- Practice disciplined listening.
- Maintain congruent communication.
- Use verbal softeners.

OWNED LANGUAGE

Taking personal responsibility is a characteristic of the Adult ego state. Personal responsibility is conveyed by the use of *owned* language. Ideas, opinions, beliefs, feelings, and preferences are "owned" by verbalizing them from a personal point-of-view rather than as external "truths" espoused from a position of infallibility. By using owned language in your communication, you increase the probability that the other person will remain open and non-defensive. Guidelines for using owned language emphasize communicating from an "I" perspective and being accountable for one's thoughts, actions, and feelings.

Think and Speak in Terms of Preferences Rather Than Shoulds

Note the difference between the following statements "*You should* talk with me first before involving other people in this decision" and "*I would prefer* that you talk to me first before involving other people in this decision." Both statements communicate your wish or desire, but the difference between "You should" and "I would prefer" is major. It is the difference between a Parent ego state communication and an Adult ego state communication. The use of "You should" and its derivatives (i.e., "You need to"; "You must"; "You have to") is invasive because the use of these pressure words amount to a form of verbal finger-pointing. Most people don't like it when you point your finger at them in the course of a conversation, and yet the use of "You" language is tantamount to the same thing: verbal finger pointing. Whether intentional or not, the use of a "You should" statement, or any other statement that uses pressure words, creates an implicit Parent-Child interaction, which may cause resistance in the other person.

Expressing your wants and wishes from an "I" perspective is more effective. When you use "I-language" (e.g., "I would prefer" or "I would like it if "), you are neither commanding nor condemning. Instead, you are simply asking for what you want. It may seem like splitting hairs, but remember the adage, "It's not what you say, but how you say it." Obviously, avoiding the use of "You should" or its derivatives, doesn't apply when using it as part of a conditional statement. For example, "You should put the package in this afternoon's mail" could be part of an "If-then" condition. As in, "If you want the package to get there by tomorrow, then you will need to put it in this afternoon's mail." Using "You should" as part of a conditional statement is actually a rational conclusion; therefore, it functions as Adult ego state communication. When used in this way, a "You should" statement is acceptable.

Sometimes well-meaning advice is delivered as a "should." For example, suppose the senior colleague in the above example said to the new staff member, "You should tell her how you feel." The colleague is giving a suggestion, but expressing it in the form of a "should" statement; therefore, it is indistinguishable from a parent-like directive. It is better using I-language statements, such as "I believe it will help if you tell her how you feel." Then, there is no confusion between a helpful suggestion from the Adult ego state, and a Parent statement of what should, need, or must be done.

Separate Your Personal Conclusions and Opinions from Facts

If you express a conclusion or opinion without owning it, such as "That idea won't work," it sounds as if you are stating an objective, undeniable fact. Statements of fact are undeniable truths, e.g., "That is a chair"; and "The sun is in the sky." However, it is easy to make statements of opinion sound like you are stating a fact, e.g., "That idea won't work." When you state your conclusions or opinions as facts, you are communicating from a Parent ego state, where conclusions and opinions are the same as undeniable truths. Conversely, expressing *owned* conclusions, opinions, and beliefs will allow you to avoid communicating in a Parent-like manner. Prior to giving your opinion, use introductory phrases that make it clear you are coming from a personal perspective. Introductory phrases (such as "From my perspective"; "The way I see it is"; "Speaking for myself, I find that") clearly separate statements of opinion from statements of fact. For example, by saying, "It's my belief that there are problems with this idea, and I don't think it will work," you will make your point using owned language while avoiding absolute statements that are characteristic of the Parent ego state. By doing so, you implicitly suggest that, based upon new information, your conclusion or opinion may change—a sign of open mindedness. It is not a question of being right; you may very well be right in that your conclusion is supported by a wealth of experience or overwhelming evidence. It is a matter of process; a matter of saying things in a way that will maintain Adult-to-Adult communication.

During a coaching conversation, while you may separate your personal conclusions and opinions from facts, the person you are helping may not. When you hear disowned language it is an opportunity for you to subtly modify their language by restating what they have said in owned language. For example, if the person says, "She doesn't care about cooperating with me," you may decide to rephrase it for the person as, "You mean it is your *belief* that she doesn't care about cooperating with you." By doing so, you compel the person to reevaluate their statement from an Adult ego state perspective.

Own Your Emotional Reactions

Life happens, and when it does, there are occasions when we have a negative emotional reaction to what we have experienced. When this occurs, it is natural to say things like "That made me mad" or "You upset me." However, this is a disowned response because it places the cause of your emotional reaction outside yourself. While you may feel frustrated or angry, the event itself did not cause your feelings, it was your thinking *about* the event that produced your emotional reaction.

When you respond to another person's behavior with negative feelings, and you wish to communicate your feelings to that person, phrase your statements about what you feel in a way that keeps the responsibility for those feelings with you. Change your language from a "You made me" response to one that describes the event followed by how *you* reacted to it. For example, "You frustrated me when you didn't follow through" becomes "I felt frustrated when I didn't get what I expected." This does not guarantee an apology or understanding by the other person, but it does remove the "finger of blame" that is injected into the conversation by making others responsible for your feelings.

PRACTICE DISCIPLINED LISTENING

Listening is not always easy; in fact, it requires discipline. Listening is much more effective when you do so from the Adult ego state and not the Parent ego state. The Parent ego state makes you susceptible to two practices that interfere with Adult-to-Adult communication: the Righting Reflex and judgmental listening. In chapter two, you were introduced to the concept of the Righting Reflex: the instinctive inclination to offer advice in the form of an answer or solution in order to correct a problem, or set things right. This tendency stems from the fact that when people perceive that something is wrong, they want to fix it. This is especially true when you attempt to help someone from your Parent ego state. The righting reflex is an example of the Parent ego state in overdrive.

When your Righting Reflex kicks in, you stop listening and interject your ideas into the conversation, often interrupting the other person in the process. This process of interrupting is called a disconfirming response (Beebe, 2005). A disconfirming response suggests that you don't care about what the other person has to say and, by extension, you don't care about the person. To avoid disconfirming responses, such as interrupting to tell the person what to do, maintain the information gathering mindset that typifies the Adult ego state. Disciplined listening requires that you keep the righting reflex under control.

Value-based judgments come from the Parent ego state. Judgments made from the Adult ego state are a product of information analyzed and logical conclusions drawn. Judgmental listening occurs when, during the process of listening, you begin evaluating what the person is saying according to criteria such as right or wrong, and good or bad—both according to your opinion. Judgmental listening takes you out of the "I want to understand" mindset. Learning to listen without making value-based judgments requires discipline, but it is necessary for Adult-to-Adult communication.

MAINTAIN CONGRUENT COMMUNICATION

Communication is very much like a song in that it has words and music. The words are what you say, and the music is how you say it. Adult-to-Adult communication is not only a product of I-language and using emotionally neutral words and phrases, but delivering a congruent message with your tone-of-voice and body language. If I say—in a sarcastic tone-of-voice—"Did you get in touch with Alan as we discussed?", it is not really a question. There is an implied "I bet you didn't" judgment indicative of the Critical Parent. If the same inquiry is made, but in a neutral, inquisitive tone, the inquiry will likely be heard by the other person as an attempt to seek information coming from the Adult ego state. Congruent communication requires that your non-verbal cues remain consistent with your message. This means managing:

- Body language (e.g., posture, body movements, and gestures)
- Facial expressions (e.g., smiles, frowns, raised eyebrows, eye contact)
- Tone of voice (e.g., pitch, volume, intensity, inflection, emphasis, and use of silence)

One way to describe Adult ego state "music" is that it is a neutral, inquisitive tone-of-voice (and body language) that signals "We are colleagues and I am interested in what you have to say." It is similar to the background music you might hear in a department store, in that it is there to enhance, but not interfere with your experience.

USE VERBAL SOFTENERS

Verbal softeners are often helpful in transforming what might be misconstrued as a Parent-like statement or inquiry into one that is being delivered in an Adult-to-Adult manner. Verbal softeners are additional words or phrases that tone down or soften the directness of a statement or inquiry and, therefore, diminish the risk that it may come across as excessively authoritative or confrontational. For example, the previous inquiry "Did you get in touch with Alan as we discussed?" was considered to be incongruent with the Adult ego state when delivered with a Parent-like tone. This can be avoided by adding verbal softeners, such as "Perhaps"; "Maybe"; "Somewhat"; "I was wondering"; "You might want to"; "I'm curious"; "You may want to consider." When using verbal softeners with that same question it would sound like this, "*I'm curious* if you *had a chance* to get in touch with Alan as we discussed?" Notice how the phrases "I am curious" and "had a chance" reduce the possibility that the speaker may come across in a Parent-like manner.

Using verbal softeners also allow you to make suggestions without sounding as if you are telling the listener what to do. In the conversation between the new staff member and her senior colleague, it may be appropriate for the colleague to make a suggestion in order to help the new staff member (e.g., recommending to her that she tell Mary how she feels when she doesn't receive the cooperation she expects). A person who is communicating from a Parent ego state might say "You should tell her how you feel," thereby creating a Parent-Child interaction. In contrast, the Adult ego state version—with verbal softeners—is phrased as, "*You might want to consider* telling her how you feel." This allows the person to decide whether to take the advice or not, and in the process, conveys to the person that she has the final control over, and responsibility for, what she decides to do.

COACHING AS A LEADERSHIP STYLE

When leading Elite Professionals, the mantle of leadership alone does not guarantee cooperation, let alone compliance. Elite Professionals respond out of respect, not out of deference to position. Respect is a product of the Idealized Influence component of transformational leadership. Leaders who exhibit Idealized Influence are admired, respected, and trusted. There is a desire on the part of followers to identify with the leader, and even emulate her if the leader is viewed as a role model. There are several behaviors that, if exhibited, will build Idealized Influence: persistence in pursuing objectives, sacrificing self-gain for the gain of others, willingness to share the limelight, celebrating followers' achievements, to name a few. However, maintaining Adult-to-Adult communication is a principal means of role-modeling respectful communication practices. Parent-Child interactions, although selectively useful, do not communicate respect.

Adult-to-Adult communication fosters a symmetrical power relationship characterized by collegial interactions. If the coaching relationship is not based upon a symmetrical power relationship, a working alliance will not flourish. Likewise, if a leader does not build collegial relationships—based on respect—his or her Idealized Influence will be reduced. A coach-like approach to interacting with others, as conveyed by Adult-to-Adult communication, can be used in all conversations, thus, serving as another means for demonstrating transformational leadership.

Chapter 5

Support-for-Thought
Intelligent Listening

By bringing a desire to help, building rapport, and communicating from the Adult ego state you are well on your way to accomplishing the stage-specific activities that are a part of Support-for-Thought. However, there is one more very important stage-related activity, i.e., clarifying the narrative of the person you are coaching. In a helping conversation, there is always a point of departure. The point of departure is a narrative or story that describes a person's current situation or problem as she sees it. However, people's stories don't arrive in a nice, neat package. They are often a loosely knit web of incomplete information, vague issues, hidden concerns, and implicit goals. In a manner of speaking, a person's narrative, as presented, is only the tip of the iceberg.

Example

Martha is one of your best staff members. She comes to you with a look of concern on her face and asks if you have a few minutes. Fortunately, it is a good time for you, and you say "Sure, what's going on?" Martha begins her story.

"I'm feeling stuck right now. I have a sense that I should be more proactively involved in advancing my career. I'm happy with what I'm doing, but I feel as if I'm missing something. I'm at a point where I feel if I don't make a concerted effort in order to advance my career in some way, opportunities will pass me by, and I'll have no choice but to stay where I am. I have to challenge myself. What do you think I should do?"

What do you do now? Where do you go from here? One answer to these questions is to better understand her story by clarifying her narrative. This requires that you become skilled in intelligent listening and understand the use of questions.

QUESTIONS ARE MAGICAL

If you could have anything in the world, what would it be? Think about it. A question like this is irresistible. It forces you to think, and even if your answer is "I don't know," you must still pause, reflect, and focus your attention on the intent of the question. In many ways, questions are almost magical because they do so many things.

Questions Are Compelling

It is virtually impossible not to respond to a good question. Questions stimulate the mind and people are compelled to answer them. Hearing a question puts people on alert and lets them know that they are expected to do more than listen; they are expected to respond. Because most people prefer talking to listening, when sincerely asked for their ideas, opinions, and thoughts, they will freely share what's on their mind. Even tough questions can be engaging, especially if you use the correct technique in setting them up. In the situation described above, Martha feels stuck in her career and doesn't know what to do. Suppose you have had several conversations to date and, even though you have helped her to come up with some actions to escape her quandary, she has not followed through on any of them, so you ask her the following question, *What's stopping you from following through on any of the actions you've come up with so far?* This is a compelling question and can stimulate her thinking about how she might be getting in her own way, but it is also a tough question.

Questions, especially tough questions, become even more compelling when you lead with a statement that sets up the question. For example, *I'd like to ask you a question you may not have considered, what do you believe is stopping you from following through on any of the actions you've come up with so far?* The initial setup really gains the person's attention (Gee, I wonder what he's going to ask me?). While the question itself may be tough, in part because the person has not thought about it before, by indicating this in advance it softens the delivery and induces interest.

Questions Direct Attention

Questions are like a spotlight in a dark room; they focus the person's attention (and therefore her thinking) toward whatever is "lit up" by that particular question. Have you ever had someone say, *"Wow, good question"* or *"I haven't thought about that before"* in response to something you've asked them? Such a reaction usually indicates that your question focused the person's attention upon something new, something she hadn't considered before; therefore, questions may also increase insight. When people are forced to provide an answer to a question they've never considered, or have only partly thought about, they are forced to self-reflect. Self-reflection is a conscious and purposive process whereby a person examines his thoughts and feelings around a particular subject. Insightful questions lead to insightful self-reflection, which increases self-awareness. For example, by asking Martha the question *"What do you believe is stopping you from following through on any of the actions that you've come up with so far?"*; her attention is directed towards uncovering the blocks that are impeding action. As she reflects on this question, it opens up the possibility that Martha will gain new insights into herself, what's holding her back, and what she really wants from her career. The question directs her attention to one area of thought while simultaneously directing it away from another. Therefore, questions become a means by which you can help people focus on thoughts and ideas that are useful while avoiding thoughts that are unproductive.

Questions Are Empowering

All questions contain presuppositions. A presupposition is an implicit belief, the truth of which is taken for granted. For example, the question *"What are your biggest challenges on the job?"* contains the implicit belief that you have challenges at work. Understanding this concept enables you to frame questions so that they contain empowering presuppositions. If you ask the person, *"What will you do once you've reached your goal?"*, you will have embedded an empowering presupposition, specifically, that you believe the person *will* reach their goal. In answering that question, the person will have implicitly accepted this empowering presupposition. On the other hand, the following question introduces an element of doubt by incorporating the words "If" and "might": *"If you are able to reach your goal, what might you do?"* A good rule of thumb is to embed empowering presuppositions into your coaching questions whenever possible.

It is also helpful to recognize questions that contain disempowering presuppositions. For example, asking a question such as *"What did she do that upset you?"* incorporates two presuppositions: (a) the other person actually did something to upset the person you are helping; and (b) the other person caused the person you are helping to become upset. Notice the difference if you were to ask *"How did you allow yourself to become upset by what happened?"* The presupposition embedded in this question is that the person "allowed" himself to become upset and is, therefore, in control of his emotions and can choose how he will react. Always be aware of the presuppositions that are embedded within your questions.

Questions Suggest Ideas

When you are engaged in a helping conversation, you will be wearing one or more of the helping hats: teaching, mentoring, or coaching. When teaching or mentoring, you are providing advice based upon what you know through your educational or personal experience. When coaching you are helping the person without *directly* offering advice, but there are still times when suggesting an idea is appropriate. In either case, it is most helpful to provide your ideas in a "coach-like" fashion and from the Adult ego state. Questions can help you do this.

You are speaking with a colleague about a problem with her schedule. She is an ICU nurse, and continually finds herself scheduled for shifts when there are events in which she would like to participate. Recently, for example, there was a dinner scheduled for the annual Christmas party and, as usual, she was assigned a shift that wouldn't allow her to attend. She is clearly frustrated and doesn't know what to do since she has already mentioned this to her nurse manager, and nothing has changed. You know the doctor who is in charge of the operating room and, based upon your past conversations with him, believe he would be a good person to talk to because he has expressed to you his desire to see the unit function well. One of the points he has made to you is that he doesn't want people coming to work angry because it can affect the attitudes in the ICU and, ultimately, creates problems that can affect patient care.

You can suggest the idea of talking to him in different ways:

"You need to talk to Dr. Smith; he's always been a champion for the unit and wants it to function well."

"Why don't you talk to Dr. Smith; he's always been a champion for the unit and wants it to function well."

"Have you thought about talking to Dr. Smith? I know that he's always been a champion for the unit and wants it to function well."

The first two statements dictate what the person should do because they contain pressure words. They can easily become Parent-like statements if delivered the wrong way. The third method, however, uses a question to suggest an idea. It cleverly plants your idea in the other person's mind where the person can then develop it as her own.

Questions Elicit Emotions

Thinking about situations evokes emotions connected to those situations. If I ask you, "What's the worst part of working with Fred?", you will need to think about any negative experiences you have had working with Fred, and in the process, you will have no choice but to re-experience any negative emotions associated with those experiences. Now, suppose I ask you to think of a time when you have been able to work with Fred in a way that was positive. Embedded within this question is the presupposition that there has been at least one time where you *have* been able to work with Fred in a more positive or productive way, and there will be a positive emotion associated with that memory. Not only will your emotional state be better, but there is also hope that if you have been able to work with Fred successfully before, you may be able to do it again. Positive emotional reactions are part of a solution-focused conversation.

A young physician in training is taking care of a patient with congestive heart failure. She knows that the attending physician will ask her penetrating questions about the patient, the disease, and the treatment options. While she believes she knows her stuff, she is worried that in front of her peers, the patient, and the professor, she will appear uncertain and less capable because of her anxiety about presenting before others. You can almost feel her anxiety as she explains her situation.

If you ask her the question, *"What makes you worried that you won't be able to perform well in that situation"* what is the effect on her emotional state? This question may be valid, but the nature of the question directs her attention to those present, or past, experiences that have led her to believe that she might not be capable. It does nothing to help her feel more confident and may actually increase her anxiety. Instead, ask, *"When was there a situation where you were in front of others but were able to do well, in spite of the circumstances?"* Not only do you imbed an empowering presupposition into the question, but you focus her attention on a time when she was successful in a similar situation. By doing so, you elicit positive emotions associated with that success.

Questions Clarify

Questions are used to clarify a person's narrative; to make a person's story less confused and more clearly comprehensible for you and for the person you are helping by filling in missing information. Clarifying a person's narrative is a key objective in the Support-for-Thought stage of the Four-square Coaching Framework. Remember Martha? She is confused about what to do in order to advance her career. Most leaders would offer reassurance and make suggestions, but before you can help Martha, you will need to build a platform of understanding about her current situation. To do that requires intelligent listening.

INTELLIGENT LISTENING
A Map Is Not the Territory

Language is the primary means by which people represent and communicate their perceptions about the world. If I say to you, "I'm having trouble working with Fred," those words represent and communicate my view about my experience with Fred. To put it another way, those words are a linguistic representation of my perceived experience. According to Korzybski, the father of general semantics, language is analogous to a map because just as a map is a representation of a territory and not the territory itself, language is only a representation of our experience and not the experience itself. "A map is *not* the territory it represents, but, if correct, it has a *similar structure* to the territory, which accounts for its usefulness" (Korzybski, 1994, p. 58). In other words, language, functioning as a map, is useful only to the degree that it accurately describes the territory it represents, namely one's subjective experience of the world.

Suppose you are using Google Maps to find a specific location. When the map first opens it defaults to a high-level view. If left there, it is not very useful for finding the location you want. People's linguistic maps function similarly; when a person begins his narrative his "map-of-the-world" defaults to a high-level view. As a result, important information is left out making it difficult to help him, or more accurately, making it difficult for him to help himself. The explanation for this phenomenon is that people generally communicate using Surface Structures (Bandler & Grinder, 1975). Surface Structure language is any communication that is missing the requisite detail to represent the person's complete linguistic representation of his experience. For example, if a person says to you, *"I'm having trouble working with Fred,"* this statement is missing important details (e.g., the kind of trouble, the reasoning that leads the person to conclude he is having trouble, what he wants from Fred that he is not experiencing, etc.). In short, the person's map is incomplete and, therefore, not accurate enough to do what maps are supposed to do (i.e., help navigate to a desired destination).

Imagine you are helping a friend drive from Lima, Peru, to Rio de Janeiro, Brazil, but the only map you have is at such a scale that it shows the cities but not the roads. From the map, you would be able see that you need to travel from the west coast to the east coast of South America, but good luck making it there. If you are to help your friend it would be essential that you recognize that the map is missing important details; namely, the specific roads and highways needed to plan and execute your trip. It is the role of a coach to recognize when important details are missing from the person's narrative and recover them.

Intelligent listening means listening for deleted information in a person's Surface Structure language and then asking intelligent questions to "zoom in" on their linguistic map so that a useful level of detail is revealed. This is a two-part process: (1) recognizing important deletions, and (2) constructing inquiries that can recover the deleted information. Fortunately, for most people this is an intuitive process once their attention is on listening for deletions and they know how to ask penetrating questions.

Recovering Deletions

The purpose of recovering deletions is to assist the other person in restoring a fuller linguistic representation of his experiences. Recovering deletions clarify the narrative and, in the process, clarify thinking—a valuable part of providing Support-for-Thought. Bandler and Grinder (1975) identified a variety of deletions, but there are four types of deletions that, when recovered, will help you fill in a person's linguistic map in order to build a platform of understanding. The author has taken the liberty of relabeling those used in this book for the purposes of clarity.

■ Unnamed references
■ Unspecified actions
■ Unchallenged pressure words
■ Unstated reasoning

Unnamed References

The easiest way to begin to understand unnamed references is to start with the most obvious. What is unnamed in the following sentence?

"They need to understand our situation."

The most obvious unnamed reference is "they." The speaker is referring to a group of people, but not naming who he or she is referencing. In all fairness, many times in the context of the conversation you will intuitively know to whom the person is referring. Nevertheless, it is not uncommon for a person to provide you a narrative which contains Surface Structure language that refers to a person or a group but without naming them. If it is important information, then recover it.

If people deleted only unnamed persons from their linguistic map, your job as an intelligent listener would be simplified, but that is not the case because there are unnamed references in people's communication that may not be as obvious. Examine this same sentence, *"They need to understand our situation."* What else is unnamed in this Surface Structure statement? What about the word *"understand"*? What is it *specifically* that they need to understand about "our situation?" Notice that this question would help to zoom in on their map so that more detail can be added. There is also an unnamed reference with respect to the word "situation." No specific situation is identified; therefore, one cannot be sure about the situation being referenced. In this simple Surface Structure statement, there were three unnamed references.

Who, specifically, needs to understand our situation?

"They need to understand our situation."

What specific situation?

What, specifically, do they need to understand about our situation?

Let's Review Martha's Narrative for Unnamed References:

"I'm <u>feeling stuck</u> *right now. I have a sense that I should be more proactively involved in* <u>advancing my career</u>*. I'm happy with what I'm doing but I feel as if I'm* <u>missing something</u>*. I'm at a point where I feel if I don't make a concerted effort in order to advance my career in some way* <u>opportunities</u> *will pass me by and I'll have no choice but to stay where I am. I have to challenge myself. What do you think I should do?"*

These intelligent inquiries will recover the unnamed references in Martha's narrative.

- In what way are you "feeling stuck right now"?
- What aspect of your career "should you be involved in advancing"?
- What specifically are you "missing"?
- What "opportunities will pass" you by?

Unspecified Actions

Another common deletion occurs when a person's Surface Structure contains words or phrases that convey an action but does not specify the behavior associated with that action. The specific words that you would listen for are called *action verbs*. Action verbs express something that a person can do. For example, "cooperate" and "help" are action verbs. Consider the following Surface Structure statement and notice the questions we would use to zoom in on the person's linguistic map to add clarity to this simple narrative.

What **do** we need to do (specifically) to help our clinical staff cooperate?

"We need to help our clinical staff cooperate with each other."

What does the clinical staff need to **do** to cooperate with each other?

The purpose of these questions is to define the *actions* that need to occur, in the opinion of the speaker. Recognizing unspecified actions becomes very important when you are helping a person move toward some goal. Most of the time, people will use statements like, *"I want to influence my direct reports in a positive way."* If you have your coaching hat on, you will recognize that it might be helpful to challenge a person to tell you what she is specifically going to *do* to influence her direct reports in a positive way. By being specific about what she is going to do, she is more likely to achieve her objective. Now, let's again review Martha's narrative for unspecified actions.

> *"I'm feeling stuck right now. I have a sense that I should be more <u>proactively</u> involved in advancing my career. I'm happy with what I'm doing but I feel as if I'm missing something. I'm at a point where I feel if I don't make a concerted effort in order to advance my career in some way opportunities will pass me by and I'll have no choice but to stay where I am. I have to <u>challenge</u> myself. What do you think I should do?"*

These intelligent inquiries will recover unspecified actions found in the phrase "I have to challenge myself."

- What can you do, specifically, to "challenge" yourself?
- How are you going to "challenge" yourself?

Did you notice that there is another word that suggests action? The word *proactively* is, technically speaking, an adverb. An adverb answers questions that begin with "how," "when," "where," and "how much." The Surface Structure, *"more proactively involved,"* is describing *how* something should occur. In this example, it is how Martha thinks she should be in advancing her career, but because it is still a Surface Structure statement it needs more clarity. Asking the question, *"How are you going to be more proactively involved in managing your career?"* will help clarify her thinking so that she creates a more useful internal map to guide her.

It is not important that you know about parts of speech (e.g., verbs, adverbs, etc.). What is important is to recognize when someone is describing an action, but does not specify the behaviors that will actually make the action happen. In other words, use your intuition, and listening skills, to guide you when the person you are coaching does not provide a complete, and useful, linguistic map. If you listen with the intent of clarifying the person's narrative, your own intuitive grasp of language will be sufficient to help the person specify behaviors that will make her statements actionable.

More Unnamed References

Let's review the statement, *"We need to help our clinical staff cooperate with each other."* We know that the words "help" and "cooperate" contain unspecified actions, but they also contain unnamed references.

What type of help (specifically)?

"We need to help our clinical staff cooperate with each other."

What (specific) type of cooperation is needed?

By recovering the unnamed references associated with action verbs, you may add even more clarity to their narrative.

"I'm feeling stuck right now. I have a sense that I should be <u>more proactively involved</u> in advancing my career. I'm happy with what I'm doing but I feel like I'm missing something. I'm at a point where I feel if I don't make a concerted effort to advance my career in some way opportunities will pass me by and I'll have no choice but to stay where I am. I have to <u>challenge myself</u>. What do you think I should do?"

The following intelligent inquiries will recover the unnamed references associated with unspecified verbs in Martha's narrative.

- In what way should you "be more proactively involved"?
- In what way do you "have to challenge" yourself?

Unchallenged Pressure Words

If you recall, pressure words are words, or short phrases, such as "should"; "shouldn't"; "must"; "mustn't"; "have to"; "need to"; and so forth. Pressure words have the power to control, direct, or restrain the individual. These words signal that embedded in the person's map-of-the-world is an internal directive that must be followed— or else. Consider this statement, "I should confront Fred about his behavior." The deleted information in this short narrative is what would happen if the person didn't confront Fred about his behavior. By challenging the person to explain what would happen if the person did or didn't follow their linguistic directive, a clearer picture of the person's internal world emerges. For example, an "I shouldn't " statement can be challenged by asking, "What would happen if you did. . .?"; or an "I have to " statement can be challenged by asking, "What would happen if you didn't. . .?" Challenging the internal directives associated with pressure words provides another way of clarifying Martha's narrative.

"I'm feeling stuck right now. I have a sense that <u>I should be</u> more proactively involved in advancing my career. I'm happy with what I'm doing but I feel as if I'm missing something. I'm at a point where I feel if I don't make a concerted effort in order to advance my career in some way opportunities will pass me by and I'll have no choice but to stay where I am. <u>I have to</u> challenge myself. What do you think I should do?"

These intelligent inquiries will challenge the internal directives associated with the pressure words in Martha's narrative.

- What would happen if you weren't more "proactively involved"?
- What would happen if you didn't "challenge" yourself?

Unstated Reasoning

Finally, when people tell you their story they are providing you with opinions and conclusions they have reached, but very seldom do they share with you their logic or reasoning behind those opinions and conclusions. Their logic is buried deep within their linguistic map, and you will have to recover it. When a person provides a Surface Structure statement such as *We need to help our clinical staff cooperate with each other,"* an important part of the map is missing: the reasoning underlying that conclusion. While the answer to that question may be intuitively obvious in the context of the conversation, there may be times when clarifying a person's reasoning underlying a stated opinion or conclusion is helpful.

> "I'm feeling stuck right now. I have a sense that <u>I should be more proactively involved in advancing my career</u>. I'm happy with what I'm doing but I feel as if I'm missing something. I'm at a point where I feel <u>if I don't make a concerted effort in order to advance my career in some way opportunities will pass me by</u> and I'll have no choice but to stay where I am. I have to challenge myself. What do you think I should do?"

The following intelligent inquiries will help recover the unstated reasoning in Martha's narrative.

- What leads you to believe that you "should be more proactively involved in advancing" your career?
- What causes you to feel that if you "don't make a concerted effort to advance" your career opportunities will pass you by?

Unstated reasoning is commonly found in a person's Surface Structure language; the challenge is to recover the reasoning that is most relevant to the discussion. Use your judgment; there is no such thing as a bad question when it comes to building a platform of understanding.

WHY NOT WHY

One type of question to avoid, especially when recovering unstated reasoning, is a question beginning with the word *why*. People's first exposure to "Why" questions are with their parents or parental figures, and those questions often came from the

Critical Parent ego state. For example, "Why did you leave your toys all over the place?"; or "Why didn't you start studying for the test earlier?" These questions were not inquiries as much as they were judgments. On an adult level, "Why" questions, especially when posed with an interrogatory voice, leaves the other person feeling as if he has to defend or explain himself. When this occurs, communication is diminished and support for thought suffers. Why questions are only useful when they are completely stripped of their negative connotations. However, because questions beginning with "why" are easily misread, you may inadvertently produce a negative reaction, even with good intentions. It is usually best to eliminate them from your stock of intelligent inquiries.

MAKING IT SIMPLE

Understanding and recovering deletions may seem complicated, but by following a few simple rules you can accomplish the task of clarifying a person's narrative in a natural, relaxed, and spontaneous manner.

1. Listen for what's not there

People's linguistic maps begin at a high-level view. Egan points out that people "offer points of view but say nothing about what's behind them or their implications. They deliver decisions but don't give the reasons for them or spell out the implications. They propose courses of action but don't say why they want to head in a particular direction, what the implications are for themselves or others, what resources they might need, or how flexible they are. "As you listen, it's important to note what they put in and what they leave out" (Egan, 2010, p. 153). In the final analysis, whether you can name a deletion is less important than knowing it's there, and using your intuitive sense of understanding about what is missing to recover the information through the use of intelligent inquiries.

2. Ask "What" and "How" questions

In the beginning of this chapter, you were asked, after hearing Martha's narrative, "What do you do now?" You now know the answer: begin to clarify her narrative in order to build a platform of understanding. Throughout this chapter, several questions were offered as a way of clarifying Martha's narrative.

- In what way are you "feeling stuck right now"?
- What aspect of your career "should you be involved in advancing"?
- What specifically are you "missing"?
- What "opportunities will pass" you by?
- What can you do, specifically, to "challenge" yourself?

- How are you going to "challenge" yourself?
- In what way should you "be more proactively involved"?
- In what way do you "have to challenge" yourself?
- What would happen if you weren't "more proactively involved"?
- What would happen if you didn't "challenge" yourself?
- What leads you to believe that you "should be more proactively involved in advancing" your career?
- What causes you to feel that if you "don't make a concerted effort to advance" your career opportunities will pass you by?

These are all "What" and "How" questions. "What" questions predominate because they are the most powerful way to clarify exactly what a client means, but there are also reasons to use "How" questions. "How" questions explore the *means by which* a person is going to do something. "When" and "Where" questions are also useful, but, generally, you need to know "What" and "How" before "When" and "Where" become relevant.

3. Use their language

The questions listed above all contain quoted material. These quotes indicate that specific words and phrases from Martha's own narrative were the foundation upon which each question was built. When you listen to a person's narrative, use her language in constructing intelligent inquiries. Using a person's own language causes her to feel understood and lets her know you are listening. This is an impossible task if your mental attention is not focused on the what the person is saying. Furthermore, using a person's specific words as part of your question makes it easy for her to respond because you are working within her linguistic frame-of-reference and that makes it simpler for her to add more detail.

4. Formulate your next question from the person's last or earlier answer

During the Support-for-Thought stage of the Four-square Coaching Framework you, as the helper, will begin to build rapport and establish a working alliance. Clarifying their narrative through intelligent inquiry is a part of this process. However, questions are not just asked and answered; questions elicit answers, which lead to further questions, and a flow of dialogue is created. Engaging in this process means following the rule of circularity. "In a true conversation each contribution builds on the last. This, ultimately, is how we know that we are being listened to: when the other person says something that connects with and develops what we have just said" (Iveson, George, & Ratner, 2012, p. 12). This circular nature of dialogue will help build and maintain rapport.

5. Inquire, don't interrogate

Clarifying a person's narrative does not mean subjecting him to an unending barrage of questions. A soft approach is required. Using questions effectively requires practice, just as does artistically performing a trumpet concerto or playing a jazz solo. Questions can be challenging, but rapport can still be maintained with the correct technique. Staying within the Adult ego state is essential because tough questions, if delivered out of a Parent ego state, can easily turn into an inquisition. There are two guidelines that will help you inquire without interrogating.

1. Use the verbal softeners that help maintain the Adult ego state. In the previous chapter, the use of verbal softeners was discussed. Remember, verbal softeners are additional words or phrases, such as "I'm curious about," that tone down and soften the directness of a statement or inquiry, and diminish the possibility that you come across as challenging or confrontational. When used as a lead-in to questions, verbal softeners engage the other person in a non-threatening way.

2. Avoid multiple questions within a single inquiry. This is sometimes referred to as the double question. For example, *"In what way do you need to be more assertive and what's stopping you from doing that now?"* A double question like this can confuse the listener because the person does not know to which question she should reply. Additionally, in picking one, the other question is left unanswered. When more than one question is included in an inquiry, the listener can also feel bombarded, making it difficult to keep up with what she is being asked. Rapport can suffer in the process.

COACHING AS A LEADERSHIP STYLE

Asking the right questions is one of the most important skills a leader can have. This skill is one means by which Intellectual Stimulation is provided to followers as part of Transformational Leadership. "Intellectually stimulating leaders help to make their followers more innovative and creative. They question assumptions, reframe problems, and look at old problems in new ways" (Bass, 2008, p. 621). The intellectually stimulating leader takes the lead in an interactive, creative process that challenges followers to "think out of the box," to address problems, and to consider alternative solutions. Intellectual stimulation requires the resourceful use of questions.

Questions are powerful. Every problem-solving activity can be described as a process of questions and answers. In fact, informed leaders would say that solving most problems is a matter of asking the right questions. As stated previously, questions direct attention. For example, recovering the unstated reasoning in a person's surface level language opens the door to challenging assumptions that may impede solution generation or creative thinking. Furthermore, drilling down into a problem by using the "what" and "how" inquiries described in this chapter with help identify and clarify the issue or problem under discussion. Finally, a hidden benefit to the use of inquiry is that it forces you—and others—to listen to the answer. Listening with an open mind can shift one's conceptual orientation (Wicker, 1985), and when combined with a non-judgmental attitude, stimulates creative thought. By using the inquiry practices discussed in this chapter, you will not only be able to clarify the narrative of the person you are coaching, but increase your ability to become an intellectually stimulating leader.

Chapter 6

Becoming a Solution-focused Leader

Diagnosis (2012) is defined as "the act or process of identifying or determining the nature and cause of a disease or injury through evaluation of patient history, examination, and review of laboratory data." Diagnosis is at the heart of the medical model. Suppose a patient complained that pains in his abdomen had become intolerable. How many doctors would simply prescribe a painkiller and send the patient home? Not a good one. A good doctor would perform a careful diagnosis that included blood work and tests, as well as a thorough physical examination. A doctor must find out what's causing the problem before offering a prescription. After all, prescribing without diagnosis can lead to malpractice.

Imagine that a colleague came to you with the following complaint.

> *"I'm really getting behind in my work. I'm so caught up in the daily minutiae that I can't seem to find the time to think about and deal with the broader issues. I know I should be delegating more, but I'm afraid that something important will slip through the cracks, and I'll be held accountable for it. Besides, I know the work better than my less experienced colleagues and by the time I explain to them what to do and how to do it, I could have done it faster and better myself. I don't know what to do."*

When this situation is posed to physicians and other healthcare professionals who are asked what they would say to the person if they were coaching him, they typically ask the following types of questions.

- *How long have you been behind in your work?*
- *What is it that prevents you from delegating more work to others?*
- *Have you had some bad experiences in the past when you've delegated work?*
- *When you have delegated, did you do it correctly?*
- *Has anything important actually slipped through the cracks and caused problems for you?*
- *Do you think that maybe you're too much of a perfectionist?*
- *Why don't you trust your colleagues more?*
- *Why is delegation such a problem for you?*
- *Are there other reasons you may be getting behind in your work?*

These questions, along with a smattering of suggestions, make up the typical coaching session, and it is easy to understand why. Healthcare professionals work from the premise that before a patient can be helped the practitioner must figure out the cause of the problem. That's true whether the practitioner is diagnosing disorders or assessing problem situation. This approach is based upon the premise that there is a necessary connection between a problem and its solution. In a clinical setting, diagnosing the problem is the appropriate first step, but in a coaching situation that approach is generally unnecessary and often counterproductive.

PROBLEM TALK

As De Jong and Berg stated: "The genetic structure of problem solving—first determining the nature of the problem and then intervening—influences the content of the interaction between practitioners and clients" (2008, p. 8). They go on to point out that most practitioners (people who are trying to help others) spend their time on the "who," "what," "when," "where," and "why" of problems; therefore, the interaction between the person being helped and the helper is largely problem-focused.

A Problem-Focused Conversation

Colleague: *How are things going in the world of quality?*

Leader: *Oh, pretty well, but I've got a problem with Rafael.*

Colleague: *What's going on?*

Leader: *He's supposed to be a senior member of the team, but I just can't seem to get him to focus on some of the strategic projects that I would like to see implemented.*

Colleague: *How long has this been happening?*

Leader: *I'd say for several months now.*

Colleague: *What have you tried so far?*

Leader: *I've tried hinting that he should put some time in thinking about where we want our quality effort to be in 3 to 5 years. I've even offered to help him sit down and start thinking through it even though that's his job—not mine.*

Colleague: *It sounds as if you've made it clear that this is a priority for you. Why do think your suggestions haven't worked?*

Leader: *I should probably have emphasized this aspect of his role when I first brought him on board. I talked about it, but may not have emphasized it enough.*

Colleague: *Why doesn't he see it for himself?*

Leader: *I don't know. Maybe he's just caught up in his own world and doesn't feel comfortable doing things that are outside of his experience. I mean, it's not like he's not motivated. He puts a lot of energy into other aspects of his work.*

Colleague: *What does he like to do?*

Leader: *I think he enjoys the direct contact with the department heads, and doing the actual teaching about quality. He's very good at it.*

Colleague: *If he's good at that you'd think that he'd want to take quality to the next level here. Could it be he's just not wired to think that way?*

Leader: *Possibly, he doesn't do very well when he has to lay things out conceptually. The last time he gave a presentation about where quality in our institution is going over the next several years he struggled with it, and I had to take over. He's good at teaching the content and interacting with the people, but not thinking about it strategically.*

Colleague: *Why haven't you been more direct with him?*

Leader: *I'm concerned that if I push him too hard he'll get upset, and it will affect what he's currently doing. I can't afford that because he's too well liked by the department heads. Plus, no one else can teach that stuff the way he does. I don't want to demotivate him.*

As you can tell from this exchange, a conversation full of problem-talk goes nowhere. The colleague is trying to help, and it's likely the leader feels listened to and appreciates his colleague's efforts, but they end up back where they started because a problem-focused conversation primarily searches for answers to:

- Questions about the problem.
- Questions about causes.
- Questions about why things are not working.
- Questions about who's at fault.

Problem talk explores the past to "get to the bottom" of a problem in the present. Its primary purpose is to understand the "why" behind a problem situation, with the assumption that such an understanding will facilitate a solution. Given the education, training, and technical background of leaders in healthcare it is reasonable that this would be the approach. There is a seductive logic in trying to understand the problem, but for the types of situations and developmental issues that require a coaching approach—such as those discussed previously in this book—problem diagnosis does not lead to a useful outcome. For example, how will problem talk and the questions associated with it:

- Help the chair of OB/GYN deal with Dr. Bernard's resistance to change, negativity, and running directly to senior management when he's unhappy with something? (chapter one)
- Assist the senior cardiologist in deciding whether to apply for the Chief of Cardiology position? (chapter two)
- Help the new nurse who feels like she doesn't fit in with the team? (chapter three)
- Help the new staff member deal with her colleague, Mary, who is being uncooperative? (chapter four)
- Help Martha, who feels stuck in her career and is not sure what to do about it? (chapter five)

It was explained in the previous chapter that questions direct attention. When you ask questions that direct a person's attention to the problem and what caused it, you often elicit a story about what the person doesn't want, things that are wrong, forces beyond her control, the burdens she is under, fault finding, and the fact that she is stuck and doesn't know what to do. Analysis of the problem makes the person an expert in the problem, but it does little good in helping the person decide what to do next. Whose fault is it that Mary is having trouble dealing with her uncooperative colleague? Whose fault is it that the chair of OB/GYN is having trouble dealing with Dr. Bernard? It really doesn't matter, because assigning blame as a means of finding the cause of the problem does nothing to help a person to look at something differently or do something differently. Until a person changes her outlook and approach, nothing will change. As Szabo and Meier so eloquently put it, "The solution does not care why the problem occurred" (Szabo & Meier, 2008, p. 10).

SOLUTION TALK

Language is the only tool we have for coaching another person. Through solution talk, we can direct the focus of a person's thinking so as to raise awareness of possibilities for the future, increase choices by developing new options, and strengthen self-confidence through the identification of competencies and resources. Solution talk is based upon a set of empirically derived principles about how people best deal with problem situations and change their behavior. For the healthcare leader who has been educated, trained, and rewarded for their problem-focused skills these principles may be a challenge, in part because they appear simple; however, simple doesn't mean less effective, or even easy. Learning to put the principles into practice will require you to have the correct mindset, master the art of solution talk, and be flexible enough to respond to the dynamics of a helping conversation with moment-to-moment decisions and tactics that maintain a solution-focused approach.

SOLUTION-FOCUSED PRINCIPLES

Principle #1: *You don't have to understand the cause of a problem to solve it.*

For the task of helping people work their way out of problem situations or pursue developmental opportunities, the processes of diagnosing problems and finding solutions aren't necessarily related. To illustrate, understanding why the new nurse in chapter three is not fitting in with the team is less relevant than figuring out what she wants to happen in the future, and how to go about obtaining it. Nonetheless, people begin their conversations talking about problems, and problems must be used as the platform upon which solutions can be built. Therefore, when a person begins a helping conversation by describing a problem, it's appropriate that you listen carefully to the situation and clarify the person's narrative. The person's story is the point of departure, from which you build a platform of understanding on which to move forward. However, you will certainly want to avoid a discussion of causes at the risk of becoming mired in the minutiae surrounding the problem. As Berg & Szabo states, "All of the facts belong to the problem, not to the solution" (2005, p. 49).

Principle #2: *Focusing on the future creates more useful energy than focusing on the past.*

What people talk about has a great influence on what they mentally attend to, and what people mentally attend to will affect their behavior. Thus, the most direct route to helping people is to start talking about their desired outcomes, and looking for a path by which they can achieve those outcomes. Focusing too much on the past can be a type of mental quicksand that prevents a person from escaping the mire of a problem situation. Establishing a desired future, on the other hand, can be a motivating experience. Think about the example at the beginning of this chapter; the person is caught up in the daily minutiae of his work and can't seem to let go of anything. If he is asked to describe what he wants to experience in the future, and the benefits to be gained (e.g., time to deal with broader issues, a better work-life balance, the ability to pursue other areas of interest), the discrepancy that is created by the difference between his current state and his desired future state creates pressure for change. People are motivated to reduce the discrepancy between what currently exists and the picture in their heads of what they want (Glasser, 1984). The combination of discomfort with one's current state and a focus on a desired future state will generate useful energy.

There is one exception to this principle: using the past to discover resources to be used in the present. Discovering personal strengths, skills, and resources used effectively in the past to help a person address a current problem situation or take advantage of developmental opportunities is a solution-focused strategy. Saleebey, an advocate of helping people focus on their strengths, says, "So what is of interest to us is how people have taken steps, summoned up resources, and coped. People are always working on their situations, even if just deciding for the moment to be resigned. As helpers, we must tap into that work, elucidate it, find and build on its promise" (2007, p. 285).

Principle #3: *Small steps lead to big changes.*

Over the past several years, there has been a push to set audacious goals (Collins & Porras, 2002). While this mantra was originally intended for companies, individuals have been encouraged to adopt this goal-focused approach as a way to achieve more in life because of the belief that establishing a "stretch goal" is a starting point for change. While it is true that it is important to dream big and establish lofty goals, as Lao Tzu, the Chinese philosopher famously stated, a journey of a thousand miles begins with a single step. In other words, a destination is reached by accomplishing a series of small goals, or steps, rather than big leaps.

Solutions are end-results. They are the product of a person taking beginning and intermediate steps to do something different that will move them toward where they want to be. Whether it is the leader who is frustrated with Rafael, or Martha who feels stuck in her career, or the chair of OB/GYN who wants to deal with Dr. Bernard's counterproductive behavior, each will have to do something differently going forward to change their circumstances. Small steps are the answer because they help the person overcome the inertia of doing nothing, provide an immediate sense of progress, and maximize the probability of success.

Small steps also lead to stable solutions. Given that the types of problems people need help with have no single textbook answer, they require a heuristic approach whereby solutions evolve from a series of small experiments. Solutions are shaped by taking a few small steps, assessing their effectiveness, adjusting the next steps based upon what has been learned, and trying out the new approach until the desired results are achieved. Solutions that emerge from this process are more stable because each piece of a solution must survive the test of effectiveness before it is combined with other pieces that result in progress.

Principle #4: *Differences make the difference.*

Gregory Bateson, the famed semanticist, wrote that in the world of communication "effects" are brought about by differences, and that what we call change is a difference which occurs across time (Bateson, 2000). It stands to reason, then, that helping people change means helping discover what they want to be *different* in their lives and then what they are going to do *differently* to achieve it. After all, it was no less than Albert Einstein who is assumed to have said, "Insanity is doing the same thing over and over again and expecting different results." While there is some debate as to whether it was indeed Einstein that coined this phrase, it does emphasize the fact that people cannot work their way out of problem situations or grow personally or professionally by maintaining the status quo. Finding differences is, therefore, crucial to change, and there are many differences to explore in a solution-focused conversation.

- What is the difference between what the person is currently experiencing and what the person wants to experience?
- How might a person need to think differently about a situation to react more productively to it?

- What does a person need to do differently to get what she wants?
- How will achieving what she wants make a difference in her life?
- What is another person doing that is different from what he wants the other person to do?
- What does the person need to do differently to increase the chances that he will get different behavior from another person?

Helping people to perceive their situations differently, think differently, and behave differently will indeed be the *difference that makes a difference.*

A Different Conversation

Using the previous example of the leader and his colleague, here is an illustration of a conversation if these solution-focused principles were followed.

Colleague: *How are things going in the world of quality?*

Leader: *Oh, pretty well, but I've got a problem with Rafael.*

Colleague: *What's going on?*

Leader: *He's supposed to be a senior member of the team, but I just can't seem to get him to focus on some of the strategic projects that I would like to see implemented.*

Colleague: *What projects specifically?*

Leader: *For one, a strategic plan for how we will implement our quality initiatives over the next few years.*

Colleague: *What else?*

Leader: *That's the most important thing for now.*

Colleague: *If he were focusing on how to implement the quality initiatives over the next few years, what would he be doing differently?*

Leader: *Well, he would be getting his team more involved in teaching the quality material so that he'd have more time to focus on the planning.*

Colleague: *Okay, you mentioned two things that would let you know he's focusing on things strategically in the way that you would like. First, getting his team prepared to do some of the teaching that he currently does, and second, having him look at some best practices in other places and how they can be applied here. Is that correct?*

Leader: *That's right. If he were doing those two things, it would be a positive start.*

Colleague: *Let me ask you a question. What might you do over the next couple of weeks that might get him started with those two activities?*

Leader: *I don't know. I've tried hinting that these are some of things I would like to see happen.*

Colleague: *Were you specific?*

Leader: *No, not exactly, I was more general.*

Colleague: *Okay, so what might you do different from what you've done so far so that he starts these first two activities?*

Leader: *Well, I guess I've not been as specific with him about what I would like, so maybe I could have a sit-down conversation with him and talk to him about the merits of getting his*

staff trained and exploring some of the best practices of other healthcare organizations in our area. At least it would be a start.
Colleague: *That's a good idea. When are you going to have this conversation?*

Note the contrast between this conversation and the problem-focused example. A solution-focused conversation addresses what the person wants to be different, and the creation of possibilities for making those differences happen. It doesn't guarantee that a specific action will succeed, but it does create movement through the use of questions that elicit participation in a conversation around building solutions. Following the solution-focused principles has several advantages:

1. A helping conversation is efficient. Concentrating on solutions, and only solutions, will enable the person to move toward action in less time. The more a person is caught up in the problem, the slower the progress.
2. The person you are helping will find it easier to work out an appropriate solution than if her thinking is problem focused. Solution-focused thinking is fixed on what she wants and how to get it as opposed to the "what and whys" of the problem; the person's entire mental resources are applied to identifying a solution.
3. The person will have an increased sense of responsibility and accountability. It is the person, through the course of your solution-focused questions, who thinks through his situation in such a way as to come up with what he really wants, and what he can start doing to achieve it. In short, the person owns the solution, and with ownership comes more felt responsibility, and, therefore, pressure to follow through on his ideas.
4. The person's confidence is increased. When a person begins to think and act with a solution-focused mindset, she becomes more optimistic about her ability to deal with problem situations and achieve her goals.

These solution-focused principles act as a compass for your helping conversations. They provide direction for how to engage in solution talk. How are they applied within the Four-square Coaching Framework? This question will be answered as you learn the stage-specific activities used in Challenge-for-Thought and Challenge-for-Action.

COACHING AS A LEADERSHIP STYLE

Problem-solving ability has historically been a defining characteristic of leadership (Cattell & Stice, 1954). The importance of leadership in leading the way for group problem-solving may be explained by understanding information processing capabilities as they apply to problems. According to Lord (1976), there are two defining aspects of human information processing that impact problem-solving: selective attention, and the limit on the number of chunks that can be retained in short-term memory—also known as Miller's law (Miller, 1956). In combination, these two aspects of information processing limit people's ability to simultaneously attend to, or rapidly store, all elements of a problem that deals with even a modest amount information. Thus, for complicated problems it is the leader's responsibility to focus attention on what is most important for solving a problem. The leader who can do this in such a way that it yields a solution is perceived by followers as an effective problem-solver.

If people are limited by selective attention and limits on what can be stored in short-term memory, then it makes sense that the best use of their cognitive abilities is to apply them toward finding workable solutions. A solution-focused approach is the natural method by which to do this. As a solution-focused leader, you are able to exhibit transformational leadership in four ways:

1. **Intellectual Stimulation:** You will change people's ways of thinking about problems. Being able to facilitate an individual, or a group, through a solution-focused discussion will provide Intellectual Stimulation by helping them examine critical assumptions, utilize different perspectives, overcome obstacles, and turn problems into solutions.

2. **Inspirational Motivation:** Your optimism about overcoming problems generally, and your personal confidence in your ability to move toward solutions while everybody else is focused on the problem will inspire others to do the same. It is important to followers that their leader has the ability to overcome crises, has a "never say die!" attitude, and demonstrates a sense of optimism about the future.

3. **Idealized Influence:** By demonstrating a solution-focused mindset, you serve as a role model for what you expect others to do in your organization. You may have heard leaders say, "Don't bring me problems; bring me solutions." Championing the solution-focused approach models the way for this to happen.

4. **Individualized Consideration:** By following the solution-focused principles, you will be able to work with individuals to create strategies for continuous improvement, and promote self-development in a way that encourages them to take the initiative.

Chapter 7

Challenge-for-Thought

Music can be considered interplay between consonance and dissonance; likewise, a coaching conversation can be considered interplay between support and challenge. Support increases rapport and creates harmony while challenge adds a discordant—but necessary—note to the conversation. Trevino (1996) makes the point that while supportive interactions between a helper and another person enhance the relationship, a healthy amount of discord facilitates change. Egan agrees with this idea when he writes, "Because helping at its best is a constructive social-influence process, some form of challenge is central to helping" (Egan, 2010, p. 211). In other words, sometimes you have to make people uncomfortable for their own good.

Challenge is the use of incisive inquiry to induce people to think about what they want, how they're going to get it, how they might be getting in their own way, and how to commit to the actions needed to achieve what they want. However, challenge does not mean confrontation. While challenge provokes people to think differently or more deeply, confrontation is a clash of opinions or ideas. Most people do not like, or cannot handle, confrontation. Confrontation produces a defensive response while challenge changes the way a person construes problems and considers solutions. Challenge is used to help while confrontation is used to dominate. While challenging another person during the conversation might be the right thing to do from a coaching standpoint, if not done properly—and in the right spirit—it may create resistance and reduce rapport. In fact, as Egan explains,

"Empathy should permeate every kind of challenge" (Egan, 2010, p. 252). Keep in mind the following guidelines for effective challenge.

1. Challenge should always be used to further the goals of the person you are helping, not as a way to exhibit power or to "one-up" the other person.
2. Challenge from the Adult ego state rather than taking a Parent-Child approach.
3. Be direct, but be tactful in the way that you challenge.
4. When challenging, be specific; specific challenges induce specific responses.
5. The targets for challenge are thought and action.

Challenging for thought and action represent two stages in the Four-square Coaching Framework. These stages are interrelated because Challenge-for-Thought creates the destination, and Challenge-for-Action the path to that destination.

CHALLENGE-FOR-THOUGHT
Designing the Future

To paraphrase William F. Buckley (1979), a leader is one who "crystallizes" what people desire. The Challenge-for-Thought phase of the Four-square Coaching Framework challenges people to think clearly about what it is they want. Thinking is an activity that is so natural, most of the time we are not even aware of it; like breathing, it just happens. Pressing a person to think about what he wants in a very conscious and deliberate way adds focus to his goal setting. The clearer people are about what they want the easier it is to chart a path to that destination, and the greater the likelihood that it will be attained. It is during the Challenge-for-Thought stage of the Four-square Coaching Framework that thinking about a preferred future is both examined and shaped so that it prepares and sustains the person in the quest for change—whether that change is achieving something better, or working a way out of an undesirable situation. This stage is comprised of two core activities.

1. Developing discrepancy
2. Constructing a well-formed outcome

DEVELOPING DISCREPANCY

Solution-focused principle #4, **"Differences make the difference,"** is at the core of this activity. The rationale for this principle can be found in several theoretical frameworks, including Solution-focused brief therapy (de Shazer, 1991) and Motivational Interviewing (Miller & Rollnick, 2002); however, one of the most intriguing explanations comes from William Glasser and his body of work named *Control Theory.* Glasser (1984) uses the analogy of a thermostat to explain how differences make the difference. He points out that thermostats operate by sensing the difference between its set temperature (the temperature it "wants") and the air temperature in the room (what currently exists). He argues that people are similar. In the view of Glasser, all behavior is a constant attempt to reduce the difference between what one wants (the pictures in our heads) and one's current reality; the greater the discrepancy between the two, the greater the motivation to reduce the difference.

One of the most important coaching activities is to focus the attention of the person you are helping on his desired future. Challenge-for-Thought directs people's thinking toward the difference between their present state-of-affairs and how they want it to be, or between their present behavior and behavior that is more congruent with their goals or values. Doing so adds specificity to their goal setting, and has the added value of creating a perceptual gap that increases motivation to change in order to close that gap. For example, when a person recognizes that her current behaviors place her in conflict with important values or interfere with the accomplishment of self-identified goals, she is more likely to experience increased motivation to change. Developing discrepancy is the first action to help point a person in the right direction; a desired future state of her choosing.

UNDERSTANDING WHAT THE PERSON WANTS

People like to complain. They like to talk about their problems. Such is the case for Suzanne, who has just received a promotion into the position of HR manager for a large hospital system. Her former leader, Dr. Williams, has always been a friend and has coached her through some tough situations, so she turns to him for help.

> **Dr. Williams:** *Congratulations on your promotion.*
> **Suzanne:** *Thanks, but you have to be careful what you ask for; you may get it.*
> **Dr. Williams:** *Wow, you sound as if you're having second thoughts.*
> **Suzanne:** *It's not so much that as the fact that I've gotten new responsibilities, but I don't have the people. So I'm supporting two large departments from an HR perspective, and I'm really, really feeling stressed out because the department heads are coming to me with all sorts of questions and issues and, quite honestly, with the few resources I have I'm not able to keep up with the activity. I'm feeling over my head. I don't want to let anybody down.*

A narrative like this is rarely useful. There is so much negativity it reminds the person of what's not going well and leads to discouragement, low energy, and a sense of being stuck. While it may be appropriate to clarify her narrative and broaden your platform of understanding, it is generally more productive to move directly into Challenge-for-Thought and begin developing discrepancy. This will redirect the person's attention from her frustrations toward an optimistic future.

Developing discrepancy can be accomplished by asking the person to answer a version of this question: "What do you want to be different from what you are experiencing now?" Metaphorically speaking, it's difficult to get people to move forward when they are looking backwards (focusing on the past), or staring at their feet (stuck in the present). Instead, they need to be looking toward their destination. By challenging people to think about a desired future state that is different from their current state, the stage is set for change and initial momentum generated.

> ## Example
>
> **Dr. Williams:** *So, tell me, Suzanne, what do you want to be different from what you're currently experiencing?*
> **Suzanne:** *I want to get a better handle on my own emotions, my stress level. My own personal stress bounces all over the place day to day.*

The purpose of the "discrepancy" question is to *challenge* people to think about what they want to be different in the future; to define a desired future state. How you ask the question may vary depending on the situation or problem you are talking about. Construct your inquiry to fit the person's specific situation.

Examples

- To assist the senior cardiologist in deciding whether to apply for the Chief of Cardiology position (chapter two), you might ask: *To make a decision, what do you need to know that is different from what you already know?*

- To help the new nurse who feels like she doesn't fit in with the team (chapter three), you might ask: *What do you want to be different about how you fit in with the team that is different from the way you fit in now?*
- To help the new staff member deal with her colleague, Mary, who is being uncooperative (chapter four), you might ask: *In what way do you want Mary to be cooperative that is different from what you are currently experiencing in the way of cooperation?*
- To help Martha, who feels stuck in her career and is not sure what to do about it (chapter five), you might ask: *If you were not stuck in your career, what would be different?*
- To help Suzanne get a better handle on her emotions and stress level (see above), you might ask: *How do you want to handle your emotions and stress differently from the way you are handling your emotions and stress now?*

DO NOT MISTAKE ACTIONS FOR OUTCOMES

When developing discrepancy, it is not uncommon for people to answer the "What do you want to be different" question with an action they want to take, rather than a desired future state that is to be gained by taking that action. For example, if the answer to the discrepancy question *"Based on what you learned, what do you want to be different about your leadership style from what it is now?"* is *"I want to do more listening than talking when I interact with my team,"* it begs the question "For what purpose?" What does the person hope to gain by engaging in the stated action? Wants and desires are different from the actions needed to realize them.

When a person answers the discrepancy question by stating an action, one option is to go with the flow and shift to the Challenge-for-Action stage, which will be discussed in the following chapter. If you take that path, you will challenge the person to think about how he is going to go about taking that action, and when and where will he start. However, another option is to ask the person how the action will help her to achieve what she wants going forward. By doing so, you can return to the Challenge-for-Thought stage to clarify her desired future state. The figure below illustrates how the second option can be diagramed on the Four-square Coaching Framework.

The top arrow indicates the conversation begins in the Challenge-for-Thought quadrant, when the colleague asks a question to develop discrepancy, and subsequently moves to the Challenge-for-Action quadrant, when the Chief Nursing Officer responds by talking about *acting* differently (i.e., doing more listening). The bottom arrow indicates that her colleague moves the conversation from Challenge-for-Action and back to Challenge-for-Thought by asking for the goal, or outcome, to be achieved by taking the action.

Colleague: *You mentioned that you received some feedback on your leadership style. Based on what you learned, what do you want to be different about your leadership style from what it is now?*

Chief Nursing Officer: *I want to do more listening than talking when I interact with my team.*

Colleague: *If you were to do more listening than talking when you interact with your team, what would you gain from that; how would that make your leadership style different from what it is now?*

Chief Nursing Officer: *I want to be the kind of leader that gets people involved. I want my team to feel like they have ownership in the changes that we are making around here.*

Understanding the purpose for the specific action moves the conversation from the Challenge-for-Action phase back to Challenge-for-Thought, where a desired future state can be specified. Although developing discrepancy is useful, it does not satisfy all of the conditions necessary to define a future state in a way that facilitates its achievement. By itself, a desired future state is equivalent to a goal (e.g., "I want to be a good leader"; "I want a more satisfying career"; "I'd like a better work-life balance"; or, as in Suzanne's case, "I want to get a better handle on my emotions, my stress level"). Goals are good, but they are basically statements of aspirations that do little to help a person actually achieve them. Goals, even ones that are stated as differences between what currently exists and what is wanted, are often ill-defined and lack the relevant detail to make future change actionable, noticeable, and indicative of success. In short, goals are often nothing more than hopes stated out loud.

It would be just as accurate to say, "I hope to be a good leader"; "I hope to have a more satisfying career"; "I hope to have a better work-life balance"; and "I hope to get a better handle on my emotions, my stress level." In order to move beyond hope to change, goals must be converted to well-formed outcomes.

CONSTRUCTING A WELL-FORMED OUTCOME

An outcome is different from a goal, or a vision of a desired future. A goal is rather general while an outcome, and especially one that is well-formed, contains elements that make the difference between wanting something in theory and enhancing the person's probability of actually achieving it. The idea of a well-formed outcome is a construct of Neural Linguistic Programming (Cameron-Bandler, 1985) and meets the following criteria:

1. A positive statement of what is wanted
2. Can be self-initiated and self-maintained
3. Includes demonstrable indicators of success

A POSITIVE STATEMENT OF WHAT IS WANTED

Suppose you are helping a friend move some furniture into his new home, and you ask, "*Where do you want this chair?*" He responds with, "*I don't want it in that corner.*" That information does little to help you know what to do with the chair. Similarly, when people think about what they do not want, it does little to help them know what they want instead.

> **Dr. Williams:** *So, tell me, Suzanne, what do you want to be different in the future?*
> **Suzanne:** *I don't want to be perceived as nonprofessional or not being able to respond and add value. I don't even think that I'm helping them at the level I want and that my leaders deserve.*

This is an example of *away-from* thinking (Hoag, 2012) on Suzanne's part, and does little to help her engage in solution-focused thinking. It is a negative representation of a future state, which is inherently confusing when establishing a destination toward which one wants to move.

AWAY-FROM THINKING

Focusing on what is not wanted, or what is to be avoided is away-from thinking. Suzanne, for example, is very clear about what is not working, and what she does not want. It's quite common for people with a problem to think and express themselves in terms of what they don't want; what they want to get *away-from*. Even when asked for what they do want, many people will often answer, "Well, I don't want this" or "I certainly don't want that." This is because people either haven't thought about what they want in any depth or because they are trapped in an away-from thinking pattern. An away-from thinking pattern can create road-blocks to progress.

Reinforcement Disappears

If people are focused on what they don't want, then in order to monitor progress they will have to pay attention to that which they want to avoid. For example, suppose a person wants less conflict with a co-worker. Assessing the person's interactions for times when there is less conflict increases the probability that the person will notice any conflict that does occur rather than times when conflict was circumvented. The effect is that a person may perceive a lack of progress even though such a conclusion may not be justified by a complete representation of events and experiences. To summarize, if a person keeps looking for what she doesn't want, she will eventually find it.

Motivation Can Suffer

As a general rule, it's more motivating to move toward something that is positive than it is avoiding something unwanted. A goal such as "not being involved in the operational details of my business" is an away-from goal. It focuses the person's attention and energy on avoiding something she doesn't want. It would be far more helpful—and motivating—for people to think of what they are attracted to, and what they do want instead. Focusing on what one wants is energizing. If a person is allowed to focus on what is *not* wanted, it may lead the person to conclude that a positive outcome is impossible, or unlikely, further reinforcing a demotivating perception that the problem or situation is inescapable.

Unwanted Behavior Is Not Replaced

It is a well-establish principle of behavior modification that to change unwanted behaviors you have to replace them with desirable ones (Martin, 1988). Replacing a negative with a positive is imperative if any individual change process is going to succeed. "Positive outcomes are not automatically accomplished by eradicating an unwanted experience. In fact, if nothing is installed to take its place, the previous unwanted experience is likely to return. I believe it would be an evolutionary step if all of our processes were directed toward what we do want, rather than having our thoughts and efforts entangled in a quagmire of complaints" (Cameron-Bandler, 1985, p. 87).

Bad Mental Habits Can Form

Thinking in terms of problems, or what is unwanted, can cause bad mental habits to form. Schwartz and Gladding (2011) explain that bad mental habits form due to a combination of three factors: (a) the neuroplasticity of the brain, (b) Hebb's law, and (c) the Quantum Zeno Effect. Neuroplasticity refers to the ability of the brain to change over time due to physiological changes of the nervous system. Physiological changes of the nervous system are subject to Hebb's law: when any two cells, or system of cells, are activated at the same time they tend to become associated and form a brain circuit which creates learned patterns of behavior. In other words, habits form because the brain learns to respond the same way every time a similar situation arises. As Schwartz and Gladding explain, "Hebb's law only works when the brain areas involved activate—and stay activated—at the same time" (2011, p. 65). This simply means that by maintaining one's focused attention on a particular set of thoughts it causes the cells to "wire together" so that Hebb's law can take effect. Schwartz and Gladding refer to this phenomenon as the Quantum Zeno Effect.

What does all this mean to you? It means that by allowing people to focus their attention on problems instead of solutions, on what they don't want instead of what they do want, on deficiencies rather than resources you are allowing Hebb's law and the quantum Zeno effect to establish mental habits that will interfere with their ability to create positive outcomes in their lives. The more a person's attention is on the negative, the harder it will be to establish a positive goal, and develop a path toward the goal that is achievable.

CHANGING NEGATIVES TO POSITIVES

> **Dr. Williams:** *So, tell me, Suzanne, what do you want to be different in the future?*
> **Suzanne:** *I don't want to be perceived as non-professional or not being able to respond and add value. I don't even think that I'm helping them at the level I want, and that my leaders deserve.*

To meet the conditions of a well-formed outcome, Suzanne must be challenged to restate what she wants in terms of something positive or desirable. Fortunately, this is easy to do through the use of an *instead question*. An "instead question" is a restatement of what is not wanted, combined with the inquiry "What would you like instead?" or "What do you want instead?"

Example:

Dr. Williams: *So, tell me, Suzanne, what do you want to be different in the future?*
Suzanne: *I don't want to be perceived as nonprofessional or not being able to respond and add value. I don't even think that I'm helping them at the level I want and that my leaders deserve.*

> **Dr. Williams:** *If you don't want to be perceived as nonprofessional, or not being able to respond and add value, what do you want instead?*
>
> **Suzanne:** *I want the department heads to be a little more patient as I go through this transition period.*

Dr. Williams does a good job of converting an away-from statement into a positive statement of what is wanted or desired. However, Suzanne's answer does not meet the second condition for a well-formed outcome: an outcome must be able to be self-initiated and self-maintained.

SELF-INITIATED AND SELF-MAINTAINED

A well-formed outcome is one that the person, by him or herself, can initiate, manage, and control. The test for this is to pose a simple inquiry to the person you are helping: *"Is the attainment of this outcome dependent on you, or others?"* A person cannot directly control the responses of other people, and yet it is common to want someone else to change or do something differently as a solution to one's problem or discontent. In spite of the best of intentions, the most one can reasonably hope for is to *influence* another person in a desired direction by behaving differently. In doing so, one can increase the probability that the other person will respond in a preferred manner. Placing the attainment of one's outcome at the mercy of others is to invite failure; therefore, when a person's outcome is for others to change, it must be reframed in such a way that it can be self-initiated and self-controlled. You can do this by asking: *"What do you need to do differently that will increase the chances that you'll get what you want from them?"*

> **Dr. Williams:** *So, tell me, Suzanne, what do you want to be different in the future?*
>
> **Suzanne:** *I don't want to be perceived as nonprofessional or not being able to respond and add value. I don't even think that I'm helping them at the level I want and that my leaders deserve.*
>
> **Dr. Williams:** *If you don't want to be perceived as nonprofessional or not being able to respond and add value, what do you want instead?*
>
> **Suzanne:** *I want the department heads to be a little more patient as I go through this transition period.*
>
> **Dr. Williams:** *OK, what can <u>you do</u> differently that will increase the chances that the department heads will be a little more patient with you as you go through this transition period?*

Dr. Williams has refocused the conversation on that over which Suzanne has direct control and can be self-initiated (i.e., her behavior). If an outcome is not defined so that it can be self-initiated and self-controlled, then the person must be challenged to rethink it. In the final analysis, the only thing people can control is their own thinking and behavior.

The Importance of Control

Whenever possible, assist people in realizing where, when, and how they can take control so as to avoid a feeling of helplessness or victimization. Personal control has been the subject of various psychological theories, but one in particular has emphasized personal control as a critical variable in an individual's personality and behavior: Rotter's locus of control theory (Rotter, 1954; Lefcourt, 1982). Locus of control theory states that people either believe they are in control of their life (internal locus of control) or that their life is controlled by environmental factors over which they have no influence (external locus of control). An internal locus of control has been determined to correlate positively with a variety of success factors. Fostering an internal locus of control is essential for the coaching process to work. The belief that you can determine your own internal state, direct your own behavior, and influence your environment sufficiently to achieve desired outcomes is a prerequisite for self-directed change and self-directed problem solving.

One's sense of personal control can also affect one's response to potential stressors. Everyone feels stress at one time or another, and when we do it is common practice to blame the stressor. For example, Suzanne attributed her stress to the fact that department heads were coming to her with all sorts of questions and issues. However, that is not the cause of her stress; it is her sense of powerlessness in response to the situation that generates a stress reaction. The role of powerlessness or lack of control as a driver of stress has long been demonstrated by researchers studying the phenomenon of learned helplessness (Maier & Seligman, 1976). Once Suzanne has a greater sense of control by identifying the actions she can take to respond affirmatively to her situation, her stress level will decrease.

A perceived lack of control can lead to decreased motivation. Suppose you are asked if you'd like to take on a new assignment; however, after exploring it further, you find out that you do not have control over the decisions needed to be successful. All things being equal, what is your most likely answer? Most people are not motivated to take on an assignment without sufficient control over the important decisions that affect their ability to succeed. When people believe that it doesn't matter what they do because they can't impact the outcome, they see their actions as futile, and they stop trying; their motivation is reduced. For all of the reasons cited above, a well-formed outcome must be under the person's control so that it can be self-initiated and self-controlled.

Let's return to Suzanne's problem situation, but in this instance her outcome is stated in the positive, and can be self-initiated and self-controlled.

Suzanne: *I've gotten new responsibilities, but I don't have the people. So I'm supporting two large departments from an HR perspective, and I'm really, really feeling stressed out because the department heads are coming to me with all sorts of questions and issues and, quite honestly, with the few resources I have, I'm not able to keep up with the activity. I'm feeling over my head. I don't want to let anybody down.*

> **Dr. Williams:** *So, tell me, Suzanne, what do you want to be different in the future?*
> **Suzanne:** *I want to get a handle on my own emotions, my stress level. My own personal stress bounces all over the place day to day.*

DEMONSTRABLE INDICATORS OF SUCCESS

Lewis Carroll wrote in his literary classic, *Alice in Wonderland,* "If you don't know where you're going, any road will get you there." While this is true, it is also true that if you don't know what it looks like when you arrive you'll never know if you've gotten there. Therefore, the conditions for a well-formed outcome require that the person identify demonstrable indicators of success. There are several reasons why specifying indicators of success is important:

- Specifying indicators of success helps to clarify what a person wants.
- Specifying indicators of success helps to define a path to success.
- Specifying indicators of success helps to make change noticeable.
- Specifying indicators of success reality tests a person's expectations.

CLARIFYING WHAT A PERSON WANTS

When Suzanne says, "I want to get a handle on my own emotions, my stress level," what does she really mean, specifically? In chapter five, it was explained that people speak in surface structure language, which is missing a lot of detail. By asking Suzanne how she will know when she is handling her emotions, and stress, in the way that she wants, you are asking her to clarify what handling her emotions and stress specifically means to her. It is analogous to asking her to write the text of a book, instead of just the chapter headings. This helps her translate a desired internal state into outward evidence of success.

> **Dr. Williams:** *So, tell me, Suzanne, what do you want to be different in the future?*
> **Suzanne:** *I want to get a handle on my own emotions, my stress level. My own personal stress bounces all over the place day to day.*
> **Dr. Williams:** *In what way do you want to get a handle on your emotions and stress?* [Use intelligent listening to clarify her narrative]
> **Suzanne:** *Oh gosh, I don't even know what to say. What do I want to do? I feel that, now, I'm showing my frustration. I want to be level in my emotions. I want to be able to deal with people, and not come across that I don't have the time to answer their questions, or that I'm putting them off. I feel as if I might be coming across that way. That might be my own thinking; I don't know whether it's true or not. So, yeah, I want to understand how to manage all of that.*

Dr. Williams: *Well, if you were level in your emotions, and you were dealing with people in the way that you want—even though you were frustrated or overwhelmed—what would you see, hear, or experience? How would you know that was happening?* [Asks for demonstrable indicators of success]

Suzanne: *I would be enjoying the interaction with the people. I would be building a relationship with them, gaining their trust; maybe even using a sense of humor. It would be a dynamic interaction where they walked away feeling good and I walked away feeling good. We would have made a nice connection, even if I couldn't answer all of their questions at that time, and I had to defer them to a meeting next week, or whatever. I would feel good. I would feel like a professional. I would feel as if I were giving it my best.*

From here, Dr. Williams can "zoom in" to recover more detail about what success looks like. For example, asking Suzanne what would be a concrete indication that she and the other person had made "a nice connection" gets to the next level of specificity, and adds detail to her narrative. Asking Suzanne to spell out what she would experience when she is successful at handling her emotions and stress level gives her desired future state definition. Furthermore, by talking about the positive indicators of success, she is unconsciously reminding herself of the benefits to be attained by taking action toward these outcomes.

It Helps to Define a Path to Success

Imagine that you have a goal of traveling to California from Texas, and a successful trip means seeing the Pacific Ocean. To experience success, the route you take will be quite different from the one you will travel if a successful trip is defined as seeing the Sierra Nevada Mountains. Once a person has spelled out a concrete picture of success, it is easier to construct a "route" to that destination than if the definition of success is vague and ill-defined. Once success is defined, it is possible to think about the necessary actions to be taken that will result in success as the person defines it.

It Helps Make Change Noticeable

People rarely achieve their picture of success in one giant leap. Change takes place over time, therefore, to keep from getting discouraged, people have to know that they are moving in the right direction. Having concrete, behavioral, and measurable indicators of success will enable them to measure their progress, and reinforces the fact that they are moving in the right direction. As the saying goes, "Success creates success" so when people can see evidence of their progress this stimulates their continuing efforts toward a preferred future.

It Reality Tests Their Expectations

When asked for concrete indicators of success, some people respond in unrealistic ways. For example, if Suzanne said that one indicator of success was that the department heads would stop asking her questions, it would not be realistic given that it is probably not going to happen. Allowing people to establish unrealistic indicators of success sets them up for failure. Well-formed outcomes must be achievable given the client's capacities and the context in which she operates.

DEFINING DEMONSTRABLE INDICATORS OF SUCCESS

As discussed in chapter five, each person has a unique map-of-the-world, a particular perception of reality. Within that map, there is an intuitive picture of what success is for any desired outcome. However, the person's intuitive definition of success must be translated into concrete indicators of what will be seen, heard, or experienced when the desired outcome is attained. There are two frames of reference that the person can use to define the demonstrable indicators of a successful outcome: Self and Other. Using both frames of reference enables people to sharpen their focus on what a picture of success looks like. Defining success from one's own perspective is generally the best starting point when asking people to tell you what they will experience when their desired outcome has been achieved. This is the approach taken by Dr. Williams when he asked Suzanne to tell him how she would know that she was being successful in handling her emotions and her stress. People can be challenged to think about how they would know that they are getting what they want by being asking questions similar to:

- How would you know if you had what you wanted?
- What will be different for you when you have achieved your desired outcome?
- If I see you in a month's time and you have dealt with the problem, or gotten what you wanted, describe what is different.
- What would be happening when you get what you want that's not happening now?

These questions, or questions like them, are designed to help people describe a picture of success that is concrete and, therefore, measureable. However, people sometimes have trouble envisioning what success would look like for them. For example, asking the Chief Nursing Officer how she will know when she has become a better leader may elicit a response such as "I don't know. I'm not sure." When a person doesn't seem to know how to describe demonstrable indicators of success, changing the frame-of-reference is often helpful. Ask the person to define a successful outcome from the *perspective of what other people might see, hear, or experience*. The Chief Nursing Officer, for example, could be asked to tell you what her staff might notice that is different when she is a better leader, or Dr. Williams could ask Suzanne, "What would your department heads see, hear, or experience if you were dealing with them in the way that you want?" You can use the same types of questions listed above, but change them to a third-party perspective. In fact, it is often helpful to obtain both perspectives in the same conversation to obtain a complete picture of a successful outcome.

John is a new nurse supervisor and needs help. His recent promotion has put him in a position of supervising a head nurse who is a good friend of his outside of work. He often finds himself in a situation where he needs to deliver a difficult message to his friend as part of his supervisory role, but he doesn't want to endanger their relationship. This leads him to tolerate behavior in his friend that he would not accept in others on the team. He believes that the other nurses on his team are noticing this, and he feels that he is losing their respect as a leader. John has sat down with his Director of Nursing, explained his situation, and asked for her advice. She has clarified parts of his story using the inquiry techniques in Support-for-Thought, and now moves into Challenge-for-Thought.

Director of Nursing: John, based upon what we've talked about so far, what would you like to be different in the future?

John: *I'd really like to find a way to become a more responsible leader in this situation rather than being viewed as a friend first.*

Director of Nursing: *If you were being a more responsible leader, rather than a friend first, what would it look like; what would you be seeing, hearing, or experiencing?*

John: *Well, I'd be coming to work thinking more objectively about what needs to be done. If there were a problem with someone, I would be able to put aside my personal feelings.*

Director of Nursing: *Think for a moment about your friend, specifically. How would you know if you were thinking objectively about what needs to be done in dealing with him, and were "putting aside" your personal feelings?*

John: *I guess I'd be focusing more on what we have to do as a team. That would be my first priority.*

Director of Nursing: *OK. What else would you be doing?*

John: *I wouldn't be looking at his work hoping there wasn't anything I needed to correct.* [Stated in the negative]

Director of Nursing: *What would you be doing instead?*

John: *Well, if there is a problem, I'd be taking it in stride.*

Director of Nursing: *How would I know that you were taking it in stride?* [Asking for a third-party perspective]

John: *If I noticed a problem, I'd be talking with him about it and offering feedback on how he could improve his work. I would still be giving him positives, but I wouldn't be afraid to challenge him if I thought it would improve the outcome.*

Director of Nursing: *What else would let you know that you're being a responsible leader?*

John: *I would be thinking that this is something that I'd do with anybody on the team. I'm not just singling him out and that this isn't personal. We can still be friends, but this is what I need to do as leader of the team.*

> **Director of Nursing:** *What would other people on the team be noticing if you were being a responsible leader in the way that you want? [Moves to obtaining a third-party perspective]*
>
> **John:** *I think they will see that I am treating everyone fairly and that no one is getting special treatment because I've known them longer, or have a personal relationship with them. Also, they will notice that I am spending more time with each of them than I have in the past.*
>
> **Director of Nursing:** *And this friend that you're talking about, what would he be noticing?*
>
> **John:** *I think he would notice that I'm being more serious in my work interactions with him and that I'm not thrown off by our friendship. I think he would notice that I'm drawing a clearer boundary between our interactions on the job and our interactions as friends off the job. I wouldn't blur the lines as much as I do now.*
>
> **Director of Nursing:** *You said that you wouldn't be thrown off by your friendship with him; such as what, specifically?*
>
> **John:** *I wouldn't be thrown off by jokes, or by him wanting to talk about personal things from off the job. For example, if he brought up something about going to a ball game, I wouldn't wander off into that conversation. I'd keep it focused on work. I'd keep it focused on the job.*
>
> **Director of Nursing:** *It seems like you have a good picture of what success looks like for you if you were being a more responsible leader in the way that you want. So let's talk about the first steps you're going to take to move toward this picture over the short term.*
>
> **John:** *Okay, that sounds good to me.*

When the Director of Nursing asked John to tell her what he wanted to be different in the future, his outcome was stated positively and could be self-initiated and self-controlled; therefore, she was able to move immediately into defining demonstrable indicators of success. During the conversation, she did several things that prepared John to take action:

1. When John starting speaking generally, she asked him to focus on the specific situation with his friend.
2. She asked "what else?" questions (Inviting) to encourage expansive thinking rather than accepting his first answer.
3. When he stated what wouldn't be happening, she used the "instead question" to elicit what *would* be happening.
4. She elicited both self and third-party criteria for success, including what John's friend would see, hear, or experience.

By following the guidelines for a well-formed outcome, including defining demonstrable indicators of success, both the Director of Nursing and John will be able to ascertain his progress relative to those indicators. This will allow the leader to reinforce his progress and to help John readjust future actions if what he is doing is not working.

KEEPING IT SIMPLE

While this chapter contains conceptual information regarding the principles under-lying well-formed outcomes, the actual steps are quite simple. Indeed, they are very intuitive, once you keep in mind the following guidelines:

1. Challenge people using incisive inquiry. Don't be afraid to make them a little uncomfortable in order to help them define what they want in a way that will assist them in taking action toward it.
2. Use intelligent listening skills to help people construct a well-formed outcome that has enough detail to be useful.
3. Keep these questions in mind as you begin to Challenge-for-Thought:
   - What does the person want to be different going forward?
   - Has the person stated what he wants in positive terms rather than stating what he does not want?
   - Is the means to achieve what he wants under his control so that it can be self-initiated and self-maintained?
   - What will the person (and others) see, hear, or experience that will indicate success?
4. Keep their outcomes realistic. It is better to break up large goals into smaller, achievable outcomes rather than risk failure by trying to do too much.

It may be tempting to simplify the purpose of the Challenge-for-Thought stage by thinking of it as merely challenging people to design and set goals. However, as stated earlier in this chapter, goals are ill-defined and can be considered "fuzzy visions" of what people want; whereas, well-formed outcomes are more actionable. Once a person has thought through and constructed a well-formed outcome, it is time to act. It is time to do something to move toward the realization of that out-come through a series of small steps. In fact, it is not uncommon that the experi-ence of taking action creates a feedback loop which causes the individual to refine what it is they actually want.

COACHING AS A LEADERSHIP STYLE

At the organizational level, leaders set the stage for success by shaping key variables that affect performance, one of which is goal clarity. The effectiveness of a trans-formational leader is due, in part, to her ability to articulate a clear and compelling vision that, in turn, is used to foster goal clarity. When leaders are able to clarify goals they set into motion a chain of events that cascade to the job level by focusing attention on what individuals need to do to achieve those goals (Pandey & Wright, 2006).

This process begins when a leader is able to get followers to envision attractive future states, a critical aspect of Inspirational Motivation (Bass & Riggio, 2006). This is similar to developing discrepancy, in that the future state becomes clear when it is communicated as to how it will be different from the present in a way that is positive and compelling. Next, the leader needs to translate that vision of the future into concrete and measureable indicators of success (i.e., definable outcomes), so leaders and followers can track their progress. These definable outcomes are the crossover mechanism between setting the vision and turning it into reality through a series of focused actions. Leaders that utilize the criteria for well-formed outcomes are able to get followers to envision successful outcomes over which they have control, which leads to a clear and optimistic vision of the future.

Connie is a nurse manager responsible for a 33-person staff, including 23 RNs and 10 patient care assistants (PCAs). She recently lost 2 RNs and, because of a hiring freeze, has not been able to replace them. As a result of the heavy workload and reduced staff, stress levels have been high and morale is low. She decided that something had to been done and decided to start with an off-site gathering for her and her staff (at least those that could attend because they were off duty).

Because she had worked with many of the people for years and her relationships were generally positive, it was not difficult to get them to open up about the problems they faced. Among them were decreased teamwork, a lack of opportunities for professional development, and a sense among the staff that their interests were being ignored, and they were not being supported by the hospital's leadership. After listing and prioritizing the problems and issues, Connie asked the team what they wanted to be different in the future. Not surprisingly, many of the ideas put forth represented away-from thinking; a list of what they didn't want. Using the principles for creating well-formed outcomes, Connie was able to turn their thinking toward positive statements of what they wanted instead, eliminate those over which she and the team didn't have direct control, and turn the discussion into defining what would constitute demonstrable indicators of success. While this was only the first step of a longer process, the team members left feeling heard, understood, and—because they could envision successful outcomes over which they had control—optimistic that things would get better.

Chapter 8

Challenge-for-Action
A Path to Doing

A coaching conversation is a balance between depth and movement. Depth provides detail and promotes understanding; it clarifies the narrative, sharpens thinking, and produces insight. Movement, on the other hand, creates progress over time, resulting in experiential change. Each stage of the Four-square Coaching Framework emphasizes either depth or movement. Support-for-Thought emphasizes depth by building a platform of understanding of people's current situations and clarifying their narrative through the deletion recovery process. Challenge-for-Thought increases depth by urging people to define what they want according to the conditions of a well-formed outcome. However, depth without movement becomes a purely intellectual exercise. A well-defined destination does not help people move from where they are to where they want to go without developing a path to that destination and taking action to reach it. Alfred Adler, the famous Austrian physician and psychotherapist, is quoted as saying, "Trust only movement. Life happens at the level of events, not of words. Trust movement" (Hutt, 2009, par. 1). It is the purpose of Challenge-for-Action to create movement by identifying and choosing action strategies that fit the opportunities, conditions, and timeframes for achieving well-formed outcomes developed during Challenge-for-Thought. The stage-specific activities for Challenge-for-Action are designed to answer three questions:

1. **What** does the person have to **do** to get what she wants?
2. **How** is she going to go about it?
3. **When** and **where** is she going to start doing it?

THERE IS NO RIGHT ANSWER

In chapter seven, Suzanne specified the demonstrable indicators of the outcome she is seeking.

> *I would be enjoying the interaction with the people. I would be building a relationship with them, gaining their trust; maybe even using a sense of humor. It would be a dynamic interaction where they walked away feeling good and I walked away feeling good. We would have made a nice connection, even if I couldn't answer all of their questions at that time, and I had to defer them to a meeting next week, or whatever. I would feel good. I would feel like a professional. I would feel as if I was giving it my best.*

For Suzanne to achieve her desired outcome, what actions should be taken? There is no one right answer to this question. There are as many different action possibilities as there are answers to the question *"What should I do to get what I want?"* Discovering the actions that will work requires a heuristic approach. The word *heuristic* is derived from the Greek word *heuriskein*, meaning to "find" or "discover." A heuristic method is one "which on the basis of experience or judgment, seems likely to yield a good solution to a problem, but which cannot be guaranteed . . . . " (Foulds, 1983, p. 929). In other words, a heuristic approach involves trying to find a solution using a good guess, educated trial and error, and common sense, but success is not assured . Feedback is obtained from what one has tried and used to refine one's approach until the desired results are achieved. Most of life's problems require the heuristic method because they contain too much ambiguity and uncertainty to yield to a schoolbook solution.

Following the heuristic approach is much like encountering dense fog on the way to a destination where you've never been. The fog makes it difficult to see very far ahead, and since you can't predict what's there (e.g. road construction, detours, etc.), you go forward based upon what you can see and as new stretches of road become visible, you modify your driving to fit the circumstances. Similarly, when people decide to take action as part of a heuristic approach, they choose their path based upon their current knowledge of the situation. The results of those actions will provide them with new information that will affect their future decisions about what to do.

As noted in chapter two, people seek help for several reasons. First, their problem situation is not a problem in the scientific sense with a clear answer that can be readily deduced using their formal training. Second, they are not being as effective as they would like to be and don't know what to do. Finally, they want to tap into their unused potential and better themselves professionally, but are not sure how to go about it. In all cases, the heuristic method is the only approach that can yield a satisfactory solution; therefore, the heuristic approach provides the model for the methods and practices used in Challenge-for-Action.

EXPERIMENTS

"Helping too often entails too much talking and too little action" (Egan, 2010, p.112). When you enter the Challenge-for-Action phase, you are moving the focus of the conversation from depth to movement. Movement requires the person take action, but due to the nature of the heuristic process, success is not guaranteed from those actions. Therefore, it reduces the degree of psychological risk if the person thinks of these actions as experiments rather than a formal action plan. As Neenan and Palmer (2012, p. 97) point out, "Experiments are a very effective way of gathering information, testing hypotheses, re-evaluating previous conclusions, responding to 'I don't know'." Reframing an action idea as an experiment rather than a step in an action plan, reduces the pressure to be perfect the first time. It sends a "let's try this and see what happens" message, thereby reducing "paralysis by analysis" so that the person can start doing something instead of waiting to figure out a flawless approach. Action, not perfection, is the goal.

> **Suzanne:** *I would be enjoying the interaction with the people. I would be building a relationship with them, gaining their trust; maybe even using a sense of humor. It would be a dynamic interaction where they walked away feeling good and I walked away feeling good. We would have made a nice connection, even if I couldn't answer all of their questions at that time, and I had to defer them to a meeting next week, or whatever. I would feel good. I would feel like a professional. I would feel as if I was giving it my best.*
> **Dr. Williams:** *What might you <u>experiment</u> with doing that will help you begin handling your emotions and stress so that you experience the kind of outcomes that you've just mentioned?*

With this question, Dr. Williams has just transitioned from the Challenge-for-Thought stage to the Challenge-for-Action stage of the Four-square Coaching Framework.

THREE TYPES OF EXPERIMENTS

There are three types of experiments, or action steps, which can start people down the path to getting what they want: Observing, Thinking, and Doing.

Observing Experiments

Observing is the only experiment a person can undertake without changing their thinking or behavior. Observing merely means that the person is attempting to gain feedback by focusing his attention on what is happening in a particular situation, with the intent that the information will help him design some thinking or doing actions in the future. For example, the colleague who feels overwhelmed by her commitments because she is unable to say "No" to requests for help, may choose to experiment with observing what happens during those situations when she is approached by others and asked to commit to projects for which she has no time. By observing how she reacts, what she does or doesn't do, what she thinks about, what others say or do that make it difficult for her to say no, she is gaining information that can be used to construct thinking and doing experiments in the future.

Observing is often a useful first step for several reasons. First, it is a low-risk experiment; it doesn't require the person to try to do something different, and yet the person will still feel a sense of movement as she prepares for action. It would be similar to the feeling one has when researching background material for a paper you are going to write; you haven't started writing, but you are moving in the right direction. Second, observing can be a vital source of information. It forces people to direct their attention to aspects of themselves and their environment that may have gone unnoticed in the past. Although people may know what they want to try, imposing a period of observation may sharpen their perspective. Noticing something different can lead to doing something different.

Finally, an observing experiment can forestall ill-considered actions. For some people, their problem is not that they refuse to act, but they act hastily, and in the process may act imprudently. It is not uncommon for people to want to act on the first idea that comes to mind rather than exploring a variety of options, and then choosing one based upon due consideration. A sense of urgency is important, but beware of false urgency (Kotter, 2008). False urgency results in doing many activities, but going nowhere; it is activity for its own sake. Experimenting with observation before designing actions can fend off the impulsiveness that false urgency can inspire.

Thinking Experiments

Experimenting with a different way of thinking is often a necessary action step in order to achieve what a person wants. Changing one's thinking requires that a person become aware of his current thinking patterns, evaluate how his thinking is helping or hurting him in a particular situation, and substitute a new way of interpreting the situation or a new set of thoughts that will help him feel or behave in the way that he wants. For example, in the last chapter, John realized that to be a more responsible leader he will need to change his thinking when giving difficult feedback to his friend by reminding himself *"this is something that I'd do with anybody on the team. I'm not just singling him out, and this isn't personal. This is what I need to do as leader of the team."* Changing one's thinking is especially important if the desired outcome is to change one's emotional state, as it is with Suzanne, who wants to reduce her stress. Dr. Williams can help Suzanne by encouraging her to experiment with changing the way she thinks about the situation in order to produce a different emotional response.

Suzanne: *I would be enjoying the interaction with the people. I would be building a relationship with them, gaining their trust; maybe even using a sense of humor. It would be a dynamic interaction where they walked away feeling good and I walked away feeling good. We would have made a nice connection, even if I couldn't answer all of their questions at that time, and I had to defer them to a meeting next week, or whatever. I would feel good. I would feel like a professional. I would feel as if I was giving it my best.*

Dr. Williams: *So, what might you experiment with changing about how you think about this situation that would be helpful, even in some small way?*

Suzanne: *I guess I could try reminding myself that the directors are not trying to make my life miserable; they are just trying to do their job.*

Dr. Williams: *How would that help you?*

Suzanne: *I don't believe I would take what they do as personally as I might otherwise.*

Dr. Williams: *That's good. Now, what else are you currently thinking that is interfering with getting what you want?*

Suzanne: *Sometimes I think that if I don't respond to all of their requests immediately I'm not doing my job.*

Dr. Williams: *If you were to experiment with thinking differently about that the next time you are being bombarded with requests, what might you try?*

Suzanne: *Well, it would probably help if I keep in mind the fact that I don't have to put everybody's requests on the high priority list all of the time. I could remind myself to step back, look at the request objectively, and decide where on my list of priorities it realistically falls.*

Dr. Williams: *How will this help you?*

Suzanne: *I think it would reduce my stress and I would be more relaxed in my interactions with them knowing that I have some control over how I will deal with their requests for information.*

Dr. Williams: *Are you willing to give this a try?*

Suzanne: *Definitely; this next week will be a rough one, and I'll have plenty of opportunities to see how it works.*

Doing Experiments

What is the answer to the following riddle? If five green frogs are sitting on a log, and four decide to jump off, how many frogs are left on the log? The answer: Five. Deciding to do something is not doing it. Taking action is the most important step in creating movement toward desired outcomes; therefore, urging the person to experiment with different actions to achieve their goal is essential to the coaching process. Deciding what to do can be a challenge for some people, but there are several ways to identify or generate actions with which to experiment.

1. Recover the behaviors associated with unspecified action verbs.
2. Identify actions stated as outcomes during Challenge-for-Thought.
3. Use the actions listed as indicators of success in a well-formed outcome.
4. Make action-specific inquiries: Three magic questions.
5. Offer suggestions.
6. Use the feedback from previous action experiments.

1. Recover the Behaviors Associated with Unspecified Action Verbs

In chapter five, you were introduced to the concept of Intelligent Listening: recognizing important deletions in the person's surface level language and constructing inquiries to recover those deletions. If you recall, one type of deletion is an unspecified action verb; a word that conveys an action, but does not specify the specific behavior associated with that action. For example, in the sentence "*I am going try to influence my direct reports in a positive way,*" the word *influence* is an action verb. Therefore, an intelligent question is "*What are you going to* **do** *to influence your direct reports in a positive way?*" By asking this question, you challenge the person to fill in the actions or behaviors that she believes will achieve her stated desire, in this case, to influence her direct reports in a positive way. Her answer can be used to construct a doing experiment by following up with the questions "How are you going to do this?" and "When are you going to start?"

2. Identify Actions Stated As Outcomes During Challenge-for-Thought

During the Challenge-for-Thought stage, the practice of developing discrepancy was introduced so that a person can think about the difference between where they are and where they want to be as a means for establishing a change goal. In the process of challenging people to define the difference, it is not uncommon that they begin to talk about what they want to *do* differently from what they are currently doing.

Lab Manager: *You mentioned that you don't feel as organized as you would like. Is that correct?*
Lab Tech: *Yeah, I seem to be doing things twice when I could get them done once if I were more organized.*
Lab Manager: *What is different about the way you would like to be organized than the way you are now?* [Challenge-for-Thought: developing discrepancy]
Lab Tech: *Well, I think that I could start making a list and using that to organize my thinking. I'm not doing that now. I could also talk to Maria to find out how she stays so organized. I bet she has some good ideas.*

In this example, the Lab Manager was attempting to create a well-formed outcome as part of Challenge-for-Thought, but the Lab Tech moved directly into the Challenge-for-Action stage by responding with actions he could take. The Lab Manager can remain in the Challenge-for-Action stage, ask him to elaborate on those actions, and then construct a doing experiment.

3. Use the Actions Listed As Indicators of Success in a Well-Formed Outcome

During the Challenge-for-Thought stage well-formed outcomes are created. One of the conditions for a well-formed outcome is that it include demonstrable indicators of success i.e., evidence by which the outcome can be determined to have been achieved. These indicators of success are stated in terms of what the person, or others, will see, hear, feel, or experience were the goal to become a reality. Often, imbedded within these indicators of success are descriptions of actions that would be taken by the person. Actions listed as indicators of success during the Challenge-for-Thought stage can be used in the Challenge-for-Action stage to create action experiments.

The Chief Medical Officer (CMO) of a large, non-profit healthcare network is an up-and-coming leader. She is a very driven, optimistic person that does a good job of surrounding herself with a strong team from whom she is able to gain a lot of loyalty. Lately, however, she has begun to get feedback that some of her leadership practices are causing problems. For example, because of her desire to get things right, she is perceived as being too much in the weeds and focusing on details that other members of her team should be handling rather than focusing on the big picture.

While optimistic, she is viewed as sugar-coating issues and discounting the seriousness of some of the problems, especially when it comes to confronting hard issues with her team. In fact, it is so important to her that her team is happy, she allows each person to march to the beat of his own drum without maintaining a consistent set of expectations for everyone. This came to a head recently when she excused some members of the team from a series of meetings because "they were working on important projects" while expecting the rest of the team to be in all of the meetings. She has turned to the CEO, a mentor of hers, to talk about how she can change her leadership behavior. He was able to help her define a well-formed outcome for the change that she wants with the following indicators of success.

- She would be backing away from day-to-day issues and letting them be handled by the team.
- The team would notice that she is very direct with them, even when discussing issues that may be uncomfortable.
- Her team will see that she is holding everyone to the same standards, and when an individual doesn't comply, the team would see that person experience the consequences.
- She would be asking more questions rather than giving the team the answers to their problems.

These indicators of success are listed as actions. By using intelligent listening and inquiry to add specificity, these actions can be turned into *doing experiments* to help her make the changes in her leadership style that she wishes .

4. Make Action-Specific Inquiries: Three Magic Questions

Asking people directly for actions they are willing to take in order to achieve their desired outcome is an obvious way to create movement. A variation on this approach is to use three questions that are almost magical in the way that they elicit different types of actions that can be tried by the person you are helping. The author refers to these inquiries as the three magic questions.

1. What are you doing that if you did more of it, would move you toward your desired outcome?
2. What are you doing that if you did less of it—or stopped doing it altogether—would move you toward your desired outcome?
3. What are you *not* doing that if you started doing it, would move you toward your desired outcome?

These three questions serve as a structure for helping people think about what to experiment with as far as doing something to achieve what they want. They are important because they operationalize three valuable ideas relative to doing experiments.

- Question #1 acknowledges the fact that people may already be doing things that are making them effective and that merely doing more of what is already working can provide additional momentum to help them achieve their desired outcome. It is much easier to urge people to experiment with doing more of something that they already know how to do rather than to do something they have never done before.

- Question #2 acknowledges the fact that people sometimes do things that simply do not work for them as far as getting what they want. In other words, they get in their own way because some aspect of their behavior is actually a roadblock to progress. To get what they want, their plan of action will have to include the reduction or elimination of behaviors that are an impediment to achieving their desired future. Recently, for example, a colleague felt overwhelmed by the commitments she had undertaken at the request of her peers. As it turned out, one of the things she needed to experiment with doing was to say "yes" less often and, for the short-term, stop saying it all together. Her acquiescent behavior interfered with the goal of creating a better work-life balance than what she was currently experiencing.

- Question #3 acknowledges that to reach a goal one may have to start doing something new, something that the person has not done before. For example, when Doug, a Vice President for Health Affairs for a prominent academic medical center on the East Coast, realized that his relationship with some of his chairs was not as good as he wanted, he decided that he needed to do something different that would help improve these important relationships. After discussing the situation with a close colleague, he decided that he would start showing more appreciation toward his colleagues than he had shown in the past, especially when a chair unexpectedly helped or supported him. This was something he had neglected to do in the past because he took their compliance for granted. Therefore, as part of his plan, he begin sending personal thank-you notes whenever chairs went out of their way to help him. While it seemed like a small gesture, it had very positive results. Doing something different does not have to be a major change in behavior. In fact, a series of small changes in behavior—over time—is the best approach.

5. Offer Suggestions

Some people believe that it is inappropriate for a person who is coaching to offer suggestions during a helping conversation. They believe that making suggestion should only be done with your teaching or mentoring hat on. However, suggestions, when delivered in a coach-like manner, can provide your client with valuable ideas and speed up the action-taking process. What does a coach-like manner sound like? As noted in chapter five, framing your suggestion as a question and delivering it from an Adult ego state enables you to offer a suggestion and maintain the spirit of the coaching. For instance, you might ask your colleague who is bemoaning the fact that she impulsively succumbs to the requests of her peers, but later regrets taking on more commitments, this question: *"Have you thought about waiting a day before you respond to a request so that you don't make an impulsive or ill-advised decision?"* You are offering a helpful suggestion, but leaving it up to the person to consider what she wants to do with it. Offering a suggestion is not the same as giving advice.

6. Use the Feedback from Previous Action Experiments

Because of the heuristic nature of the problems and issues discussed in a coaching conversation, deciding on the actions that will lead to desired outcomes is an educated trial-and-error process. After people do what they think will help them achieve their goal, they assess the efficacy of their actions, and next steps are determined from what has, or has not, worked. These new actions are usually the product of follow-up coaching conversations in which progress is the subject of discussion. During these conversations, it is appropriate to ask the following questions:

- Did the person actually do what he said he was going to do?
- If not, what stopped him, and what does he need to do differently to follow through next time?
- If so, how did the actions work?
- Based upon what happened, are there other things the person might want to do more of, stop doing, or starting doing (three magic questions) to achieve what he wants?

COACHING AS A LEADERSHIP STYLE

The purpose of the Challenge-for-Action stage of the Four-square Coaching Framework is to promote action in pursuit of one's goals and objectives. Doing does not always lead to success, but there is no success without the doing; action makes things happen. In leadership, action is also a key to success. The leader who is action-oriented—the active leader—is usually associated with greater satisfaction and effectiveness among their followers. Conversely, less activity is negatively related to the performance and satisfaction of followers (Bass, 2008). There are at least two reasons why action-oriented leadership has been proven to be a central factor in effective leadership generally and transformational leadership specifically: (a) the active leader is task oriented, and (b) their action orientation creates a sense of urgency.

In recent years, much of the emphasis on leadership has been on the social and interpersonal skills necessary to create productive working relationships with peers and followers. This is evidenced by the number of writings touting the importance of emotional intelligence and related concepts to the leadership role. However, early studies of leadership (e.g., Medow & Zander, 1965) focused on a different dimension: task orientation. Task-oriented leaders believe that they must be proactive in pursuing what they want through their actions. They describe themselves as taking initiative and persistent in overcoming obstacles. Consequently, followers perceive them as dependable in the pursuit of objectives. The characteristics associated with action-oriented leaders place them at the high end of the activity dimension in Bass's transformational leadership model as contrasted with less effective leaders who are described as passive (e.g., wait for things to go wrong before taking action, etc.). Therefore, transformational leaders are, by definition, active and take an action-oriented approach to leading.

The qualities of a transformational leader have been shown to be uniquely appropriate for leading organizational change efforts (Eisenbach, Watson, & Pillai, 1999). For example, in order to pull or attract followers to different change possibilities, the leader must craft an appealing vision that takes into consideration the underlying needs and values of the key stakeholders (Inspirational Motivation). However, embedded within the action-oriented approach of a transformational leader is another competency that is linked to fostering change in organizations: the ability to create a sense of urgency. Leadership and change expert John Kotter believes that creating a sense of urgency is essential in bringing about change (2008). However, he also states that a sense of urgency is not the natural state of affairs in most organizations; therefore, it must be created by leaders within the organization. Leaders create a sense of urgency by modeling action-oriented behavior in their day-to-day activities (Idealized Influence) and challenging others to act in order to overcome the inertia that results from the complacency that Kotter believes afflicts organizations. Challenge-for-Action is not only a stage in the Four-square Coaching Framework, it is a means for creating the requisite sense of urgency that is the first step in any organizational change process, and for becoming an action-oriented leader.

Chapter 9

Challenge-for-Action
Go Slow to Go Fast

There has been a movement in science for the last couple of decades away from the perception that scientific progress is the result of sudden flashes of insight and giant leaps of movement. Instead, it is argued that most discoveries are the result of continuing, persistent, methodical practices and study. This approach to scientific research is termed "Slow Science." In his article, "Fast Science vs. Slow Science, Or Slow and Steady Wins the Race," Eugene Garfield writes "important discoveries generally are made by those who doggedly plug along in a field that is ripe for discovery and who are intellectually prepared to recognize and exploit unexpected results" (1990, p. 380). Similarly, in the field of behavioral change and solution-focused endeavors, it is the person who makes small and consistent progress over time that is most likely to achieve sustainable results. Change is rarely easy and generally requires a gradual progression of small steps toward the desired result. When helping a person to decide on new actions, the author suggests following the Law of Least Change: "*What is the least that can be done and still make progress?*" By asking the person this question, you introduce the strategy of making small changes over time and follow Solution-focused Principle #3: "*Small steps lead to big changes.*" There are several advantages to this approach.

OVERCOMING INERTIA

Have you ever tried to change your thinking or behavior only to realize that you've slipped back into your old patterns? Have you ever vowed to change only to realize that you've never gotten around to it? The problem: inertia, the resistance or disinclination to motion, action, or change. What causes it? There are several possibilities, but competing priorities and feeling overwhelmed by what has to be done are heavy contributors.

Professionals in healthcare face a tremendous amount of job pressure, and the time it takes to deal with the day-to-day necessities often leaves no room for the discretionary attention and energy needed to do the things one would like. Most people, for example, have vowed to improve their health by exercising more, but it is common to find that at day's end, once again, there has been no time for it. This problem is exacerbated when the actions that need to be taken are perceived to be overwhelming, e.g., getting in the car, driving to the gym, changing clothes, competing for equipment, and then fighting the traffic home. For change to occur, something needs to happen to get the ball rolling—even slightly. Following the Law of Least Movement reduces the barriers to action.

MAXIMIZING REINFORCEMENT

When people try to do too much too fast, they may become disillusioned if they do not experience the success they expect. Suppose, for example, that Suzanne (chapter eight) created a long list of actions that she thought would help her handle her emotions and stress level during her conversations with department heads, but when she tried to follow her long list it was too much and she became disillusioned. This is not an uncommon experience because change is a heuristic process, and there will inevitably be some actions that are tried that don't work. It is best not to compound the problem by trying to do too much too fast. Instead, create early successes through successive approximations.

The method of successive approximations was first articulated by the father of behavioral psychology, B. F. Skinner (1953). Essentially, this method involves a process of developing complex behaviors by sequencing a series of less complex behaviors such that they build upon one another until success is reached. This approach will facilitate individual change efforts. For instance, when planning an action sequence that will result in a behavioral change goal, start with a simple behavior that can easily be accomplished and leads to an early success experience. Follow it with the next logical behavior, and so on until the final goal is reached. As a person goes through this process, their behavior progresses in successive increments and is continually reinforced; it is the behavioral equivalent of "success breeds success."

INCREASED OPTIONS

A third rationale for encouraging people to take small steps toward their desired outcome, is that it allows them to learn from doing, and in the process, discover options they may not have heretofore considered. It has been previously noted that people choose actions based upon their current assessment of their situation and what it will take to get what they want, but they follow a heuristic path. The key to using the heuristic process successfully is to take small steps and use the feedback from one's actions to adjust behavior accordingly. "Once a person makes a small change, then everything tends to look different from this changed perspective" (Berg & Szabo, 2005, p. 19). This is a strategy that is consistent with action learning whereby a person studies her own actions and experience in order to improve in some way (Marquardt, 2004). Taking small steps gives a person time to reflect upon and learn from experience so that she generates better ideas, makes better decisions, and takes more effective actions in the future. Ultimately, it is a quicker path to sustainable change.

To summarize, small steps lead to big changes because they maximize the probability that a person will make consistent progress over time. Additionally, taking an incremental approach is consistent with the heuristic process. Designing actions that are comprised of a series of small steps helps a person overcome inertia, maximizes reinforcement by yielding early successes, and increases a person's options because of the action learning component of this strategy. In short, going slow to go fast makes sense.

WHERE ARE THEY NOW?

When people decide to take action to achieve a meaningful outcome, it is beneficial to know where they are starting from in relation to their desired outcome. Using a travel analogy, suppose California is your destination, and you are starting from Texas. That will be a different travel plan than if you were starting from New York or Colorado. How you organize your trip, and your expectations for how long it will take to arrive, will vary depending on your starting point. One of the first activities in the Challenge-for-Action stage of the Four-square Coaching Framework is to help people make an assessment of where they are relative to the outcome that they want to achieve. Fortunately, it is easy to do using a simple technique called *scaling* (Berg & de Shazer, 1993).

Dr. Williams: *Suzanne, it sounds as if you have a good idea of what you will experience when you have a handle on your emotions and stress. Now, I have a question for you, "On a scale of zero to ten, with ten being that you are handling your emotions and stress in the way that you want—even if it's not perfect—and zero being the opposite, where, on that scale, are you now?"*

```
0   1   2   3   4   5   6   7   8   9   10
```

This simple zero to ten structure, with ten representing their desired outcome (but not perfection), and zero being the opposite is a simple, visual structure that allows the person to convert intuitive thoughts and feelings into something more concrete and useable. Since each scaling question is handcrafted to the situation, it can be used to access people's perception of almost anything: for example, the distance between where they are now and where they want to be; the resources they have used to get to their present place on the scale; the indicators that tell them where they are on the scale; measures of self-confidence, their degree of investment in changing, and their evaluation of progress along the way. Solution-focused scaling is one of the most flexible coaching tools available to you, and once a person identifies where she is on the scale, you will have several options as to how to proceed.

Dr. Williams: *Suzanne, it sounds as if you have a good idea of what you will experience when you have a handle on your emotions and stress. Now, I have a question for you, "On a scale of zero to ten, with ten being that you are handling your emotions and stress in the way that you want—even if it's not perfect—and zero being the opposite, where, on that scale, are you now?"*

Suzanne: *As I think about it, I guess I would have to say that I'm probably at a six on the scale.*

Once a person provides an intuitive rating of where they are starting from using the numerical scale, the information can be used in several ways:

- To highlight what is going right.
- To plan the person's next small step forward.
- To elicit concrete indications of progress.
- To remind the person of what she has already accomplished.

Highlight What Is Going Right

Suzanne's answer tells you that, while she wants to do better, she is obviously doing something right in handling her emotions in order for her to rate herself a six. In fact, any number that is not a zero tells you that they are doing something positive. Therefore, the first question you might ask is, "*Given that you have rated yourself a six, you must be doing something right that would keep it from being lower. What are you doing that's helping you rate yourself at that level?*" Identifying what the person is currently doing that is working—even a little—can be a starting point from which to build additional action steps. It is quite common that people will be so preoccupied with what they want to be different in the future that they fail to note that there are already positive things happening in the present, and something must already be working for them if they have a positive rating as a starting point. By identifying what they are already doing that is working, you are following a very simple, solution-focused axiom for designing actions: If something is working, do more of it (de Shazer et al., 2006).

What if the person says zero? This is definitely a rare answer. In fact, the author does not recall anybody rating themselves a zero as a starting point, but if they do, it is a sign that they are deep in the midst of a troubling situation, and are trying to dig themselves out. Show empathy, and ask what they are doing to cope with this situation given that their current rating would suggest that they perceive themselves very far away from their goal. As soon as possible, move to the next step; that is, what can they do to move up the scale?

Plan Their Next Small Step Forward

When helping a person design action experiments, remember to follow Solution-focused Principle #3: *"Small steps lead to big changes."* Scaling makes it easy to do this by asking people what they would have to do to move up the scale a small amount. Generally, it is best if a person thinks about what it would take to move up one or two points, but no more. For example, *"What would you have to do to move up from a six to a seven, or maybe an eight, on the scale?"* These small steps then generate actions which can be either doing more of what is currently working, or trying something different. While simple, this is not necessarily easy when working with Elite Professionals. These people are used to ambitious action plans. They are impatient, and their achievement need drives them to want to succeed at whatever they take on as quickly as possible, but the nature of the heuristic process requires that they go slow to go fast. Too often they are inclined to overreach with their action steps, and it can lead to failure and discouragement. You can help them resist succumbing to their achievement-driven instincts.

Elicit Concrete Indications of Progress

In chapter seven, the rationales for helping people specify what they want to be different in their future (developing discrepancy) were provided. Once discrepancy has been developed, a goal can be converted to a well-formed outcome, which includes asking the person to specify demonstrable indicators of success. The idea of describing demonstrable indicators of success also applies to the technique of scaling. Asking people to identify the indicators that will tell them when a specific point on the scale has been reached helps them to quantify signs of progress for each step along the way. Answers to questions such as *"What will tell you that you have moved one point up the scale?"* or *"How will you know when you have reached a seven or eight on the scale?"* elicit measurements by which they can judge their own progress and provide a clear target for their action experiments.

Remind Them of What They Have Accomplished

Scaling can also be used to measure the results of actions taken. Checking in with the person to assess how things are going and to determine the next steps to be taken is a necessary part of the coaching progression. By asking for a new estimation on where people are on the scale relative to where they started, it is possible to document, and reinforce, any movement that has occurred. For example, when a person says, *"I think that I'm now at a seven whereas before I was at a six,"* the person is compelled to notice her own progress, and recognizing her progress reinforces her efforts. Once progress is identified, inquiries can be made about what the person did to make that progress, setting the stage for the next round of action experiments.

INTRODUCING THE SCALE

Scaling can be introduced, in general, as follows:

> *"Imagine a scale from zero to ten with ten being when you have reached your desired outcome and zero being the opposite. Where, on that scale, would you say you are now?"*

In place of the words "your desired outcome" you can restate the specific outcome formulated during the Challenge-for-Thought stage. While ten represents the achievement of the stated outcome, it should not be presented as a state of perfection. Additionally, it is best to leave zero relatively vague allowing people to define what it means for their individual situation, hence the phrase *"with zero being the opposite."* The possibilities for the use of scaling are many, but as a rule of thumb it is best introduced as part of the Challenge-for-Action stage after the person has developed a well-formed outcome during Challenge-for-Thought.

Dr. Williams: *Suzanne, it sounds as if you have a good idea of what you will experience when you have a handle on your emotions and stress. Now, I have a question for you, On a scale of zero to ten, with ten being that you are handling your emotions and stress in the way that you want, even if it's not perfect, and zero being the opposite, where, on that scale, are you now?*

Suzanne: *As I think about it, I guess I would have to say that I'm probably at a six on the scale.*

Dr. Williams: *Given that you have rated yourself a six, you must be doing something right that would keep it from being lower. What are you doing that's helping you rate yourself at that level?*

Suzanne: *I think I'm keeping my emotions to myself. I don't think I'm letting my stress show when I'm with the department heads.*

Dr. Williams: *That's good. What are you doing to stay under control when you're with the department heads?*

Suzanne: *I think one thing that is helpful is that I'm reminding myself that even though things are stressful right now, due to the lack of resources, this will change. I believe that I will have additional people available to me over the next six months. So I guess I think, "This too shall pass."*

Dr. Williams: *Great. It sounds like that's important for you to keep doing. Now given that you're at a six on the scale compared to where you want to be, what can you experiment with doing over the next week or two that will help move it up to a seven, or possibly an eight?*

Suzanne: *Well, if I were to reach out and maybe be proactive, especially with some of the top leaders that have a lot of challenges it would enable me to meet on my own terms. That would probably relieve my stress because I could carve out the time and work it into my schedule as opposed to being reactive. That's what's happening right now; my phone rings, an e-mail pops up, or I'm asked to attend a meeting, and I'm not prepared. When those things happen, it elevates my stress, so being proactive with a few targeted executives would help.*

Dr. Williams: *I like that idea. It seems like it would help to put you back in control as opposed to just reacting to unexpected events.*

Suzanne: *Yeah. I think that would really make a big difference.*

Dr. Williams: *Are there some opportunities coming up in the next few days where you'll be able to do this?*

Suzanne: *Yes, absolutely.*

From this point in the discussion, Dr. Williams can pinpoint what those opportunities are and how, specifically, Suzanne is going to act on her idea. In follow-up discussions, he can review her progress and talk about additional action experiments that will continue the small steps toward her desired outcome.

Scaling is a core technique in any solution-focused approach. It has been proven effective in a variety of settings; however, some leaders feel awkward utilizing what seems to them an "artificial" technique. As illustrated by the uses described above, scaling can be very beneficial when employed during the Challenge-for-Action phase of the Four-square Coaching Framework. The author suggests that it is worth experimenting with; however, if you decide otherwise, at least keep in mind the concepts upon which scaling is based as you help a person design actions to achieve goals.

USE THE PAST IN ORDER TO PREPARE FOR ACTION IN THE FUTURE

Ideas for action experiments can emerge from any of the techniques discussed in this and the previous chapter, but a fruitful source of ideas is the person's own history; from his or her success stories. Although being solution-focused means looking to the future and finding solutions, it doesn't necessitate ignoring the past when it can be used as a springboard to action in the present. Most people have previously solved many problems and probably have some ideas of how to deal with their current situation (Szabo & Meier, 2008). Accessing people's past successes often produce insights which stir them to action because they are able to use what has worked before. However, to use the past as a resource, people must draw upon experiences that mirror their present situation in some way.

> **Dr. Williams:** *Has there ever been a time when you've been in a similar situation where you have felt frustrated and been under this kind of pressure, but you were able to handle your emotions and stress in the way that you want to now?*
>
> **Suzanne:** *(Laughs) Yeah, actually yes. Yeah, it's happened before.*
>
> **Dr. Williams:** *Can you give me a specific example of when you've been able to do that?*
>
> **Suzanne:** *It would have been when I transitioned into a new role, probably about three years ago. There was a lot of new learning that I had to do. I needed to learn a great deal of new information, and then of course the same thing happened. I became stressed out about it, and started doubting whether I was providing the right information to others. So yeah, I can recall having similar feelings.*
>
> **Dr. Williams:** *And yet that turned out such that you felt successful handling your stress, correct?*
>
> **Suzanne:** *Yes, I felt good during that time. I was able to reach a balance.*
>
> **Dr. Williams:** *What were you doing or thinking that helped make you successful?*
>
> **Suzanne:** *Actually, and it's a phrase I like to use, but I haven't thought about it in a long time, "It's not just about me." So I'm not just focused on my concerns and feelings; instead I put myself in the place of the other person. In this example, I remember putting myself in the place of a leader I was trying to support. It's sort of a shifting the focus away from me and, actually as I'm saying this, I'm realizing I'm so caught up in my own little world now that I'm worrying about this, I'm worrying about that, and I'm thinking that I've got all of this work, et cetera, et cetera. So perhaps if I shift myself out of that mode that might help minimize stress and help me handle my emotions.*
>
> **Dr. Williams:** *I think that's a great insight.*
>
> **Suzanne:** *Yeah, actually I think it will help a lot.*
>
> **Dr. Williams:** *Is there anything else you did?*
>
> **Suzanne:** *It's another thing that I've forgotten while feeling so stressed, and that's to maintain my sense of humor. Sometimes you've got to let things go a little bit, and strike a more pleasant and congenial conversation with someone. Does that make sense?*

At this point, Dr. Williams supported Suzanne's ideas, and paraphrased the two things that Suzanne came up with from her past that might help her better handle her emotions and stress in the way that she wants. Suzanne responded that shifting the focus would take the weight off her shoulders and that she was anxious to experiment with doing this over the next week or two to see how much it would help. By accessing past learnings that are applicable to her present situation, Suzanne has identified small steps that she can take toward her goal. Use the following guidelines when employing this technique:

1. A success story can be a time when someone was even a little successful.
2. Ask for details to clarify the person's narrative.
3. Use stories where the person actively did something to produce the successful outcome, as opposed to success being the result of external factors.
4. Compliment the person whenever possible to reinforce her ideas.

5. Paraphrase useful solutions so that they standout during the conversation.
6. Help the person translate what he did or thought during his success story to his current situation.

CHALLENGE-FOR-ACTION SUMMARIZED

The Challenge-for-Action stage of the Foursquare Coaching Framework is designed to help an individual answer three questions.

1. **What** do I have to **do** to get what I want?
2. **How** am I going to go about it?
3. **When** and **where** am I going to start doing it?

■ The actions that are generated during this stage are best thought about as experiments because solution generation in coaching is a heuristic process; which means using your best guess as to how to proceed, learning from what happens, and adjusting your approach moving forward.
■ There are three types of action experiments: observing, thinking, and doing.
■ Changing one's thinking is often the first step toward achieving what is wanted.
■ The three magic questions are useful for helping the person decide what to do to move forward.

1. What are you doing that is helping, and you should continue doing, or do more of?
2. What are you doing that would be helpful if you did less of it, or stop doing it altogether?
3. What are you not doing that, if you started doing, would be helpful?

■ Go slow to go fast; small steps lead to big changes.
■ Scaling is a useful technique to pinpoint where people are now compared to where they want to be. Scaling helps to:

1. Define what people are doing right that causes them to choose their current point on the scale,
2. Identify what can be done to move up one or two points on the scale, and
3. Measure the results of actions taken.

■ Use the past to prepare for action in the future. Success stories can provide action ideas with which to experiment.

COACHING AS A LEADERSHIP STYLE

When people think of leadership, they often think of extraordinary responses to situations, or of people who are endowed with unique attributes that cause them to stand out from others. Consequently, much of the literature touts leadership as something very significant and quite special, representing leaders as charismatic figures who do the extraordinary and, in the process, inspire others to great deeds. The German sociologist Max Weber was the first to introduce the concept of charisma to the study of leadership. Weber's concept of charisma was of a mystical and personally magnetic savior with extraordinary capabilities. According to Weber, the charismatic leader is "set apart from ordinary men and treated as endowed with supernatural, superhuman, or at least . . . exceptional powers and qualities . . . (which) are not accessible to the ordinary person but are regarded as of divine origin or as exemplary, and on the basis of them the individual concerned is treated as a leader" (1968, p. 63). While Weber's work was a topic of interest to political scientists and sociologists, it wasn't until the 1970s and mid-1980s that the concept of charisma become inextricably linked to leadership.

As investigations into charismatic leadership began to appear in the organizational literature, variations on the charismatic theme emerged. For some, it implied visionary thinking and innovation (Sashkin, 1988). For others, it was transformational, and even heroic, because the leader was able to use his personality to instill faith in his followers, appeal to moral ends that raised the moral consciousness of others, and turn previously dormant followers into active ones (Burns, 1978). Still others conceived of leadership as *inspirational* rather than charismatic (Downton, 1973), such as when followers identify with, and are drawn to, the leader's goals and purposes, but not necessarily to the leader per se. Finally, there were those that believed that leadership is a compilation of all of the behaviors associated with charismatic, visionary, heroic, transformational, and inspirational leadership because of their high correlations with each other (House & Podsakoff, 1994). These explanations, however, have not strayed far from Weber's original concept in that they too seem to imply that one must be an exceptional individual responding to exceptional situations. There are some leaders that certainly fall into that category, but most people in leadership roles are not there to save the world. So, if leadership is not "'a savior like' essence in a world that constantly needs saving" (Rost, cited in Barker, 1997: 348), then what, for all practical purposes, is it?

MUNDANE LEADERSHIP

Alvesson and Sveningsson suggest that there be a rethinking of leadership as a set of ordinary or "mundane" practices. This, however, does not mean that leadership itself is ordinary or mundane, but rather that leadership is a matter of doing little things each day to stimulate the voluntary motivation that is the goal of all leaders. As Alvesson states, "In many cases, the meaning and significance of leadership may be more closely related to the mundane than to the carrying out of great acts or the colorful development and implementation of strategies and changes" (Alvesson & Sveningsson, 2003, p. 1437). In other words, leadership is about consistent actions on a daily basis that may seem inconsequential, but the actions are the *differences that make a difference* (Solution-focused Principle #4).

The "doing the little things" approach to leadership mirrors the stage-related activities that correspond with the Challenge-for-Action stage in the Four-square Coaching Framework. Just as you challenge the people you are coaching to specify what they are going to do differently to get what they want, and encourage them to do the little things that lead to success, you can challenge yourself to engage in mundane leadership by asking, "What small actions—doing, thinking, or observing—can I experiment with today to be a better leader?" It is the little things that you do on a daily basis that make the difference; small steps lead to big changes.

Chapter 10

Support-for-Action

Readiness for Change

There is no change without action, but there is no action without the desire to act. The desire to act is dependent upon a person's *readiness for change*, and, as Hettema, Steele, and Miller point out, "Anyone who aspires to help others change will quickly discover that people are often less than 'ready, willing, and able' to do so" (2005, p. 92). It is often assumed that when people seek out coaching there is an impetus to change, and that, in most cases, is a valid assumption. However, hesitancy about change is natural, and people come to a helping conversation with a wide range of readiness. The purpose of the Support-for-Action phase of the Four-square Coaching Framework is to evaluate a person's readiness for change and enhance her willingness and commitment to act in pursuit of desired change goals. By evoking a thoughtful dialogue about a person's desire to change, you can facilitate the creation of the necessary psychological incentives to maximize the probability that change will occur. The stage-specific activities for Support-for-Action are designed to:

1. Assess the person's readiness for change
2. Strengthen the person's commitment to the outcomes defined during Challenge-for-Thought, and increase his willingness to carry out the activities generated during Challenge-for-Action

READINESS FOR CHANGE

The phrase "ready, willing, and able" communicates that there are at least three components related to individual change, but for accuracy, the phrase should be restated as "Recognition, Importance, and Confidence." *Recognition* is the extent to which the person is aware of the need for change; the need to have something in his personal or professional life change from what it currently is. *Importance* is the extent to which the person attaches enough personal value to the need for change that she becomes committed to doing something about it. Importance determines the intensity with which the person will pursue change goals. *Confidence* is the extent to which the person believes that she is able to change. It is the person's belief that she has the capability to make the changes she desires and control the conditions that will allow her to succeed. Evaluating the person on each of these factors will provide a measure of the person's chance for success in reaching her change goals. When there is a high level of readiness, the requisite support for action is present.

RECOGNITION

"Self-recognition of the need to change is an essential first step; without it, no change can occur" (Hicks & McCracken, 2009, p. 82). The odds of helping people change either themselves or their circumstances are small to nonexistent when they do not see the need for a change. Fortunately, most coaching conversations occur because you are helping a person deal with a problem situation or achieve a desired developmental goal. Therefore, it is rare to find yourself in a situation where the recognition for change is not a pre-existing condition. The lack of recognition that change is needed is more likely to become an issue when:

1. You are in a leadership position and must change the counterproductive behavior of a direct report.
2. You are trying to help someone who doesn't see how he is getting in his own way.
3. You have put on your mentor hat during a helping conversation and are obliged to encourage a person to change in a way that he is unaware of or that he resists.

In chapter two, Dr. Rhymer put on his mentoring hat when asked for advice by the Cardiologist who was considering applying for the Chief of Cardiology position at their system's heart hospital. With his mentoring hat on, Dr. Rhymer freely gave his opinion about the challenges the Cardiologist would be facing, offered advice about how he thought the Cardiologist ought to deal with those challenges, and shared his evaluation of the person's capability to do the job; all perfectly acceptable actions when mentoring another person. However, suppose Dr. Rhymer also believed that the Cardiologist would need to change the way he comes across to others if he is to be successful in the position under discussion, but the Cardiologist is not aware of his detrimental interpersonal style; the lack of recognition of the need to change becomes a potential roadblock.

One of the most researched models of individual change is the Transtheoretical Model (TTM) of change developed by James Prochaska and Carlo DiClemente (1983). TTM offers an integrative framework for understanding intentional behavior change. The model describes individual change as a progression of stages and provides strategies to guide the individual through those stages.

1. Precontemplation: There is no intention to change; the individual is unaware or underaware of the need for change.
2. Contemplation: The person is aware that a problem exists and is thinking about changing, but has not yet made a commitment to action.
3. Preparation: The individual is intending to take action in the immediate future or may even begin taking small steps toward the change goal.
4. Action: The person is fully involved in making a change as evidenced by her commitment of time and energy.
5. Maintenance: The person has consolidated the gains attained during the actions stage, and the change is considered stable.

As is the case with the Cardiologist, a person who does not recognize that a change is needed is in the precontemplation stage of change. According to Prochaska, Norcross, and DiClemente (2005), precontemplation exists when a person has no intention to change himself or his circumstances because he is either unaware of a problem (*"As far as I'm concerned I don't have anything that needs changing"*), or underaware of a problem (*"I guess I'm a little too aggressive, but it's nothing that I really need to change"*). In other words, a person may realize that there's something there, but it's not a big enough issue, in his minds, for concern. This is illustrated in the following conversation between Dr. Rhymer and the Cardiologist.

Cardiologist: *I am thinking about applying for the chief's position, but I'm not sure what the situation is over there or what they're looking for, and I have some concerns. Do you think it's something I should do?*

Dr. Rhymer: *I'll be glad to help, but first tell me more about your concerns.*

Cardiologist: *Well, my foremost concern is whether they will be open to my leadership.*

Dr. Rhymer: *I see. Well, in my opinion the most immediate challenge will be coming to terms with Dr. Hanson, chief of cardiac surgery. He's been in that role for a long time and, as you know, he's very opinionated. He really doesn't listen to anyone's ideas except his own and can be difficult to deal with. He'll be retiring next year though, so you'll only have to work with him—or around him—for a few months. Given your style how do you see that working out?*

Cardiologist: *I don't see a problem. He's very assertive, but I can stand up to him. They've needed strong leadership over there for some time.*

Dr. Rhymer: *True, but is it possible that you may also come across too strong at times?*

Cardiologist: *I guess I am a little outspoken, but it's nothing that causes me problems. Frankly, that's the problem around here, people don't speak their mind.*

As a mentor, Dr. Rhymer has a challenge: He sees the need for the Cardiologist to change in order to be successful in the chief's position, but it is obvious to him that the Cardiologist does not realize the magnitude of the problem. When a person is in the precontemplation stage, it is difficult to help them. "Precontemplators process less information about their problems, devote less time and energy to reevaluating themselves, and experience fewer emotional reactions to the negative aspects of their problems" (Prochaska et al., 2005, p. 229). To help the Cardiologist, Dr. Rhymer must move him from low to high on the recognition continuum so that he reaches the contemplation stage.

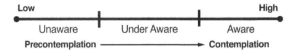

The Recognition Continuum

Contemplation is a stage in which people are aware that the status quo is not acceptable; either because a problem exists or their current circumstances are not providing them the satisfaction they desire. Once they have reached this stage, they begin to think seriously about doing something to change their condition, but they have not yet made a commitment to take action. To shift from precontemplation to contemplation on the recognition continuum, a change in awareness about themselves or their situation is required. Shifting a person from the low end of the recognition continuum to the high end can be a challenge because you are likely to encounter resistance. To detect resistance, listen for resistance talk.

Resistance Talk

Resistance talk is easy to identify; it is "speech that signals movement away from a particular kind of change" (Miller & Rollnick, 2002, p. 49). Resistance talk is present when the person speaks about:

1. *Contentment with the status quo (does not want to change)*
   "I'm satisfied where I am in my career, right now." [Content with the status quo, implicit advantages in not changing]
2. *Reasons for sustaining the status quo and/or the disadvantages of change*
   "If I take a leadership position it will inhibit my clinical work, which I love." [Disadvantages of change]
3. *Need for the status quo (Have to stay, no viable choice)*
   "If I don't take on the extra assignments, nobody else will do it." [Indirectly expresses intention not to change]
4. *Commitment to the status quo (not going to change)*
   I'm not as insensitive as some people think. [Indirectly expresses intention not to change]
   I'm not going to start delegating more because I don't think they will do as good a job as I will. [Directly expresses intention not to change]

When you hear resistance talk, you can be certain that the person is low on the recognition continuum with regard to the subject under discussion. Resistance talk is a sign. It is an indication that you need to slow down, proceed with caution, and be patient with where the other person is coming from; a tactic that is often easier said than done, especially if you have a strong desire (or investment in) the person changing in some way. If you push for increased recognition because it is obvious to you that change is needed, you may unintentionally intensify a person's refusal to acknowledge a need for change since he has not yet come to that conclusion himself. When helping people who have low recognition of the need for change, there are two general guidelines to follow. First, start from their awareness of the need for change, not from what is obvious to you. Second, do not try to "break down" their resistance; instead, work at the edge of their resistance to "dissolve" their unwillingness to consider that change is needed (Dimond, Havens, & Jones, 1978). There are two kinds of resistance that you are likely to encounter: uninformed resistance and rebellious resistance.

UNINFORMED RESISTANCE

Uninformed resistance is an unwillingness to consider the need for change because of a lack of knowledge. It is a blind spot in the person's awareness; the person does not see what others see about her or she does not understand the significance of what she is being asked to do. It's analogous to driving toward a cliff without knowing it's there or underestimating its drop and, consequently, not recognizing that a change in direction is needed. In the case of the cardiologist, it is underestimating how his behavior negatively affects those around him and how the consequences of his lack of understanding could adversely affect his ability to perform the role of chief. To help people overcome a potentially serious blind spot, expose them to information that can trigger an "aha" moment; a moment that will cause them to contemplate a change. Education and feedback are the means by which this task is accomplished.

Education

You never sell, you only educate. Attempting to sell people on something they need to do is often met with resistance while educating people so that they come to their own conclusions about its importance gains buy-in. When people are exposed to new and relevant information that decreases blind spots, the educational process becomes the method of influence. Providing information, from a source the person respects, gives the person a new perspective from which to reevaluate the need for change.

Dr. Wells is the Technical Director of Radiology for a large community hospital system. Her Director, Dr. Sato, is concerned that her inability to build relationships and influence through persuasion is undermining her capacity as a leader since her command and control style is being rejected by those under her direction. Dr. Sato suggested that a more collegial-oriented managerial style might work better than the directive style she now relies upon, but received only a blank stare in return. It's obvious to Dr. Sato that Dr. Wells is low on the recognition continuum with regard to changing her leadership style.

Dr. Sato considers Dr. Wells an "up and comer" and passes off her style as a function of her relative inexperience in a leadership role and her drive to succeed. However, she does acknowledge that Dr. Wells needs to modify her style if she is going to be successful in the long term, but is unsure how to help her realize that change is needed. It was decided that perhaps an educational approach to raising awareness was needed.

A local university was selected that offered an executive level leadership development program for high potential healthcare leaders, and Dr. Wells was offered the opportunity to attend the program. Dr. Wells was honored to be selected for the program and eagerly attended the first class: Motivational Leadership. At first, like many elite professionals, she was convinced that her strong suit as a leader was her personal drive and strong need for achievement; after all, it had gotten her to this point in her career. However, as the class progressed, she began to view the role of the leader differently. She began to understand that her ultimate success was not going to be dependent on her personal efforts, but the efforts of those around her. In other words, influence, not personal achievement, would be the key to her success. Upon examining her current leadership style and its negative impact on the motivation of those upon whom she depends for the department's success, she realized that she had work to do; a change was needed.

It is not uncommon in healthcare to use education as a means to induce change. In fact, an important part of the role of a healthcare professional is to educate their patients about the effects of lifestyle choices harmful to their health in an effort to move them from precontemplation to contemplation on the recognition continuum. Education is an effective tool in overcoming uninformed resistance so long as the information is directly relevant to the person's situation, and it is delivered by a respected source. Books written by experts in their field and seminars or classes taught by highly regarded professionals are obvious sources that meet these conditions. However, do not underestimate the impact of mentoring as an educational tool. Mentors educate people by imparting relevant information gleaned from their own personal or professional experience. When combined with the interchange of ideas and questions that typify the mentoring process, mentoring may very well create an "aha" moment that moves a person from precontemplation to contemplation.

Using education as a means of dealing with uninformed resistance is fairly straightforward. Far more challenging is attempting to increase recognition through the use of feedback. Fortunately, there is a long history of research that specifies the guidelines for giving feedback in a manner that is effective, and increases the probability that it will be accepted by the person receiving it.

Feedback

According to McShane and Von Glinow, "Feedback is any information that people receive about the consequences of their behavior" (2005, p. 153). Although feedback can be considered a form of education, there is usually a different subjective reaction to information when it comes from the observations of other people rather than an objective, impersonal source, such as a workshop or a book. Feedback that originates from other individuals (e.g., one's superior or peers) is referred to as evaluative feedback (Podsakoff & Farh, 1989). Dr. Wells, for example, is receiving evaluative feedback when she is told that her direct reports indicate that her style is too controlling. If this is a blind spot, the feedback will come as a surprise and may trigger a defensive response. No matter how accurate the feedback, if Dr. Wells becomes defensive, it will not be accepted and will have no constructive impact.

The probability that a person will have a productive response to feedback will be determined by three factors: (a) how accurately the feedback is understood, (b) the degree to which it is accepted as valid (an accurate portrayal of his behavior), and (c) the recognized value of what is learned from the feedback (Ilgen, Fisher, & Taylor, 1979). These factors are influenced by both the source of the feedback and the content of the message itself. Following specific guidelines will generate a positive response to all three factors; however, it is beneficial to remember two overarching principles. First, you must have rapport with the person because a helping conversation is fundamentally a relationship-driven experience, and a person's reaction to feedback will be as much a reaction to you as to the information itself. Second, avoid coming across as evaluative or judgmental. If people believe or feel as if they are being judged, defensiveness is a natural reaction. Communicate from the Adult ego-state, not the Parent ego-state.

1. Comment on Their Behavior, Not Their Intentions

Triggering any action or behavior is an intention, therefore, "as unbelievable as it may sometimes seem, every person's behavior makes sense to them" (Daniels, 1994, p. 32). When Dr. Wells *tells* a colleague how she wants something done as opposed to discussing it with him, her behavior is congruent with some specific intention (e.g., to have it done in a way that she is comfortable with because she knows, or believes, it will work). However, giving feedback about a person's intentions is problematic. Imagine if Dr. Sato said, *"I want to talk to you about the way you treat your colleagues. You seem to want to have everything done your way because you don't trust them, and this is causing problems within your team."* A person's intentions are private and unspoken; therefore, her interpretation could well be wrong. While she may be correct, the feedback is not likely to be well-received. Ascribing motives to the behavior of other people puts them on the defensive, causing them to focus their energies on justifying their actions rather than to reflect on their behavior. The opportunity for self-assessment will be lost, and the degree to which the feedback is accepted as valid will be diminished.

When providing feedback on a person's behavior, describe what you have observed objectively and in a neutral tone. Think of yourself as providing a *verbal video* of what you have seen, without judgment. Present the natural, logical consequences of the person's behavior based upon cause-and-effect reasoning, or what you have directly observed. For example, when Dr. Wells takes over tasks that are the responsibility of others, it is appropriate to describe what she is doing and point out that she may be unintentionally sending a message that she does not trust others to do their work. Be descriptive and non-evaluative and, as always, maintain an Adult ego-state.

2. Be Behaviorally Specific

Chapter five addressed the importance of specifics and the fact that Surface Structure language is vague and unhelpful in critical conversations because it does not contain the requisite level of linguistic detail to build a platform of understanding. Feedback needs to be specific so that it is perceived accurately. A positive response is dependent on the person being able to pair the feedback with specific behavior about which the feedback is intended (Ilgen et al., 1979). If Dr. Sato says to Dr. Wells, *"You're heavy-handed in the way you get things done with your colleagues,"* not only does it risk coming across as judgmental, but without more specifics the feedback is not particularly useful (e.g., What, specifically, does Dr. Wells *do* that comes across as "heavy-handed?"). Without a specific behavioral reference, the term "heavy-handed" may mean something totally different to Dr. Wells than to Dr. Sato and, therefore, has the potential for starting a "that's not true" argument. Another advantage of behavioral specifics is that "in most cases people will not only find the behavioral statement the easiest to listen to, but it's also the one they are most likely to take action on" (Reynolds, 1997, p. 157). Behavioral specifics avoid the global label trap. Global labels are words or phrases that categorize the whole person instead of particular aspects of their behavior (e.g., "You're overbearing"). Such feedback labels the person rather than

something the person is doing in specific situations. Global labels make it difficult for people to respond objectively to what they hear and invariably provoke
a defensive response. Global labels are inherently judgmental and are indicative
of the Parent ego-state.

3. Make It Relevant

A person may understand the feedback, but not its relevance. Feedback is relevant only when the person recognizes it as personally or professionally important. Importance, as a component of readiness for change, is discussed in chapter
eleven; however, it is worth noting that the value a person places on the information determines whether he will act upon it. If Dr. Wells is given feedback that
doctors are complaining about her leadership style, but she does not attach any
significance to those complaints, there will no motivation to act on the feedback.
In some instances, the information provided by the feedback is already known
(e.g., Dr. Wells may already be aware of her behavior and its effect on people). If
Dr. Wells fails to act on what she already knows, it is because she does not perceive a problem and, therefore, the information is not relevant to her. The only
way to move her from precontemplation to contemplation on the recognition
continuum is to reframe the information. Reframing means introducing people
to a different, and often novel, way of viewing some aspect of self, others, their
problem, or their situation (Corcoran, 2005). In order to overcome Dr. Wells's
reluctance to change her behavior based upon what she knows about how people
react to her style, Dr. Sato will have to help her view the situation differently.
She might do this by explaining that she is weary of the complaints of doctors
about Dr. Wells's style and, therefore, even if it not important to Dr. Wells it is
important to her that a change is made. Dr. Wells may then reinterpret the situation as a relationship issue with her boss rather than a difference of style issue
with her colleagues.

4. Ensure Credibility

All feedback originates from a source, and while the source is not part of the feedback it is often difficult to separate the two (Ilgen et al., 1979). Therefore, acceptance of the feedback is as much dependent on the source of the feedback as it is
on the content of the feedback. The most influential characteristic of the source is
its credibility. Credibility determines how much influence the source of the feedback has on the person receiving it. Credibility is judged on the basis of three factors: competence, familiarity and trustworthiness. Competence, as an influencer,
is a function of expert power (French & Raven, 1959). The source has expert
power if the person or persons providing the feedback is perceived as possessing
the required skill, knowledge, qualification, or capacity to provide the evaluative

feedback. Imagine having no expertise in art, and yet giving feedback to an artist on her work. It is doubtful that the feedback would be accepted. Similarly, imagine Dr. Wells's reaction to critical feedback about her leadership style if Dr. Sato, herself is perceived to be an incompetent leader.

Competence is also evaluated on the basis of familiarity (i.e., Does the source of the feedback possess sufficient data upon which to provide accurate observations?). If Dr. Sato is removed from the day-to-day interactions between Dr. Wells and her colleagues, then she will not be perceived as being familiar enough with Dr. Wells's style to give credible feedback. Although she might give feedback about what others have told her, being a third-party source is awkward. Not only does it leave one vulnerable to the "You don't really know" response, it makes it difficult to be behaviorally specific because of the lack of firsthand observations. Therefore, the source of the feedback must have a generous length of record regarding the behavior of another to give evaluative feedback that will be accepted.

Finally, credibility is also a function of trustworthiness (i.e., "Can I trust what this person is telling me?"). If Dr. Wells believes that Dr. Sato is not trustworthy, it might very well raise several questions (e.g., "Is she ignoring some information to my detriment?"; "Is she disguising her true intentions?"; "Is she distorting the facts?"). It would create a level of suspiciousness that would interfere with Dr. Wells's receptivity to the feedback, even if the feedback were accurate. Without trust, there is a natural resistance to the influence of another. "Trust exists when we make ourselves vulnerable to others whose subsequent behavior we cannot control" (Kouzes & Posner, 1990, p. 146). The willingness to be vulnerable is dependent upon the motives ascribed to the other person. Without the perception of good intentions, there is no trust. Feedback from a coach or mentor is often accepted because trust and, therefore, credibility are generally present by virtue of the relationship itself.

UNINFORMED RESISTANCE SUMMARIZED

- Resistance talk is speech that signals no intention to change.
- Uninformed resistance is an unwillingness to consider the need for change because of unawareness or under awareness about something that, unless attended to, will have a negative impact on one's professional or personal life.
- Uninformed resistance is indicative of the precontemplation stage on the recognition continuum. Overcoming uninformed resistance may be accomplished by providing information that will increase a person's awareness of the need for change.
- Education is one way to provide the information needed to increase recognition of the need for change. Formal education (e.g., classes and workshops) and informal education (e.g., teaching and mentoring) are all a means by which a

person may acquire the information that will move them from precontemplation to contemplation on the recognition continuum. A stronger dose of information may be provided in the form of evaluative feedback.

- Evaluative feedback provides information about the consequences of one's behavior, and is derived from the observations of other people.
- The following guidelines can help you use feedback to increase recognition of the need for change:
  1. Comment on people's behavior, not their intentions
  2. Be behaviorally specific
  3. Make it relevant
  4. Ensure credibility

REBELLIOUS RESISTANCE

Rebellious resistance differs from uninformed resistance in that the person often has a great deal of awareness about his or her behavior and its impact on themselves or others, and still refuses to acknowledge that a change is needed. Miller and Rollnick (2002) maintain that this happens for two reasons: (a) The person has a heavy investment in the behavior and is unwilling to give it up, or (b) the person's personality is such that he is independent and doesn't like being told what to do. Rebellious resistors are outspoken, and their dialogue is full of resistance talk (i.e., arguing, rationalizing their behavior or adamantly stating that they have no reason to change and will not consider it). The challenge in dealing with rebellious resistance is to help people shift some of their energy into contemplating change rather than using their energy to resist it. If this challenge is met, then the same determination used to resist change will be applied to making the change and lead to a successful outcome.

Rebellious resistance is often encountered during the treatment of addictive behavior (e.g., the problem drinker who knows about the dangers of heavy drinking and fully confesses to drinking, but swears it is not a problem because *"I don't drink any more than my friends do"*; *"I have a good job and family, how could my drinking be a problem?"*; *"I don't ever feel that drunk, I can handle it. Besides, it makes me feel good."* Some of the most effective techniques for contending with rebellious resistance, and increasing readiness for change can be derived from methodologies that have been developed for the clinical setting. Practices derived from the field of Motivational Interviewing (Miller & Rollnick, 1991, 2002; Rollnick & Miller, 2008) are especially useful for coaching or mentoring situations. Motivational Interviewing (MI) was originally developed as a treatment for problem drinkers, but has been adapted to address motivational change issues in a wide variety of settings. The principles and practices derived from MI are well suited to deal with rebellious resistance.

A Quiet Conversation about Change

Rebellious resistors oppose change because they do not see the need for it and will openly say so. They appear to have all the answers, and a conversation with them feels like a "point-counterpoint" argument. Consequently, when the stakes are high or you have a strong personal or professional investment in them changing, it is quite natural to fall into the trap of attempting to set them straight in order to promote their well-being. That is exactly the opposite of what the principles and practices of MI would have you do. The more you try to argue with rebellious resistors as to why change is needed, the more they will argue why it is not. So, what's the alternative?

The goal of a conversation with a rebellious resister is to have a quiet conversation about change that, by using some specialized skills and obeying certain principles, induces *him* to tell you how and why change would be beneficial. Consistent with the core principle of coaching, this approach is a collaborative, person-centered conversation that relies on a style that guides rather than directs in order to elicit and strengthen recognition of the need for change. To hold such a conversation with a rebellious resistor, one must adhere to the following principles and techniques:

1. Resist the Righting Reflex

When one comes from the Parent ego state, the urge to correct another's misconceptions or course of action so as to set things right becomes almost automatic and reflexive. As explained in chapter two, this inclination is labeled by Rollnick, Miller, and Butler (2008) as the Righting Reflex. Although the intention underlying the righting reflex is commendable (to provide corrective action as a means of helping), it has a paradoxical effect on the conversation when dealing with a rebellious resister. Instead of eliciting recognition of the need for change, it usually causes people to defend the status quo and diminishes the prospect that their level of recognition will increase, thereby having the opposite effect from what was originally intended. In fact, according to MI principles, if you are arguing for change and the other person is arguing against it, you are in the wrong role; your role is to promote a discussion that will encourage *the other person* to voice the arguments for change, not you.

2. Reflect Resistance

As discussed in chapter three, the use of reflection as a communication technique signals verbal attention. It is an overt indication that you are listening and attempting to understand the other person and, therefore, is a technique used in fostering Support-for-Thought; however, it is also a means by which you can respond to rebellious resistance. Miller and Rollnick offer two ways to reflect resistance that are very useful when encountering resistance: simple reflection and amplified reflection. Simple reflection is an acknowledgement of the other person's disagreement or perception by making a statement that *reflect* –in your own words—what the other person said, but indicates no agreement or disagreement. Simple reflection is a way of engaging the resistance with nonresistance; a good principle to follow with a rebellious resistor.

Dr. Jacobs, the medical director in chapter two, who is seen as a know-it-all by his colleagues.
Dr. Jacobs: *I don't see the need to avoid giving advice when I know that it can help them.*
Simple Reflective Response: *You see your approach as helpful, which is really your intent. Is that correct?*

Dr. Rajiv, the nitpicker in chapter three, who judges, rather than develops, the younger physicians.
Dr. Rajiv: *What if I tell you that you're wrong; I really do listen to what they are saying. I don't think I'm all that judgmental; after all, someone has to tell them the truth.*
Simple Reflective Response: *So, you're actually telling them things they need to hear without intending to be judgmental, and at the same time, doing more listening than what it might appear to others.*

The purpose of simple reflection is to avoid responding with an immediate counter argument, signal that you are listening, and remove any possibility that you are judging what the person is saying. It is a neutral response on your part. Amplified reflection is similar to simple reflection, in that it is a statement that *reflects* what the person has said, but it differs in that it is amplified or slightly exaggerated so that it encourages the person to back off from her original statement enough to consider an alternate point of view. There are cautions to be heeded with this stratagem: First, the exaggeration should not be too extreme, or else the overstatement itself will elicit a defensive reaction; and second, amplified reflection must be done thoughtfully and without sarcasm or it may elicit a hostile response. Below are two examples of this technique using the statements of Dr. Jacobs and Dr. Rajiv. Notice that the use of amplified reflection makes it difficult to agree 100 percent with the reflection itself, hopefully prompting a "Well, no" reply that opens the door for a follow-up question about whether a change would be worth considering.

Dr. Jacobs: *I don't see the need to avoid giving advice when I know that it can help them.*
Amplified Reflective Response: *So, you're going to give advice whether or not other people want it or resist it.*

The most natural reply is a version of, "*No, of course not!*" The follow-up question would be, "*So is it worth considering when your advice is helpful and when it isn't so that you can be more effective?*"

Example

Dr. Rajiv: *What if I tell you that you're wrong; I really do listen to what they are saying. I don't think I'm all that judgmental; after all, someone has to tell them the truth.*

Amplified Reflective Response: *Let me see if I have this correct; you're listening to other people, even though they don't think you are, and there is absolutely no judgment in your responses.*

The hoped-for response would be, "*Well, there might be a possibility that I come across that way at times, but they need the feedback.*" The follow-up question would then be, "*If a small change in your approach would make them more receptive to what you have to say, would that be worth considering?*"

3. Emphasize Personal Choice and Control

Think of the last time someone tried to force you to do something against your will. What was your reaction? Most probably, you responded by pushing back, by asserting your own freedom of choice, which is a natural reaction to a threatened loss of choice. This response has a name: psychological reactance (Brehm & Brehm, 1981). Psychological reactance occurs when an attempt at social influence is perceived as threatening one's autonomy, one's ability to form opinions, or to do what one wants to feel free to do (Silvia, 2005). The intensity of the reaction will be directly proportional to the importance the individual places upon the choices that are eliminated or threatened. Therefore, since rebellious resistance is a product of the heavy investment people have in their current behavior, pressing them to recognize the need for change will most probably result in psychological reactance. To avoid this possibility, deflect the reactance by making statements emphasizing their personal choice and control over what happens.

Dr. Jacobs: *I don't see the need to avoid giving advice when I know that it can help them.*

Personal Choice Response: *And you don't have to, it really is your decision. What I'm suggesting is that you may even be more influential and helpful if you change your style, but in the final analysis it really is up to you.*

Dr. Rajiv: *What if I tell you that you're wrong; I really do listen to what they are saying. I don't think I'm all that judgmental; after all, someone has to tell them the truth.*

Personal Choice Response: *You're correct! Someone does need to tell them the truth; however, it's also true that people will be more or less open to the truth depending on what they experience from you during the conversation. I'm only asking that you take a closer*

> *look at how you're coming across—if you want to. That's what I'd do if I were you, but I'm not making that decision, you are.*
>
> *Dr. Wells, the command and control leader who needs professional development in order to develop a more collegial style.*
> **Dr. Wells:** *Why are you telling me about this leadership program? Are you saying that I have to attend?*
> **Personal Choice Response:** *Absolutely not! It's just information for you to consider. I think there are some advantages in attending classes to increase your leadership skills. I know they have helped me in the past, but you can make up your own mind.*

4. Agree with a Twist

Another very useful technique in responding to rebellious resistance is to suggest initial agreement, but with "a slight twist or change of direction" (Miller & Rollnick, 2002, p. 105). This allows you to disagree without being disagreeable and reduces the dissonance between you and the other person while giving you the opportunity to influence the direction of the conversation. When you *agree with a twist*, you are offering a different point of view without appearing confrontational. To use this technique, respond to rebellious resistance with a reply that contains three components:

1. A direct statement of support, followed by a generalization extracted from their original point with which any reasonable person would agree;
2. Your suggestion (or counter point) made as a statement of curiosity and referencing their specific situation; and
3. A question asking for their thoughts about what you said.

To illustrate, suppose the person you are coaching makes the following statement, *"I'm not going to delegate more of the work because when I do, people don't get it right and I end up having to do it myself in the end."* You believe that he needs to learn to delegate more and is not aware of how his own need for perfection is getting in his way, but his statement is a clear indication of rebellious resistance. You decide to agree with a twist and say, *"You have a point* [direct statement of support], *when people are given tasks and those tasks have to be redone by someone, it's inefficient and frustrating* [a reasonable generalization of their statement]. *Thinking about your specific situation, I'm wondering if it's possible that your own need for perfection might have a hand in this* [your point made as a statement of curiosity about their specific situation]. *What do you think* [a question asking for their thoughts]?

This approach allows you to push back against rebellious resistance, but without adding fuel to the flames. As with any technique, it must be done with intent to help, be timed appropriately, and delivered with skill; otherwise, it will be perceived as manipulation. Here is another example of agreement with a twist.

> **Dr. Rajiv:** *What if I tell you that you're wrong; I really do listen to what they are saying. I don't think I'm all that judgmental; after all, someone has to tell them the truth.*
>
> **Agreement with a Twist:** *You're correct! People do need to be told the truth if they are going to do a good job and improve in the process. Thinking specifically about your situation, I am curious as to whether the young physicians will be more open to the truth if you change your style slightly so that they do not confuse your feedback with judgment. What do you think?*

In summary, to respond to rebellious resistance resist the Righting Reflex, use both simple and amplified reflection, emphasize personal choice and control, and agree with a twist. Employing these practices during a conversation with a rebellious resister enables you to roll with their resistance, thereby improving the odds that the person will move to contemplation on the recognition continuum. The following is an example illustrating all four techniques described above.

> ### The Situation
>
> *Dr. Jacobs is a medical director in a physician-owned group that provides emergency medicine services to local hospitals. His colleagues view him as a "know it all" who constantly intervenes to provide answers to their problems immediately upon hearing about their situation. By his way of thinking, he is saving them time because he has the experience and knows what to do, and in all fairness, his answers are often correct. He cannot understand why they get upset when he is offering what are clearly workable solutions to their difficulties. He is proud of his ability to get to the heart of a problem and provide a solution.*
>
> **Leader:** *John (Dr. Jacobs' first name), I noticed that you were trying to help one of our physician residents, Jerry Anderson, and he didn't seem to be reacting very positively to your advice.*
>
> **Dr. Jacobs:** *You know Jerry; he's just insecure, like many of our younger residents.*
>
> **Leader:** *You're correct there. Many of our young physicians are insecure and can use some advice from time-to-time. In this instance, I'm wondering whether some of his reaction is due to the fact that you were giving him advice he didn't ask for. Does that make sense?* **[Agreement with a Twist]**
>
> **Dr. Jacobs:** *I don't see the need to avoid giving advice when I know that it can help them.*
>
> **Leader:** *And you don't have to, it really is your decision. What I'm suggesting is that you may even be more influential and helpful if you change your style, but in the final analysis it really is up to you.* **[Emphasizing Personal Choice and Control]**
>
> **Dr. Jacobs:** *I don't think it's my style. Some of these young residents are so insecure that any attempt to help is a threat to them, but that's not going to stop me because I know I can help them. After all, I have a lot of experience they can take advantage of.*
>
> **Leader:** *So, it's important to you that they take advantage of what you know, given your experience.* **[Resists the Righting Reflex,** *and instead uses* **Simple Reflection]**
>
> **Dr. Jacobs:** *Exactly. I know Rick [the medical director], and I know Jerry. When Jerry mentioned he was having problems with Rick I thought he could use some advice.*

> **Leader:** *Let me see if I have this correct, you thought he could use some advice even though he didn't ask for it.* [**Amplified Reflection**]
> **Dr. Jacobs:** *Look, sometimes these young residents need advice, but don't ask for it. I'm not going to stop trying to help just because they don't ask for it.* [Defensive response]
> **Leader:** *You have a good point; people don't always ask for advice, even when they would benefit from it. However, in this particular situation, I'm wondering whether your eagerness to help Jerry by giving advice that is not asked for is really accomplishing what you want. What do you think?* [**Agreement with a Twist**]

The key to success with Dr. Jacobs is to be patient, roll with his resistance, and work at the edge of that resistance to dissolve it until he starts to contemplate the need for change. Notice that the final question, i.e., "What do you think?" is a wide-open question, and may give rise to an opportunity for a discussion with Dr. Jacobs about when his advice-giving is effective, and when it's not. By responding to resistance with non-resistance, eventually there will be an opening in the conversation to more directly address the issue at hand, and perhaps even to provide feedback about how Dr. Jacobs' behavior is being perceived. If the conversation is handled properly, it will yield a dialogue and not an argument.

RECOGNITION OF THE NEED FOR CHANGE IN REVIEW

- Recognition is the first of three necessary ingredients for change to occur. When people are low in recognition, they are in the precontemplation stage. People in this stage are not considering a change because they are either ignorant of the problem, or in denial because they do not believe their behavior is a problem.
- When attempting to increase someone's recognition of the need for change, it is common to meet resistance. The presence of resistance is signaled by *resistance talk*. Resistance talk is any speech that indicates movement away from change (i.e., contentment with the status quo, reasons for sustaining the status quo, statements of need for the status quo, and commitment to the status quo).
- When you hear resistance talk, roll with it. Your goal is not to confront it directly, but to work around the edges of resistance until it is dissolved.
- There are two kinds of resistance: uninformed resistance, and rebellious resistance. In both cases, the goal is to have a quiet conversation about change in order to move the person from precontemplation to contemplation on the recognition continuum. There are many techniques that are useful in this process, but they are all designed to promote self-analysis and introspection, encourage the person to rethink his behavior, and examine the drawbacks of the current behavior.
- If resistance can be dissolved, the person will move to contemplation where the need for change is considered.

COACHING AS A LEADERSHIP STYLE

Organizational change efforts naturally breed resistance because people are being asked to modify their behavior in some way. It is easy for a leader to interpret resistance as an indication that either people are refuting what needs to be done or that mistakes were made by the leader in her change efforts. Whichever the case, it may lead to feelings of frustration or even anger. Rather than responding in a counterproductive manner, use the principles and practices described in this chapter for overcoming resistance to organizational change just as you would use them to overcome resistance to individual change. Appropriate leadership behavior is central to the organizational change process because it is the responsibility of those who are driving the change to overcome any resistance to the change. Implementing organizational change strategies that reduce resistance is a complex process; however, the initial steps in creating organizational change are similar to the steps for facilitating individual change; namely, roll with resistance and build recognition of the need for change.

To roll with resistance, leaders must first reframe their thinking about resistance. It is worth noting that resistance in organizations serves a positive purpose: It maintains equilibrium until the reasons for change are both clear and compelling; otherwise, organizations would be entirely unstable. Leaders need to anticipate resistance and prepare rationales and approaches to address the anticipated resistance instead of fueling it. Additionally, organizational change causes individuals to experience a reaction similar to any emotionally stressful experience (Kyle, 1993). It is emotionally stressful because it involves going from the known to the unknown, and individuals vary in terms of their ability and willingness to handle that change (Darling, 1993). Therefore, in order to lead an organization through major change, leaders must be able to deal with the affective responses of employees and their resistance talk (speech that signals movement away from change).

- *We've been successful, so why do we need to change now?*
- *We are already swamped, how can we do this too?*
- *Isn't this just the latest fad, like everything we do here?*
- *Who's responsible if this fails?*
- *We're unique; it won't work here.*
- *It sounds good to me, but others here won't buy it.*

As with the rebellious resistor, it is important to have a quiet conversation about change with organizational stakeholders so as not to exacerbate their already emotional state. When encountering resistance talk—and the emotions associated with it—remember to resist the Righting Reflex, focus on those areas where they have control, and "agree with a twist" when needed. Additionally, the leader must craft an appealing vision of the change and why it is necessary (Ford & Ford, 1994). This process is no different from helping an individual move from precontemplation to contemplation on the recognition continuum. Until the person embraces the reasons for making a change they will not contemplate doing anything about it. Likewise, until the members of an organization understand and buy-in to the rationale for the change they will not become willing participants in the change process. The transformational leader that uses the coaching practices described in this chapter to build readiness and deal with resistance will be a step ahead in achieving his or her organizational change goals.

Support-for-Action
Importance and Confidence

> It's Sunday morning. As you get ready to start the day, you decide to check your weight as it's been awhile since you've weighed yourself. You step on the scale, and a number appears. "That can't be right," you say to yourself. So you step down and then step back on the scale, only to find the first reading was correct; you are several pounds heavier than you want to be. You vow that you're going to cut back on your calories, but that night as you are out to dinner with friends the desert tray is brought by the table and you just can't resist the piece of cinnamon-pumpkin cheesecake. You say to yourself, "I know I need to cut back, but this looks so good"—and it is!

Does this sound familiar? It is an example of sufficient recognition of the need for change, but insufficient motivation to follow through with behavior necessary to make the change. One would think that recognition of the need for change would be enough to start the change process; unfortunately, that is not the case. Without the remaining pieces of the puzzle (i.e., Importance and Confidence), any attempt to change one's self or one's situation will stall. One way to conceptualize the process is to think of recognition as the green light that gives one permission to proceed, and Importance and Confidence as being the gas pedal that, when pushed, delivers the propelling force that moves the car through the intersection. Importance and Confidence work together to provide the motivation to act so that one can achieve one's desired outcomes.

MOTIVATION TO ACT

"How do you know if someone is motivated to do something?" Typical answers to this question are: *"They are energized and excited to do it." "They do it really well." "You don't have to ask them twice, they do it the first time." "They show initiative." "They are persistent and work hard at it." "They seek out the task."* While these answers are correct as far they go, they are incomplete. The simple answer to the question is *"Because they do it."* All behavior is motivated behavior, and yet when this fact is revealed to people, their first response is normally, *"That can't be true. I've done plenty of things that I wasn't motivated to do."* The reason for their response is that motivation, although exhibited to some degree and in some form by people daily, is generally a misunderstood phenomenon. However, if a distinction is made between two types of motivation, extrinsic and intrinsic, the impetus for any action becomes clear.

Extrinsic Motivation

When a person is moved to do something for instrumental purposes only, they are said to be extrinsically motivated. For example, a physician who takes on an administrative leadership role merely because it adds to her income stream, and not because it is inherently attractive to her, is doing so for its instrumental value. Similarly, a physician who attends a remedial coaching program at the direction of their state's medical board is extrinsically motivated because he is doing it for the instrumental purpose of avoiding sanctions. Both represent motivated behavior, but in one case the instrumental outcome is tangible gain, and in the other it is the avoidance of unwanted consequences. Thus, extrinsic motivation does propel action, but the impetus to act has a perceived locus of external causality (deCharms, 1968). Consequently, when the external motives to act cease to exist, motivation disappears, as well as the associated actions. Clearly, extrinsic motivation cannot be depended upon as an enduring impetus for behavioral change.

A special case of extrinsically motivated behavior deserves to be mentioned because it frequently occurs in healthcare settings. Power relationships abound in healthcare organizations, and because they do, it is tempting for those in a one-up position to use their power advantage as leverage so as to induce behavioral change, especially when it is perceived as being for a person's own good. Power advantage refers to "the extent to which the recipient believes the source influences the contingency between the recipient's behavior and his or her receipt of valued out-comes" (Ilgen, Fisher, & Taylor, 1979, p. 359). In other words, a request to behave differently from a person with perceived influence in the organization can generate behavioral compliance by the recipient, even in the absence of personal acceptance that change is needed. This method of motivation, however, is innately unstable as a determinant of long-term change because the actions are the result of feeling pressured, rather than a personal commitment. The purpose of Support-for-Action is to ensure that action experiments derived from the Challenge-for-Action stage are supported by the personal commitment that can only come from intrinsically motivated behavior.

Intrinsic Motivation

Intrinsic motivation refers to doing something for its inherent interest or satisfaction; for its own sake (Alexander, Ryan, & Deci, 2000). There is plenty of evidence that humans are endowed with intrinsic motivational tendencies. Children, for example, will engage in "play behavior" with no goal in mind, other than the pure enjoyment of the activity itself. Csíkszentmihályi and Csíkszentmihályi (1988) state that there is adult play as well, and it can lead to an even greater sense of satisfaction called the "flow experience," where action and awareness merge into a state of completely focused intrinsic motivation. Maslow (1943) described these intrinsically motivated occurrences as peak experiences. He hypothesized that they were a natural product of our need for "self-actualization" as human beings. Although the desire to express ourselves through intrinsically motivated activities may be an essential part of our nature, research shows that intrinsic motivation is exhibited only under specifiable conditions: The goal must have *importance*, and the individual must have *confidence* in their ability to attain it.

According to the expectancy-value model of motivation (Fishbein & Ajzen, 1975; Eccles, 1983; Wigfield, 2000), intrinsically motivated behavior is in response to a person's beliefs and values about the goal toward which she is working. Specifically, the individual must believe that the activity or goal has *attainment value* (DeBacker & Nelson, 1999). In other words, it must be important to the individual so that the investment of time and effort toward goal attainment is justified. Let's reexamine the scenario of Dr. Francis (chapter three) with this idea in mind. Dr. Francis is an excellent emergency room physician. Her chair is encouraging her to assume some formal leadership responsibilities. While interested, she is also uncertain whether this is something she really wants. During a coaching session, Dr. Francis identified several actions to be undertaken in order to increase her leadership-related responsibilities. However, whether or not she will be intrinsically motivated to carry out those activities depends on the inherent value, or importance, she places upon her goal. If she does not truly value taking on more leadership responsibility, then the chances that she will follow through with actions related to that goal are small, regardless of how well-intentioned they may be. Dr. Francis will more than likely leave the coaching conversation with good intentions, but during a follow-up discussion when she is asked to report on her progress, it will not be surprising to hear "I just haven't gotten around to it yet." Indeed, this may be a case of responding to the extrinsic pressure of her chair rather than intrinsic motivation on her part. As part of Support-for-Thought, it is the coach's responsibility to test for and discuss *Importance* as one factor in the motivation equation needed to support the person's actions and goals.

A second factor that produces variability in intrinsic motivation is addressed by the concept of *Confidence*. Confidence is a by-product of self-efficacy: A self-evaluation of one's competence to execute a course of action successfully that is deemed necessary to reach valued outcomes (Bandura, 1982). Self-efficacy reflects the two-fold belief that one has the capability to undertake the needed actions for goal attainment, and the requisite control or influence over those variables that can affect the outcome of their efforts. When a person has confidence in the fact that they are able to act and succeed, it affects four major psychological processes that influence success generally (Bandura, 1994), and the ability to achieve their change goals specifically: cognitive processes, motivational processes, affective processes, and selection processes.

1. Cognitive Processes

When people have confidence in their ability, they are able to visualize success scenarios that support their change efforts. When people lack such confidence, they are more likely to visualize failure and dwell on the many things that can go wrong. It is difficult to carry-out the actions needed to achieve well-formed outcomes while fighting self-doubt.

2. Motivational Processes

Intrinsic motivation is self-generated, and since people form beliefs about what they can or cannot do, their commitment to a planned course of action will be affected by the confidence they have in being able to carry out the plan and its associated activities. Confidence determines the goals one sets, how much effort is expended toward those goals, how long one perseveres in the face of difficulties, and one's resilience to failure.

3. Affective Processes

Whether people perceive a situation as a "threat" or a "challenge" is determined by their belief in their ability to cope effectively with that situation. If people lack confidence in their ability to cope or succeed, then they will perceive the situation as threatening and experience the stress and anxiety that accompanies such an appraisal. On the other hand, confidence dispels anxiety and facilitates emotional responses that positively support one's efforts.

4. Selection Processes

People avoid activities and situations they believe exceed their coping capabilities. The greater the belief a person has in their capabilities the wider range of options they will consider *selecting* in pursuit of their desired goals. Since success is achieved through choice-related processes, it makes sense that the more choices a person will consider the greater the chances they have in achieving success. If a person refuses to experiment with different actions to gain what they want, their paths to accomplishment are limited. One of the main goals of any coaching process is to increase the choices a person perceives as available to them.

Returning to Dr. Francis and her situation, let's focus on the impact of *confidence*, and how it can affect her motivation to take on increased leadership responsibilities. In this scenario, let's assume that Dr. Francis has attached importance to the goal of stepping into a leadership role, but she has never felt comfortable "in the limelight" and, therefore, lacks confidence in her ability to lead. She has always preferred a participative role and following the lead of others to being in charge and assuming a position of authority where she may be required to exert her will over others. Although she is able to make decisions assertively as a physician, she is much less sure about her ability to do so in a leadership position. If this lack of confidence cannot be overcome, it will reduce the intrinsic motivation needed to achieve her goal, even though the goal may have professional or personal value. If her chair is coaching her through this situation, then he can expect that movement toward her goal will be slow. Her lack of confidence requires that she take on small challenges initially so that she can experience early success. Additionally, failures, even small ones, are likely to be perceived as proof that she is not up to the task; therefore, keeping setbacks in perspective and viewing them as teachable moments is essential.

AMBIVALENCE: THE DILEMMA OF CHANGE

Ambivalence about change is a common experience. Even when a person has recognized the need for change and has moved from precontemplation to contemplation, she may not have yet taken action. In other words, contemplation is not a commitment to act. This point in the change process is analogous to standing on the edge of a cliff, but not making the leap. Some people stand on the edge of the cliff for days, others for weeks, and still others for months and years until they can resolve the "I want to, but I don't want to" dilemma. Ambivalence can be thought of as a manifestation of an approach-avoidance conflict. An approach-avoidance conflict occurs when a person has a single goal or wish that is both desirable and undesirable at the same time. Everyone has experienced the ambivalence that results from approach-avoidance conflicts as evidenced by the following types of thoughts and concerns:

---

*"I want to eat that piece of cheesecake, **but** I don't want the extra calories."*

*"I want to take on more leadership responsibilities, **but** I don't want to give up my clinical work."*

*"I want to expand my professional horizons, **but** I don't want to give up time with my family."*

*"I want to apply for that position, **but** I don't want to work under that manager."*

*"I want to give more presentations, **but** I'm not very good at them and I don't want to look foolish."*

Notice that ambivalence is clearly indicated by the word "but" in the middle of each of the statements. It is common for a person to encounter ambivalence in the form of these "I want to, but" conflicts, even if the person is at the high end of the recognition continuum. When ambivalence is present, it signals a problem with either *importance* or *confidence*, or both. When Importance and Confidence are sufficient for the task, the person will exhibit both a willingness to act and an emotional or intellectual commitment to that course of action. According to Miller and Rollnick (2002), it is useful to think of each of these two dimensions simply as being either high or low. This produces four possible combinations, which they say can give you an idea of where people are with respect to their readiness for change, and where to focus if readiness is lacking.

1. **Low Importance and low Confidence.** These people might recognize the need for change on an intellectual level, but have not attached any self-interest to actually making the change, nor do they feel that they could succeed in making a change if they tried. There is no commitment or willingness present; thus, no action is likely to occur. There are some instances where people with low confidence may attribute low importance to change as a defense mechanism because they are insecure about their ability to achieve it.
2. **Low Importance and high Confidence.** These people are willing to act because they have the confidence to do so, but the commitment is not there. They see no personal value in the change goal. Action taken from this quadrant, if it happens at all, will most likely be driven by extrinsic pressures and is, therefore, unreliable. Occasionally, extrinsically motivated action will yield results that cause the person to see the value of change, causing them to reappraise its importance.
3. **High Importance and low Confidence.** The only thing holding these people back from taking action is the lack of self-efficacy. They don't believe they will be capable of achieving their goal or taking action, not because it isn't important to them, but because they are afraid that they lack the knowledge, skills, or abilities to do so. However, if importance is high enough, they might be willing, with enough encouragement, to try. Occasionally, they will perceive themselves as having the capability to take action, but believe that the circumstances are such that there are external barriers over which they have no control and action is futile.
4. **High Importance and high Confidence.** If recognition is present, there is nothing holding back a person in this quadrant. Assuming that the person has acknowledged during the Challenge-for-Thought phase that she wants something to be different for herself, recognition will be a given. Now the task is to ensure that what the person wants is truly important and that the person feels confident in executing the requisite actions to attain it.

ARE THE COSTS AND CONSEQUENCES ACCEPTABLE?

It is human nature to seek equity. Equity theory was first proposed several decades ago by John Stacy Adams (1963) as a variable in determining employee job satisfaction. According to Adams, equity is the perception that one is treated fairly relative to comparable others within the organization. Equity is determined by comparing one's ratio of inputs to outcomes to that of others. Inputs are anything the person might invest in a task (e.g., effort, time, education, experience); outcomes are anything he or she receives in return that has tangible or psychological value. When there is perceived equity, it is logical that he or she feels satisfied and is, therefore, motivated.

As equity theory evolved, it became evident that perceptions of equity are not only evaluated through comparisons with others, but are determined by one's internal standards as to what is the appropriate ratio of inputs to outcomes (Porter, Bigley, & Steers, 2002). In other words, benefits gained are relative to the costs of attaining those benefits. It is, therefore, reasonable to expect that when there is ambivalence, the question of equity has not been answered in the affirmative. The costs and consequences of pursuing one's goal may not match the importance of that goal, and until equity perception exists, motivation will suffer. It is during the Support-for-Action stage that ambivalence is resolved. When a person has reached a point on the recognition continuum where they are contemplating moving to action, they are at a tipping point. According to the TTM model of Prochaska and DiClemente, it is during the contemplation stage that a person becomes aware of the potential benefits of taking action, but they also become aware of the costs. Questions like "Why do I want to do this?"; "Can I actually do it?"; "Does the benefit outweigh the costs, or risks?"; "How important is this to me?" are all a part of a cognitive appraisal process surrounding ambivalence that takes place during the contemplation stage.

THE AMBIVALENCE APPRAISAL PROCESS

Cognitive appraisal has long been at the heart of many psychological theories. One of the first theorists to advance the idea of cognitive appraisal is Richard Lazarus, who, with his colleague Susan Folkman, proposed that stress and other emotional responses were the product of an automatic, often unconscious, intuitive appraisal of an individual's real-time experience and the meaning attached to it (Lazarus & Folkman, 1984). Building on this idea, a person at the upper end of the recognition continuum contemplating whether to take the next step in pursuit of their change goals likewise goes through an appraisal process, most of which is also intuitive, unconscious, dynamic, and relies on subjective judgments. However, unlike the cognitive process described by Lazarus and Folkman, the goal of this appraisal process is to resolve ambivalence associated with issues of Importance and Confidence.

According to the TTM change model, if ambivalence during the contemplation stage of change can be resolved, then people will begin to experiment with small action steps toward change. Prochaska and his associates labeled this the "preparation stage" (Prochaska, Wright, & Velicer, 2008). In addition to experimenting with small steps, this stage may also include collecting information about change before taking more direct action. Consider the case of Dr. Wells, the high potential technical director who could benefit from some formal education on leadership. Let's assume that she has recognized the need for changing her style and is contemplating taking steps to do so. She will have resolved ambivalence and moved into the preparation stage of action if she begins, on her own volition, to research leadership programs that will furnish the knowledge and skills she seeks to reach her change goals. The actions that flow from preparation are also in keeping with the Solution-focused Principle #3: *Small steps lead to big changes.*

Once an individual has taken the first tentative steps toward his change goals and experienced some success, he begins to take bigger and more confident strides toward his change destination. This is the "action" stage of the TTM model and is an example of "Success begetting success." When a coaching conversation is in the Support-for-Action phase, progress is acknowledged, reinforced, and supported so that there is a continued effort towards change. However, action toward change will not occur until ambivalence is resolved and a decision to move forward is made by the individual. Just as a decision is the bridge between wishing and acting, resolving ambivalence is the bridge between the recognition of the need to change and the motivation to act.

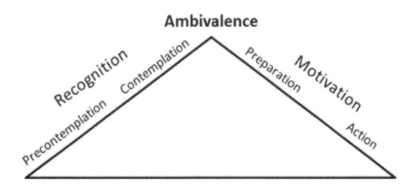

The stage-related activities of Support-for-Action are designed to resolve ambivalence in favor of action, assuming that change is compatible with a person's personal values and aspirations. In other words, the leader's role, as a coach, is to help remove ambivalence as a barrier to action in support of the person's well-formed outcomes, but it is not to persuade a person to resolve ambivalence in the direction of action if it is not aligned with the person's wishes and goals. Since the ambivalence appraisal process is automatic, often unconscious, and intuitive, it raises the question "How can you help a person when the decision process is transparent, even to them?" Fortunately there is a way: Eliciting and responding to Change Talk. "The strength of the client's perception of the importance of change and confidence in achieving it is presumed to underlie his or her commitment to change and to be evident in speech" (Amrhein et al., 2003, p. 862). In the language of Motivational Interviewing, this type of speech is called Change Talk.

CHANGE TALK = SUPPORT-FOR-ACTION

The primary purpose of Support-for-Action is to strengthen an individual's commitment to outcomes defined during Challenge-for-Thought and to increase his motivation to carry out activities generated during Challenge-for-Action. This purpose is achieved by "spotlighting" statements that confirm the *importance* of change or that indicate *confidence* in the person's ability to make it happen. This strategy is based upon the premise that people can talk themselves into change if they engage in self-motivating speech, or, in other words, when they hear themselves acknowledge the value of change and express belief in their own capabilities (Rollnick, Miller, & Butler, 2008).

Importance

Importance is the measure of worth a person assigns to his change goals and activities. High importance produces strong commitment because it means that the change is linked to personal values and aspirations; therefore, the time and effort required to make it happen is justified (equity perception is positive). Importance is revealed when people articulate their own reasons for change by:

1. Talking about the disadvantages of the status quo.
2. Talking about the advantages of change (their desired future state).

As discussed in chapter seven, when there is a difference between what people want, the picture in their head, and what they are currently experiencing, they are motivated to close the gap. Statements about the disadvantages of the status quo acknowledge concern or discontent with the present circumstances and imply a discrepancy between what exists and what they would like to be different. Statements about the advantages of change emphasize the appeal of the desired future state, even though their current situation may not be unpleasant.

> *"One thing that could come out of this is that I would have a lot more time to think strategically about what needs to be done in our department, rather than just firefighting problems."* [Advantages of the change]
>
> *"I can see that, in the long run, the pace that I'm working is going to do me in if I don't make a change."* [Disadvantages of the status quo]
>
> *"I'm getting things accomplished, but, not in a way that's going to make me a better leader."* [Disadvantages of the status quo]
>
> *"I think that by improving my teaming skills, I will be seen more positively by my director, not just my colleagues."* [Advantages of the change]

Importance can also be conveyed indirectly through expressions of desire or need. *Expressions of desire* begin with phrases such as "*I want*"; "*I would like*"; or "*I wish.*" Desire implies that, although unstated, there are advantages for the person in making a change for the better.

"*I want to* do more delegating of tasks."
"*I would like to* have a better work-life balance."
"*I wish* I could be a leader, not just a manager."

Expressions of need begin with phrases such as "I have to"; "I need to"; or "I should." If you recall from chapter four, these are pressure words and signal that there is an internal directive that must be followed "or else." For example, the statement "*I need to confront Fred about his behavior*" indicates that not doing so would sustain the status quo, which is undesirable.

"I like my autonomy, but *I have to* be more of a team player."
"I've never really thought that much before about how I'm coming across to others. This is serious; *I need to* turn this around."
"I really *should* do a better job of listening so that I'm not perceived as so judgmental."

In chapter five, it was asserted that people communicate in surface-level language; thus, most statements of desire or need are just the tip-of-the-iceberg as the majority of information about those desires and needs is beneath the surface. The critical deletion in such statements is the unstated reasoning, i.e., the logic that specifies what is to be gained from what they want or the negatives of the status quo that cause them to believe they "have to" or "need to" do something to change it. Change Talk spotlights the advantages of change and disadvantages of the status quo so that people hear their own self-motivating speech.

Clinical Research Manager: *"I want to do more delegating of tasks."* [Expression of desire]
Department Administrator: *"What would that do for you?"* [Recovering the reason for that desire; making the advantage of delegating explicit]
Clinical Research Manager: *"One thing that could come out of this is that I would have a lot more time to think strategically about what needs to be done in our department, rather than just firefighting problems."* [States an advantage that would come from the change]

> **Clinical Research Manager:** *"I need to have a better work-life balance."* [Expression of need]
> **Department Administrator:** *"What's wrong with the way it is now?"* [Asks for them to argue against the status quo]
> **Clinical Research Manager:** *"I can see that, in the long run, the pace that I'm working is going to do me in if I don't make a change."* [States a disadvantage of the status quo]

A person's narrative may contain many statements of desire or need. These are wonderful opportunities for strengthening the person's perception of the importance of change. These statements can be used as springboards from which to elicit Change Talk. For example, Martha, from chapter five, is feeling stuck. She states that she "should" be more proactive in advancing her career than she has been in the past. By asking her for specifics about the advantages of being proactive and disadvantages of maintaining the status quo, Martha is induced to talk, out loud, about the value of being proactive in advancing her career, as well as the disadvantages of not doing so; thereby, engaging in Change Talk.

> ### Martha's narrative: (the underlined statements are opportunities for eliciting Change Talk):
>
> *"I'm feeling stuck right now. I have a sense that I should be more proactively involved in advancing my career than I have been in the past. I'm happy with what I'm doing, but I feel as if I'm missing something. I'm at the point where I feel that if I don't make a concerted effort to advance my career in some way, then opportunities will pass me by, and I'll have no choice but to stay where I am. I have to challenge myself. What do you think I should do?"*
>
> ### Inquiries to elicit Change Talk:
>
> ***"What might happen if you're not more proactively involved in advancing your career?"*** [Elicits the disadvantages of the status quo]
> ***"What are you missing, specifically?"*** [Elicits disadvantages of the current state by taking about what is missing that is important to her]
> ***"What's to gain if you challenge yourself?"*** [Asks for her to specify the advantages of challenging herself] or ***"What will happen if you don't challenge yourself?"*** [Specifies the disadvantages of the status quo]

Confidence

When a person has confidence in their capability, perceived self-efficacy is present. "Perceived self-efficacy refers to beliefs in one's capabilities to organize and execute the courses of action required to manage prospective situations" (Bandura, 1995, p. 2). Support-for-Action involves assessing and strengthening a person's perceived self-efficacy by listening for and reinforcing indicators of confidence. Statements of confidence are based upon the person's perception of his ability and his conviction that he can use this ability to act on his change goals. Confidence, as an expression of Change Talk, is revealed by:

1. Statements about present capability.
2. Statements of strong intention.

STATEMENTS ABOUT PRESENT CAPABILITY

There are three types of statements that indicate present capability: (1) declarative affirmations; (2) references to past successes; and (3) statements of possibility. While they all represent Change Talk that signals confidence, they vary with respect to strength of conviction.

- **Declarative affirmations** are easy to recognize because they are direct statements of self-efficacy. They are the strongest expressions of confidence and include statements such as:

> *"I can be very assertive when I want to."*
> *"I certainly am able to sit down with Rafael and have a conversation with him about his priorities."*

- **Past indicators of success** inspire confidence because they are proof that the person has demonstrated capability. In chapter nine, it was advised that past successes be used as a resource for designing current actions. Past successes are also a part of Change Talk. When people point out that they can do something because they have done it before, it is an expression of confidence.

> *"I had a similar situation in the past where I had to be very assertive, and it worked."*
> *"I was in a similar situation once where I was being bombarded with questions that I couldn't answer because I was new to my job, but I was able to deflect them without making the other person feel as if I were putting him off."*

■ **Statements of possibility** also indicate confidence in present capabilities; perhaps not as strong as declarative affirmations or references to past successes, but confidence nevertheless. A statement that something is possible or likely to happen implies that it is within one's capabilities. Inherent in a statement of possibility is an expression of optimism that change or action is conceivable.

> *"I might be able to start delegating tasks that, even though I enjoy them, I know can be done by others who are just as capable."*
>
> *"I think I can start pulling back in some of the meetings so that I don't come across as a know-it-all by appearing as if I have all the answers."*

STATEMENTS OF STRONG INTENTION

■ **Statements of strong intention** reveal confidence. When people use phrases such as *"I will"*; *"I am going to"*; *"I intend to"*; they are implying that they have the capability and control over the necessary variables to act in pursuit of desired outcomes. Such an assertion reflects a strong belief in their capability, is a testimony to their commitment, and portrays a sense of optimism that change can happen.

> *"I'm going to improve my relationships with my colleagues so that I'll have more social influence with them."*
>
> *"I intend to manage my emotions so that my personal stress doesn't bounce all over the place."*
>
> *"I will be more assertive with my teammates in meetings so that I don't get stuck with all of the tasks that no one wants to do."*

Confidence, whether conveyed as statements of present capability or strong intent is one form of Change Talk; expressions of the importance of goal attainment, the other. Whether a person will continue to engage in Change Talk or veer away from it, will depend on your response to it. Responding to Change Talk is contingent on your ability to recognize it. When Change Talk is present, it can be responded to in a way that enhances the person's willingness and commitment to act in pursuit of their goals. The field of Motivational Interviewing has many techniques for responding to Change Talk (Rosengren, 2009). The four major techniques can be characterized by the acronym "E.A.R.S": **e**laborate, **a**ffirm, **r**eflect, and **s**ummarize.

RESPONDING TO CHANGE TALK: USE YOUR E.A.R.S.

Coaching is an activity that takes place because someone wants help. In chapter two, coaching is defined as *the process of facilitating self-determined and self-directed problem solving or change within the context of a helping conversation.* During the

Support-for-Action phase, anything you can do to enhance intrinsic motivation is not only welcome, but part of your role. When you elaborate, affirm, reflect, and summarize Change Talk, you are selectively responding to people's narratives, and by doing so, helping them reinforce their perceptions of Importance and Confidence; thus, building their readiness for change.

Elaborate Change Talk

In chapter five, the reader was introduced to the magic of questions, and the fact that questions are the means by which deleted information is recovered. Additional information is generated as people elaborate on their surface-level language. Therefore, responding to Change Talk with a "What" or "How" question will cause the person to elaborate on Importance and Confidence as it relates to the action experiments planned during Challenge-for-Action or well-formed outcomes developed during Challenge-for-Thought. The purpose of elaboration is to focus people's attention on the advantages of achieving their desired outcome, disadvantages of the status quo, and their capability to achieve what they want; thereby, enhancing motivation to act.

"I want to do more delegating of tasks." [Statement of desire]

"How does that help you?"

"I would have a lot more time to think strategically about what needs to be done in our department, rather than just firefighting problems." [Elaborates on the advantages of changing]

"What else does it do for you?"

"I think it would help with my work-life balance?" [Additional advantage]

"How, specifically, would it help with your work-life balance?"

"I wouldn't be staying at work after hours because I would be focusing on what's important, and letting go of less important, but time-consuming tasks." [Elaborates on the additional advantage]

"What would be a concern for you if you don't do more delegating of tasks?"

"I'm afraid that some of my good people will get frustrated because they're not getting a chance to show what they can do." [A disadvantage of not changing—of maintaining the status quo]

"And that's a problem because. . . . ?"

"They might start looking for other opportunities." [Elaborates on the disadvantage of the status quo]

"How confident are you that you can actually 'let go' of some of the tasks you like to do when others can do them just as well?"

"I know I can do it because I've been able to do it in the past, once I've made up my mind." [References a past success—builds confidence]

"Tell me about that time in the past and how it gives you confidence going forward now." [Elaborates on the past success]

The conversation, instead of moving on to other subjects, has entered a loop, and a good one. It is deliberately spiraling around the Change Talk dimensions of Importance and Confidence. Asking the person to elaborate on their Change Talk statements causes them to engage in enhanced reflective thought and internal dialog about the positive reasons for change, and why they are capable of it. Change Talk is magnified because it is voiced, *out loud*, by the person himself. The leader, by differentially responding to the person's statements with inquiries that increase Change Talk, is helping to stimulate intrinsic motivation in support of the desired change.

Affirm Change Talk

Whether with animals or people, reinforcement works. When you reinforce Change Talk, two things happen: It produces a favorable reaction in people, further increasing their belief in what they said, and it makes it more likely that they will make similar comments in the future. Reinforcing Change Talk is simply a matter of *affirming* what you hear by making a positive comment about what you hear them say. Affirming Change Talk is analogous to adding seasoning to food; too little of it and the food will lack flavor, but too much of it spoils the taste. Therefore, affirming statements should not be overused lest they lose their impact. Instead, use them judiciously so that they retain their reinforcement value. Affirming statements include phrases such as "You have a good point"; "I like what you said because . . ."; "I think that's a very good idea"; "You're right, it is important to [restate their idea]." You may also compliment the person directly: For example, "That's very perceptive of you to see that." Let's reexamine the previous example, but with affirming statements added in bold. For illustrative purposes, there are more affirming statements than may actually be needed.

"I want to do more delegating of tasks."

"How does that help you?"

"I would have a lot more time to think strategically about what needs to be done in our department, rather than just firefighting problems."

"That's a smart idea. I can see how firefighting problems would get old after a while. What else would delegating tasks do for you?"

"I think it would help with my work-life balance?"

"That certainly would be a good thing. How, specifically, would it help with your work-life balance?"

"I wouldn't be staying at work after hours because I would be focusing on what's important, and letting go of less important, but time consuming tasks."

"What would be a concern for you if you don't do more delegating of tasks?"

"I'm afraid that some of my good people will get frustrated because they're not getting a chance to show what they can do."

"And that's a problem because?"

"They might start looking for other opportunities."

> **"It sounds as if you're thinking ahead; that's smart.** How confident are you that you can actually 'let go' of some of the tasks you like to do when others can do them just as well?"
>
> *"I know I can do it because I've been able to do it in the past, once I've made up my mind."*
>
> **"That's great; you've actually done it before.** Tell me about that time in the past and how it gives you confidence going forward now."

Affirming statements indicate to people that you think they are on the right track and, therefore, reinforces their Change Talk. When mixed with questions that push for elaboration, affirming statements "soften" the question-answer exchange so that people are not likely to feel that they are being put on the spot. Affirming statements facilitate the flow of Change Talk.

Reflect Change Talk

Reflection is a long-standing communication technique that evolved from the client-centered counseling approach of Carl Rogers (2007). In its most simplistic form, reflection is the process of restating what another person is saying, using your own words. This simple technique can be used for a variety of purposes, depending upon the stage in the Four-square Coaching Framework. For example, during Support-for-Thought, reflection was introduced as a means for reassuring people that you are listening while also inducing elaboration as a means of adding clarity to their narrative. During Challenge-for-Thought and Challenge-for-Action, reflection confirms the accuracy of what they want and what they will do, respectively. Reflection, as used in Support-for-Action, defuses resistance and will magnify statements of Change Talk.

During the person's narrative, you choose what to reflect and what to leave unsaid. When you hear Change Talk, *selectively* reflect only those statements which you deem most influential in providing Support-for-Action. This brings those statements to the forefront of the conversation, which has two advantages: It compels people to hear reasons of importance and expressions of confidence a second time as the Change Talk is reflected back to them, and it often compels people to elaborate on the reflection itself.

> *"I know I can do it because I've been able to do it in the past, once I've made up my mind."*
>
> **"So, you feel confident because you have, in essence, a track record of success already in doing this."**
>
> *"Exactly. I've been able to look at what's on my plate and decide which things I can let others do, and once I let go of something I'm pretty good at staying out of their way."* [An elaboration stimulated by the previous reflection]

Summarize Change Talk

Summarizing is a technique used in both the Support-for-Thought and Support-for-Action stages of the Four-square Coaching Framework. Therefore, summarizing can occur at different points in the conversation, and for different purposes. When used during Support-for-Thought, its purpose is to demonstrate verbal attention and clarify the key points of the discussion. When used during Support-for-Action, its purpose is to highlight Change Talk. Summarizing Change Talk has three advantages:

1. Summaries, as with reflection, allow people to hear, yet once again, their own Change Talk.
2. Summaries, as with affirming, reinforce the importance of the material you have chosen to summarize.
3. Summaries subtly encourage people to elaborate on the Change Talk being summarized.

Summaries highlight a collection of statements made by the person regarding any aspect of Change Talk, i.e., the disadvantages of the status quo, the advantages of change, confidence in her abilities, or declarations of intent to change or carry out actions in support of desired outcomes. Because summaries occur at intervals during the conversation, there may be many statements of Change Talk from which to choose. Therefore, it is up to you to choose those statements which will best support their perceptions of Importance and Confidence regarding the change goal and its attainment. Normally, summaries are delivered in "bullet-point" fashion and use as much of their exact language as you can recall. To ensure that you are accurate with your summary, conclude with a question such as "Does that sound right to you?" "Have I got this right?" or "Have I missed anything?" so that people can confirm what they have just heard. Ending with these questions also serves to invite them to correct or add to the collection of summary statements they have just heard.

> *"Based on what you've said so far, let me see if I can capture your main points and you tell me if I'm correct. It sounds like it's important to you that you start delegating tasks for several reasons. First, it will give you more time to think strategically, instead of just firefighting. Second, it will help your work-life balance. Third, you're afraid that your good people will seek other opportunities if they're not given more challenges. Not only do you believe that this is important to you, but you also are confident that you can do this because you've done it before. Have I got this right? Have I missed anything?"*

ELICIT CHANGE TALK

Change Talk may happen at any time during the coaching conversation. In other words, even when the conversation is in another stage you can quickly jump to Support-for-Action to elaborate, affirm, reflect, or summarize Change Talk. For example, the primary purpose of Challenge-for-Thought is to assist the person in developing a well-formed outcome in support of what she wants in the future, but if, during that discussion, the person were to allude to the importance of that outcome, or her ability to achieve it, seizing this opportunity to respond to Change Talk would be appropriate. As a general rule, **when you hear Change Talk, respond to it.** In fact, it's not even necessary to wait for it at all. If there is a natural opportunity to *elicit* Change Talk, do so. Suppose, for example, that the Nurse Manager from chapter three is building a platform of understanding (Support-for-Thought) by listening to her new nurse discuss her concerns about fitting in with the team. During the narrative, the Nurse Manager senses an opportunity to elicit Change Talk; there are two techniques she can use.

1. **Ask an open-ended question about Importance or Confidence.** For example, *"What makes it so important to you that you change this situation?"* [Elicits the advantages of change]. *"What kinds of problems are caused by this situation?"* [Elicits the disadvantages of the status quo].
2. **Use reflection to elicit Change Talk.** For example, *"As I listen to you, it sounds to me as if this is something that's really important to you. The status quo seems unacceptable."* [This reflection directs the person's attention to the disadvantages of the status quo and the advantages of change. As the person goes into more detail, you can respond to further Change Talk by using your E.A.R.S.: elaborating, affirming, reinforcing, and summarizing.]

CHANGE TALK IN REVIEW

There is no change without action, and there is no action without the motivation to act. However, people are often ambivalent with regard to their motivation, even though they may recognize that change is needed. Ambivalence is caused by an approach-avoidance conflict; for example, "I want to change, but do I want to put the time, energy, and effort into achieving it" [Importance]; or "I want this, but do I have the capability to make it happen?" [Confidence]. The ambivalence appraisal process is automatic and intuitive. Readiness for change is enhanced if this process is made explicit and ambivalence is positively resolved. Eliciting and responding appropriately to Change Talk is a means by which to help the person resolve ambivalence.

Change Talk is defined as any speech that moves the person in the direction of change and is focused on two aspects of readiness for change: Importance and Confidence. Importance is revealed when a person articulates the disadvantages of the status quo or the advantages of his desired future state. Confidence is expressed by statements affirming the person's capability to act or statements of strong intent to achieve his goal. If Importance and Confidence are high, the person will be intrinsically motivated to take action; otherwise, readiness for change is questionable.

Change Talk is elicited by asking open-ended questions about Importance and Confidence or by reflecting back implied statements of Importance or Confidence. Change Talk can occur spontaneously at any point in the conversation, and is responded to by using the techniques of elaboration, affirming, reflecting, and summarizing, a.k.a. "E.A.R.S." Change Talk is a means to increase or enhance a person's intrinsic motivation to change. A high level of motivation ensures that a person is ready to pursue the well-formed outcome developed during Challenge-for-Thought and follow through with the actions identified during the Challenge-for-Action stage of the Four-square Coaching Framework.

COACHING AS A LEADERSHIP STYLE

Like never before, healthcare is going through revolutionary as well as evolutionary change. Responding to regulatory, economic, and competitive shifts by simply being more efficient and relying on past organizational behavior and processes will not work as they may have in the past. Healthcare leaders will have to display transformational leadership by not only crafting an appealing vision of the change that is needed for their organization, department, unit, and so forth, but by communicating how the current change differs from previous change initiatives. That, however, should not be difficult given the publicity surrounding the economic and political realities of healthcare. The difficult challenge will be to stimulate the intrinsic motivation needed by the people, at all levels of the organization, who will actually be charged with changing their behavior and implementing the required organizational processes that will operationalize the vision.

The stage-related activities of Support-for-Action are designed to enhance individual motivation as it relates to achieving one's desired outcomes by heightening the importance of change and boosting one's level of confidence in making the change. These factors, Importance and Confidence, are the same factors that must be addressed by healthcare leaders responsible for ensuring that readiness for change exists in their part of the organization. For example, transformational leaders do more than just create a vision; they are able to communicate the *importance* of that vision to their part of the organization as well as link its importance to each individual in a way that is meaningful and motivating. When people have a personal stake in the outcome, their commitment to the change effort is high.

Perhaps a more challenging task than persuading people the vision is worth pursuing is developing the *confidence* that it can be attained. This speaks to the credibility of the vision; people must believe that it is possible to succeed in its pursuit. The traits of the Elite Professional were spelled out in chapter one, and one of the characteristics is that, while motivated by a meaningful challenge, an Elite Professional must perceive the challenge as achievable; otherwise they become demotivated. Confidence that the goal is achievable can be fostered in at least two ways: behavioral modeling and providing individual support. A part of Idealized Influence as a component of transformational leadership is being perceived as a role model. Developing confidence in goal attainment starts with demonstrating your own personal excitement and energy for the desired future state, showing confidence in your abilities to make it happen and, as importantly, expressing confidence in your team's ability to succeed.

A second method of developing and maintaining people's confidence is to help them act or perform in the face of change. As pointed out in the previous chapter, change has an affective component for most people; therefore, they may need emotional assistance in accomplishing their tasks. Transformational leaders, through the process of Individualized Consideration, can provide such assistance by demonstrating empathy—the ability to listen and understand their feelings and concerns as they go through the change process. Simultaneously, the transformational leader expresses her confidence in each person's ability to perform effectively and meet the challenges before them, and providing help when needed.

The linkage between leadership and coaching in support of change should be obvious. The factors strengthened by coaching in order to provide support for individual change, namely Importance and Confidence, must also be addressed in support of organizational change. Furthermore, as people go through the organizational change process, they will need the same personal support afforded an individual being coached or mentored for reasons of problem resolution or professional development. The methods and techniques of coaching are indispensable to demonstrating effective leadership during change.

Chapter 12

A Coaching Roadmap
Putting It All Together

Coaching is a process with a purpose. That purpose is to facilitate self-determined and self-directed problem solving or change. The process, a coaching conversation, is similar to a journey in the sense that it is intended to help a person "travel" from one place to another. Whether it is to resolve a problem situation, or to better oneself personally or professionally, the journey takes the person from where he is now to where he wants to go. As described in chapter two, your role in this process is that of a guide who can help the person make the journey successfully. To do that, it helps to have a map of the terrain so that you know where you are in the process. You can use the map to find the best path to the destination they choose, or to get back on the path if you become lost; the Four-square Coaching Framework is the map.

THE FOUR-SQUARE COACHING FRAMEWORK SUMMARIZED

 Support-for-Thought

"Every head is a world" states a Cuban proverb. To coach people, you must understand their world as it relates to the problem situation at hand or the developmental experience they are seeking. Understanding is a product of clarity, which is increased as unexpressed details in their narrative are recovered. As clarity is increased, a platform of understanding is built; new insights are gained; and a person's thinking is refined. Support-for-Thought doesn't just happen; it is the result of three factors: (a) the establishment and maintenance of professional rapport, (b) adult-to-adult communication, and (c) the ability to listen and engage in intelligent inquiry. Rapport builds the relationship so that the person is free to think out loud; adult-to-adult communication promotes dialogue and collegiality; and intelligent listening creates a more robust narrative. When there is

Support-for-Thought, the conditions exist for constructing well-formed outcomes, designing actions, and strengthening a person's readiness to act.

 Challenge-for-Thought

A journey must have a destination. However, the people you help may not always know where they want to go, they may only know that they don't want things to be the same as they are now. Challenging them to think about their current situation and what they want to be different helps them define their destination. Challenging people's thinking assumes that Support-for-Thought is present. The goals of the Challenge-for-Thought stage are to: (a) develop discrepancy, and (b) construct a well-formed outcome. Discrepancy establishes the difference between what they are experiencing currently and what they want to be different in the future. Constructing a well-formed outcome ensures that the destination they choose is a road *to* somewhere, as opposed to an unspecified location that merely leads them away from where they are now. A well-formed outcome also includes the criteria for a successful trip, the demonstrable indicators of success. Finally, the outcome is defined in such a way as to maximize the probability that people have direct control over the actions and circumstances needed to complete their journey.

 Challenge-for-Action

A successful journey requires movement. Challenge-for-Action shifts the focus of the conversation from depth (understanding their current situation and what it is they want to be different in the future) to movement (designing the actions that will help them attain their desired outcomes). People may have a clear idea of what it is they want; however, without action, desire remains a wish that will never become reality. Challenging people to think about what they have to *do* to get what they want is the first step in creating movement toward their destination. Helping them decide what it is they might do, and then gently pressing them on *how* they are going to do it and *when* and *where* they will start, promotes action. The types of problems, issues, and concerns that are the subject of any coaching conversation do not lend themselves to formulaic action plans because they require a heuristic approach. Deciding on actions means making the *best guess* about what should be done to achieve a desired outcome. Those action ideas are tried, and feedback obtained so that people can travel toward their destination through a series of small but effective steps. Challenging people to "experiment" with taking action removes the roadblock of trying to decide on the perfect plan and is consistent with the heuristic nature of solution-focused coaching.

Support-for-Action

People cannot complete their journey without taking action, but there is no action without the desire to act. The desire to act is dependent upon a person's readiness for change. The purpose of Support-for-Action is to evaluate a person's readiness for change and enhance his willingness and commitment to act in pursuit of desired change goals. Readiness starts with the recognition of the need for change. Unfortunately, recognition alone does not indicate sufficient readiness to support action; there must be plenty of motivation. Motivation is determined by the degree of importance attached to the change goal (the desired outcome) and by the level of confidence the person has in her ability to act and succeed in its attainment. When a person speaks positively about the importance of what she wants and expresses confidence in achieving it, she is engaging in *Change Talk*. Eliciting and responding to Change Talk is a way of enhancing the motivational component of readiness for change. Change Talk can be elicited through the use of open-ended questions and reflection. Change Talk can be responded to by using your E.A.R.S.: elaboration, affirming, reflecting, and summarizing. Change Talk is also a means by which any ambivalence a person may have about pursuing his goal can be resolved.

A FLUID PROCESS

Due to the heuristic nature of the issues addressed by the coaching conversation, helping people work through problem situations, enhance their professional development, or advance their career is a "messy business." The path taken on this journey is not necessarily a straight line, nor is the journey usually completed in a single conversation. As described in chapter two, when you put on the coaching hat, your role in this process becomes that of a guide, someone who can help people navigate through a confusing jungle of ideas, thoughts, needs, wants, goals, and actions that confront them until they reach their destination. As a guide, being able to plot your initial course and adjust to the changing landscape of the conversation is vital. The Four-square Coaching Framework is a conceptual structure that leads you through the coaching conversation but is not a rigid set of sequential steps—or stages. Although there is a seemingly logical progression that begins with Support-for-Thought and ends with Support-for-Action, the coaching conversation is a fluid process. The unpredictable nature of the coaching conversation suggests that the Four-square Coaching Framework is best used as a coaching blueprint (a map) that will tell you where you are in the conversation and what remains to be discussed.

The conversations below demonstrate how the coaching conversation can move through all, or part of, the Four-square Coaching Framework. It can start in any quadrant and move through the other quadrants more or less in order, or it can switch quadrants with a single statement by the person being helped or an inquiry by the person doing the coaching. By picturing all four quadrants and knowing where you are at any point in the conversation, you are able to recognize what has been covered and what territory remains to be traveled. In these examples, graphic symbols represent each of the quadrants and allow you to track each example conversation as it progresses.

= Support-for-Thought

= Support-for-Action

= Challenge-for-Thought

= Challenge-for-Action

MANNY: MANAGER OF NURSING BUSINESS OPERATIONS

Manny has been talking with his Nursing Director about the stress he is under and the fact that he brings a lot of it on himself because he is not good at setting boundaries with other people. He has asked for a few minutes of his leader's time in order to bounce his thoughts off her.

Director: *You mentioned that you wanted to talk about a couple of things. What's on your mind?*

Manny: *I'd like to bounce some ideas off of you. I'm not very good at setting boundaries for myself. I need to improve that.*

Director: *What kind of boundaries specifically?* (Clarifying the narrative)

Manny: *I am too willing to take on additional work. I don't speak up enough in my meetings, in my team meeting and my departmental meetings. I don't resist enough when decisions are being made that will create a lot of new work for me and my team.*

Director: *Anything else around this idea of setting boundaries?* (Clarifying the narrative)

Manny: *No, I think that sums it up. It's just an inability to say no when I have too much work on my desk, and I'm being asked to take on more.*

Director: *So what is different now that causes you to want to make a change?* (Eliciting Change Talk: Importance; dissatisfaction with the status quo)

Manny: *Well, you know that I'm working with different people now, and there are some very strong personalities in my department. Frankly, I feel like I'm just not assertive enough with some of the people that surround me on the committees.*

Director: *How do you know that you are not assertive enough?* (Elaborating Change Talk: Importance; dissatisfaction with the status quo)

Manny: *I usually leave a meeting having not resisted enough on ideas that I know probably were not in the best interest of my department. Also, I leave with a bunch of additional tasks that leave me feeling quite overwhelmed.*

Director: *Are there other times when you don't feel that you're assertive enough?* (Eliciting dissatisfaction with the status quo)

Manny: *I think that I'm not assertive enough even within my own team. I look at myself and think that my personality is such that I don't delegate enough. I'm simply too willing to say, "Yes, I'll be the one to do that"; and that is everywhere in my life generally, and with my family for sure. Now it's just looking at that for what it is and realizing that this is my fault. I've gotten to this place where I feel overwhelmed, stressed out, and not working at the level I would like because I don't draw boundaries well.*

Director: *So, this is not just something that you want to do for professional reasons. It sounds as if you're saying that this is important for personal reasons also.* (Reflecting Change Talk: Importance)

Manny: *Definitely, very much so.*

Director: *Have there been situations in the past where you have been assertive in the way that you want to be, going forward?* (Eliciting a past success

Manny: *Well, yes, there have been times—as I think about it—that I did not say "Yes" immediately. I was more aware that when people said "Will you do this?"; "Will you take that on?"; or "Will you participate on this committee?"; I simply said "I'll get back to you on that." I think that helped me limit my tasks a little bit better.*

Director: *How did that help you limit your tasks a little bit better?* (Elaborating Change Talk: Confidence)

Manny: *I wasn't impulsive with my decision by reacting to the pressure of the moment. I went away and thought about it. This allowed me to make a more considered decision, and many times I would be able to be assertive and say no.*

Director: *So going forward, this is not something that you've never done before so that means that you are perfectly capable, right?* (Reflecting Change Talk: Confidence)

Manny: *Yes, I just think I've fallen into some bad patterns.*

Director: *Okay, that makes sense. I mean, we all fall into some bad patterns from time to time. Let me see if I can summarize what you've said. First, you said that being assertive by setting boundaries is really important to you, for both personal and professional reasons. Second, you know that you are capable of this because you've been able to be assertive and set boundaries in the past. Is this correct?* (Summarizing Change Talk)

Manny: *Yes, I think that's accurate.*

Director: *OK, the question I have for you now is, "Based on what you have said, what do you want to do differently going forward to start setting boundaries for yourself?"* (Shift to Challenge-for-Action)

COMMENTARY

The conversation begins with some clarification of the narrative (Support-for-Thought). Very little time is spent building a platform of understanding because the person began the discussion by stating his problem and that he believes improvement is needed. Consistent with Solution-focused Principle #1: *You don't have to understand the cause of a problem to solve it*, the conversation quickly navigated to the Support-for-Action quadrant where the importance of changing was established (even though a well-formed outcome has not yet been created). The director also elicited a previous success experience proving the person is capable of doing what he wants to do (confidence building through Change Talk). This past success will be available for use in the Challenge-for-Action quadrant as a basis for identifying what has worked in the past that might work in the present as an action experiment. Building upon what has worked in the past is often a good starting point for designing actions during the Challenge-for-Action stage. The director's final question shifted the conversation to Challenge-for-Action. The conversation to this point can be mapped as follows:

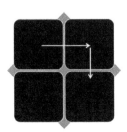

Challenge-for-Action is the next step in the discussion, but Challenge-for-Thought has not been addressed. With this map as a guide, the director knows that once questions associated with Challenge-for-Action are answered (for example, "What are you going to start doing differently?"; "How are you going to go about it?"; "When and where will you start?"), the conversation can shift to Challenge-for-Thought, an unexplored quadrant. In fact, it is quite common to turn the person's answer to the question "What are you going to start doing differently?" into a springboard for developing discrepancy in Challenge-for-Thought by asking the question "What will be different for you in the future when you start doing [name the actions]?" This creates a smooth transition from Challenge-for-Action to Challenge-for-Thought.

The move to the Challenge-for-Thought quadrant during this conversation is optional. Once action experiments have been identified during the Challenge-for-Action stage, there may or may not be time or need to move into Challenge-for-Thought. However, if the director decides to develop discrepancy and create a well-formed outcome, she may do so by asking questions similar to the following:

- How will you know that the actions you are taking will be successful?
- How will the way you set boundaries in the future be different from what you do now?
- What will you see, hear, or experience that will let you know you have been successful?
- What will other people notice about how you set boundaries that will be different from what they see now?

Let's examine another conversation where the path taken is different.

GLEN: CHIEF OF RADIATION SAFETY

Glen has been in the role of Chief for six months. During that time, he has begun to realize that it is more difficult than what he thought it would be. He is beginning to wonder if he has the personality for the job. His colleague Martin, whom he has known for many years, has made the leap from supervising ten employees to being responsible for sixty employees in his role as Anatomic Pathology Manager. Glen attends several institutional committee meetings with Martin, and Martin seems to be adapting well to the change in responsibility. Glen turns to him for advice, but Martin puts on his coaching hat instead.

Glen: *Martin, I've been watching you in your new role for the last several months, and you seem to be adapting really well. I'm curious how you've done it; things are not going as smoothly for me.*

Martin: *What's not going as smoothly for you?* (Clarifying the narrative; building a platform of understanding)

Glen: *Let me give you an example. I attended the Radiology and Institutional Clinical Practice Committee the other day, and it was very contentious. Emotions ran high; people became very partisan and in my opinion, disingenuous. I felt uncomfortable; I don't handle those situations very well, but I need to be able to given my new role.*

Martin: *What else is not going "as smoothly" as you would like?*  (Clarifying the narrative; building a platform of understanding)

Glen: *I think I internalize things too much.*

Martin: *In what way?* (Clarifying the narrative; building a platform of understanding)

Glen: *If I'm in a conversation and the person complains about something that's happening, I feel responsible; in fact, I tend to take it personally. I've also noticed that when I offer my solution to a problem and people push back, I see it as some kind of slight. I know that's probably overreacting, but that's what happens. I guess, in some ways, I'm just too sensitive. I'm used to patients and residents accepting what I have to say without question and appreciating it. People don't do that now, even though I'm the chief in my area.*

Martin: *So what do you want to be different in the future?* (Developing discrepancy)

Glen: *I think the main thing is I want to stop overreacting.*

Martin: *If you weren't overreacting, what would you be doing instead?* (Establishing a positively-stated outcome)

Glen: *Good question. I'm not sure.*

Martin: *OK, Let me ask you this: What's the downside of overreacting? When you overreact what problems does it create?* (Eliciting dissatisfaction with the status quo)

Glen: *The biggest problem is that it causes people to want to be even less cooperative, but it's their cooperation I want. So I kind of create a vicious cycle; the more I push for them to cooperate, the more they resist, and the more I push.*

Martin: *So what you're doing now is not working because you're pushing too hard, but when you don't get what you want you're just doing more of it instead of doing something different? Is that correct?* (Reflecting dissatisfaction with the status quo)

Glen: *Yeah, that's exactly what's going on.*

Martin: *So what does that mean in terms of what you want to be different in the future?* (Developing discrepancy

Glen: *Now that I think about it, I guess what I want to be different is how I interact with people so that I can build better relationships. If I had those relationships, then I don't think I'd get the resistance I do now, or at least I'd have a better chance of gaining some cooperation. I think that would smooth things out.*

Martin: *How specifically would that "smooth things out"?* (Elaborating advantages of changing)

Glen: *I would have less conflict, and so I would feel less stress. I think that's part of the problem; I feel tense all of the time and this might help me go about things in a more relaxed way.*

Martin: *What would people notice when you are going about things in a more relaxed way?* (Well-formed outcome: indicators of success)

Glen: *I would be less focused on me and more interested in what they have to say. Also, I think they would see me as being a little more under control in the conversation; I tend to be overly excitable at times.*

Martin: *What else?* (Well-formed outcome: indicators of success)

Glen: *I think they would see me giving up some things and not just trying to have everything my way. Also, I have a tendency to try and go directly from point A to point B without letting people know my reasoning. I just assume that it's obvious and they'll agree. So they would hear more of the thinking behind what I'm requesting or the conclusions I've reached.*

Martin: *You have mentioned several things that people would see you doing. For example, you mentioned giving in a little more so that people don't feel it's a one-sided deal with you, and sharing a little more of your reasoning for your requests so that they have a better understanding of why you are making the request. You also mentioned doing a better job of staying under control during your conversations.* (Summarizing)

Do you have an opportunity coming up where you could experiment with doing these things in the near future? (Challenge-for-Action)

Glen: *As a matter of fact, I do. I'm going to be meeting with someone from ENT next week. They want to purchase an ultrasound machine to use it for neck exams, but this would compete with us here in Radiology. I'm going to handle the conversation differently than I normally would to see if we can figure something out together.*

COMMENTARY

This conversation won't make everything go smoothly for Glen, but it's a start. By thinking about how he is going to approach his conversations differently, and improve his relationships in the process, he is beginning to head in the right direction. Several aspects of this conversation are different from the previous one. First, a little more time was spent in the Support-for-Thought quadrant, building a platform of understanding about his current situation. Second, from Support-for-Thought, the conversation proceeded directly to Challenge-for-Thought in an attempt to develop discrepancy and build a well-formed outcome; however, the first effort failed. Glen's initial response to the question *"What do you want to be different in the future?"* produced an away-from answer (*"I want to stop overreacting"*), and so Martin attempted to generate a positive statement of what Glen wants (*"What would you be doing instead of overreacting?"*). The conversation stalled when Glen responded with *"I'm not sure,"* but by moving to Support-for-Action and asking about problems created from his overreaction, Martin was able to return to Challenge-for-Thought and develop discrepancy by asking Glen what he wants to be different from what he is experiencing with the problems. Furthermore, by going to Support-for-Action and asking about the problems his current behavior were creating (establishing dissatisfaction with the status quo), Martin was able to highlight the importance of change.

Another difference between this conversation and the previous one is the recurring movement between Challenge-for-Thought and Support-for-Action. This is not uncommon as the relationship between a well-formed outcome and the establishment of its importance (as well as the person's confidence in achieving it) is similar to the relationship between action experiments and the readiness to act. Finally, it should be noted that the indicators of success listed by Glen in response to the question *"What would people notice when you are going about things in a more relaxed way?"* can be used as a springboard for developing action experiments. As discussed in chapter eight, action experiments can stem from actions/behaviors listed as indicators of success in a well-formed outcome, which is exactly what happened in this conversation. Using the Four-square Coaching Framework as a map, the conversation progressed as follows:

This map illustrates the fluid nature of a helping conversation generally, and a coaching conversation specifically. Furthermore, since coaching often happens over time, future conversations will flow from preceding ones. For example, once Glen has had the opportunity to meet with the representative from ENT, a follow-up conversation answering these questions would be appropriate.

- Did Glen actually do what he said he was going to do?
- If not, what stopped him and what is he going to do differently in the future to ensure that he acts on his intentions?
- If he did do what he said he was going to, how did it work?
- Based upon what happened, what can be learned? What might he do more of, stop doing, or start doing?

As you might expect, there are other paths that could have been followed during the conversation between Glen and Martin. For example, suppose Glen would have begun the conversation with the statement *"Martin, I would like to start building better relationships so that I can have more productive conversations with the people I interact with in my new role."* Martin might respond with *"How would those relationships be different from what you're experiencing now?"* [Developing discrepancy]. In this instance, Glen and Martin would be starting the conversation in the Challenge-for-Thought quadrant and would move to other quadrants from there. If this were the case, Martin would be choosing Movement over Depth. The salient point is that you have a choice of many paths within the Four-square Coaching Framework. As long as you know where you are within the framework and the quadrants yet to be explored, you can navigate a course that will be successful.

FROM COACHING TO MENTORING . . . AND BACK AGAIN

Chapter two introduced the concept of three helping hats: teaching, mentoring, and coaching. All three hats may be worn at some point during a helping conversation, but only one hat can be worn at a time. It is important to know which hat you are wearing, especially when you are switching between coaching and mentoring within the same conversation. The following example illustrates how Martin could have shifted from coaching to mentoring and back to coaching. Let's pick up the exchange in mid-conversation.

> **Glen:** *If I'm in a conversation and the person complains about something that's happening, I feel responsible; in fact, I tend to take it personally. I've also noticed that when I offer my solution to a problem and people push back, I see it as some kind of slight. I know that's probably overreacting, but that's what happens. I guess, in some ways, I'm just too*

sensitive. I'm used to patients and residents accepting what I have to say without question and appreciating it. People don't do that now, even though I'm the chief in my area.

[Martin shifts to mentoring.]

Martin: I've gone through the same thing, and I found that the more I expected people to respond to me because I had some authority the more disappointed I became. What helped me, and maybe it's something you might want to consider, is to remember to ask myself this question "How would I get this done if I didn't have any authority?" This forced me to realize that I had to develop better relationships with the people who were important to my success so that I might do a better job of persuading others, rather than dictating to others. Does that make sense?

Glen: Yeah, that's really helpful.

[Martin shifts back to coaching.]

Martin: So what does that mean in terms of what you might want to be different in the future?   (Developing discrepancy)

Glen: I think I have to start building better relationships than the ones I have now. If I had those relationships, then I don't think I'd experience as much resistance, and because I wasn't dictating, I'd have a better chance of gaining some cooperation. I think that would smooth things out.

Martin: What would people notice if you were building better relationships with them? (Well-formed outcome: indicators of success)

COACHING REQUIRES MORE THAN A MAP

The Four-square Coaching Framework is a process map. It is a structured way to think through a coaching conversation so that the person being helped is able to engage in self-determined and self-directed problem solving or change efficiently and effectively. By following the map, you will be able to guide people through a discussion that:

1. Clarifies their current situation without deteriorating into problem talk
2. Translates a desired future state into attainable outcomes
3. Designs actions that move them toward what they want
4. Enhances their readiness to act and make the changes they desire

By using this map, you will know where you are in the discussion at any point in time and be able to make considered decisions about the best path to their destination. Furthermore, you can use the Four-square Coaching Framework to bring the conversation back on task if it becomes confusing, or loses direction. Finally, you can use this map when popcorn coaching opportunities present themselves to choose where the focus of the conversation should be to provide the most help in the least amount of time. Just having a map, however, does not necessarily make you a good coach. It provides the process knowledge that can guide you through a coaching conversation, but that knowledge must be accompanied by the skills, abilities, and personal attributes that, when taken together, make the coaching process work.

RAPPORT

Coaching is a relationship-driven experience. A harmonious relationship built on trust and mutual respect provides the underpinnings for a productive coaching conversation. Rapport creates a connection with the other person that yields the level of comfort and acceptance necessary for direct and honest communication. The kind of communication that will withstand the constructive tension that occurs naturally when a person is challenged to specify what he wants and what he will do to achieve it. Rapport is established through positive regard, empathy, and genuine attention. As you navigate the Four-square Coaching Framework:

- Maintain an attitude of positive regard by accepting and respecting the person you are coaching as a person.
- Display empathy by showing your willingness to understand, from the person's point of view, his thoughts, feelings, and struggles.
- Give the person your genuine attention; monitor your body language, stay mentally focused, and use the verbal techniques of inviting, reflecting, and summarizing.

ADULT-TO-ADULT COMMUNICATION

During any helping conversation, especially coaching, you must communicate from the appropriate ego state. Remember, an ego state is the way in which you manifest your personality during a conversation as displayed by your attitude, tone, and the type of statements you make. People communicate from three ego states, the Parent, Adult, and Child, and all three ego states are useful in day-to-day interactions; however, coaching requires that you stay within the Adult ego state. The Adult ego state avoids the judgmental attitude and sense of superiority inherent in the Parent ego state and conveys a "let's think through this together" attitude. It utilizes words and tone that signals a collegial, rather than a power-up, relationship. Communicating from the Adult ego state seeks to produce a reciprocal response. Adult-to-Adult interactions maximize problem-solving and solution-focused thinking. The guidelines for communicating from the Adult ego state are:

1. Use owned language by communicating from an "I" perspective and being accountable for your thoughts, actions, and feeling responses.
2. Practice disciplined listening, by avoiding judgment, limiting interruptions, and controlling the Righting Reflex.
3. Maintain congruent communication so that your adult ego state language is matched by the corresponding body language, facial expressions, and tone of voice.

INTELLIGENT LISTENING

Intelligent listening is the ability to listen for, and recover, deletions contained in people's surface structure language in order to add clarity and understanding to their narrative. Four types of deletions were described: (a) Unnamed References; (b) Unspecified Action Verbs; (c) Unchallenged Pressure Words; and (d) Unstated Reasoning. The guidelines for intelligent listening are:

1. Listen for what's not there. Use your intuition to identify what is not being made explicit by the person's narrative.
2. Ask "What" and "How" questions to recover any of the four types of deletions, and avoid "Why" questions.
3. Use the person's language when constructing a question so that you are working within the person's frame-of-reference.
4. Formulate your next question from the person's earlier answers or statements. It creates continuity within the conversation.
5. Inquire; do not interrogate. Although you will be pressing the person to add clarity to her narrative, maintain rapport.

SOLUTION-FOCUSED THINKING

Instead of focusing on people's problems and their causes, solution-focused thinking concentrates on the future: What does the person want that is different from what she is currently experiencing? What is she going to do differently to achieve it? Solution-focused thinking is the foundation upon which the Four-square Coaching Framework is built. Solution-focused thinking follows four principles:

1. You don't have to understand the cause of a problem to find a solution. The more attention given to a problem, the less will be available for the solution.
2. Focusing on the future creates more useful energy than focusing on the past. People can change their future, but they can't change their past.

3. Small steps lead to big changes. Going slow to go fast is the best way to ensure steady progress.
4. Differences make the difference. Helping people define what they want to be different and what they will do differently to achieve it is magical.

CHANGE TALK

Change Talk is speech that indicates movement toward change or action. It is present when a person speaks about the *importance* of his goals and outcomes or actions that need to be taken in pursuit of those goals and outcomes. It is also present when a person indicates *confidence* in his ability to achieve what he wants or speaks of his capability to take the actions required for goal attainment. Change talk can be elicited through the use of open-ended questions, and it can be responded to by using your E.A.R.S.

1. Elaborate Change Talk by asking "What" and "How" questions.
2. Affirm Change Talk by giving positive reinforcement when you hear it.
3. Reflect Change Talk so that the person hears it again out loud.
4. Summarize Change Talk so that the person's specific comments about Importance and Confidence are emphasized.

Your goal, through the use of Change Talk, is to help people to "talk themselves" into taking action in pursuit of the changes they want to make or to attain the outcomes they desire.

LEADERSHIP AND COACHING

Elite Professionals do not want to be managed; they want to be led by a leader who is a role model, has a compelling vision for their part of the organization and can communicate it, overcomes problems and obstacles, and is available to provide guidance and help when needed. Transformational leaders satisfy these requirements and, in return, are rewarded with extra effort and commitment from those who follow them. The component of transformational leadership most aligned with coaching is Individualized Consideration; however, coaching competencies help to operationalize all components of transformational leadership, including Intellectual Stimulation, Inspirational Motivation, and Idealized Influence.

As with coaching, leadership is a relationship-driven experience. Through Individualized Consideration, leaders personalize their relationships with colleagues and followers and pay particular attention to each person's needs for achievement and growth. The Support-for-Thought competencies of rapport building,

Adult-to-Adult communication, and Intelligent Listening are required to demonstrate this component of transformational leadership.

Intellectual Stimulation is used to encourage followers to think creatively, approach old problems in new ways, and try new approaches. This is also the goal of Challenge-for-Thought and Challenge-for-Action from a coaching perspective. The competencies associated with solution-focused inquiry (e.g., developing well-formed outcomes, designing action experiments, etc.) and used during the coaching process can be effective with both individuals and groups to provide Intellectual Stimulation as part of transformational leadership.

Inspirational Motivation is the result of articulating a clear and compelling vision that excites people and fosters goal clarity. However, it is not enough just to have a vision of the future. That vision must be translated into real-world outcomes. Challenge-for-Thought does that on an individual level by developing discrepancies and well-formed outcomes. Those same practices, when used organizationally, assist in translating a vision into something concrete around which planning and execution can occur. When the vision drives organizational change, the competencies needed to build and maintain readiness for individual change during Support-for-Action will assist the transformational leader in facilitating that change.

Finally, Idealized Influence is the means through which leaders are respected and admired. Transformational leaders behave in ways that cause others to identify with them and want to emulate them. When leaders demonstrate Inspirational Motivation, provide Intellectual Stimulation, and show Individualized Consideration, they are modeling attributes that also create Idealized Influence. In the final analysis, the common thread among all of these components of transformational leadership is that the mind-set and competencies needed to navigate the Four-square Coaching Framework, as described in this book, are as indispensable to the practice of transformational leadership as they are to the process of coaching.

References

Adams, J. S. (1965). Inequity in social exchange. *Advanced Experience in Social Psychology, 62,* 335–343.

Alexander, P., Ryan, R., & Deci, E. (2000). Intrinsic and extrinsic motivations: Classic definitions and new directions. *Contemporary Educational Psychology, 25* (1), 54–68.

Alvesson, M., & Sveningsson, S. (2003). Managers doing leadership: The extra-ordinarization of the mundane. *Human Relations, 56* (12), 1435–1459.

American Hospital Association. (2010). Accountable Care Organizations: AHA Research Synthesis Report. American Hospital Association Committee on Research.

Amrhein, P. C., Miller, W. R., Yahne, C. E., Palmer, M., & Fulcher, L. (2003). Client commitment language during motivational interviewing predicts drug use outcomes. *Journal of Consulting and Clinical Psychology, 71,* 862–878.

Avolio, B. J., & Yammarino, F. J. (Eds.). (2002). *Transformational and charismatic leadership: The road ahead.* Boston: JAI.

Bandler, R., & Grinder, J. (1975). *The structure of magic.* Palo Alto, CA: Science and Behavior Books.

Bandura, A. (1982). Self-efficacy mechanism in human agency. *American Psychologist, 37* (2), 122–147.

Bandura, A. (1994). Self-efficacy. In V.S. Ramachaudran (Ed.), *Encyclopedia of human behavior* (Vol. 4, pp. 71–81). New York: Academic Press.

Barker, R. (1997). How we train leaders if we don't know what leadership is? *Human Relations, 50,* 343–362.

Bass, B. M. (2008). *The Bass handbook of leadership: Theory, research, and managerial applications* (4th ed.). New York: The Free Press.

Bass, B., & Riggio, R. (2006). *Transformational leadership* (2nd ed.). New York: Psychology Press.

Bateson, G. (2000). *Steps to an ecology of mind: Collected essays in anthropology, psychiatry, evolution, and epistemology.* Chicago, IL: The University of Chicago Press.

Beebe, S. A. (2005). *Communicating in small groups: Principles and practices* (8th ed.). Boston, MA: Allyn & Bacon.

Benjamin, A. (1981). *The helping interview* (3rd ed.). Boston, MA: Houghton Mifflin Company.

Berg, I., & de Shazer, S. (1993). Making numbers talk: Language in therapy. In S. Friedman (Ed.), *The new language of change: Constructive collaboration in psychotherapy* (1st ed.). New York: Guilford.

Berg, I. K., & Szabo, P. (2005). *Brief coaching for lasting solutions*. New York: W.W. Norton & Company.

Berne, E. (1964). *Games people play*. New York: Grove Press.

Berne, E. (1972). *What do you say after you say hello?: The psychology of human destiny*. New York: Grove Press.

Boyatzis, R. R. (1982). *The competent manager*. New York: John Wiley.

Brehm, S. S., & Brehm, J. W. (1981). *Psychological reactance: A theory of freedom and control.* (1st ed.). New York: Academic Press.

Buckley, W. F. (1979, September 22). Let's define that "leadership" that Kennedy says we need. *Press-Bulletin (Binghamton, NY)*, p. 4A.

Burley-Allen, M. (1982). *Listening: The forgotten skill*. New York: John Wiley & Sons.

Burns, J. M. (1978). *Leadership*. New York: Harper & Row.

Cameron-Bandler, L. (1985). *Solutions*. San Rafael, CA: FuturePace.

Cattell, R. B., & Stice, G. F. (1954). Four formulae for selecting leaders on the basis of personality. *Human Relations, 7*, 493–507.

Cherniss, C., & Goleman, D. (Eds.). (2001). *The emotionally intelligent workplace: How to select for, measure, and improve emotional intelligence in individuals, groups, and organizations.* San Francisco, CA: Jossey-Bass.

Collins, J., & Porras, J. (2002). *Built to last: Successful habits of visionary companies*. New York: Harper Collins Publishers.

Corcoran, J. (2005). *Building strengths and skills: A collaborative approach to working with clients.* New York: Oxford University Press.

Csíkszentmihályi, M., & Csíkszentmihályi, I. S. (Ed.). (1988). *Optimal experience: Psychological studies of flow in consciousness.* New York: Cambridge University Press.

Daniels, A. C. (1994). *Bringing out the best in people: How to apply the astonishing power of positive reinforcement.* New York: McGraw-Hill.

Darling, P. (1993). Getting results: The trainer's skills. *Management Development Review, 5* (5), 25–29.

DeBacker, T .K., & Nelson R. M. (1999). Variations on expectancy-value model of motivation in science. *Contemporary Educational Psychology, 24*, 71–94.

deCharms, R. (1968). *Personal causation*. New York: Academic Press.

De Jong, P., & Berg, I. K. (2008). *Interviewing for solutions* (3rd ed.). Belmont, CA: Thomson Brooks/Cole.

DeLong, T .J., Gabarro, J. J., & Lees, R. J. (2007). *When professionals have to lead: A new model for high performance.* Boston, Massachusetts: Harvard Business School Press.

de Shazer, S. (1991). *Putting difference to work*. New York: Norton.

de Shazer, S., Dolan, Y. M., Korman, H., Trepper, T. S., McCollum, E. E., & Berg, I. K. (2006). *More than miracles: The state of the art of solution focused therapy.* New York: Haworth Press.

Diagnosis. (2012). In ahdictionary.com. Retrieved from http://www.ahdictionary.com/word/search.html?q=diagnosis&submit.x=21&submit.y=23.

Dimond, R. E., Havens, R. A., & Jones, A. C. (1978). A conceptual framework for the practice of prescriptive eclecticism in psychotherapy. *American Psychologist, 33* (2), 239–248.

Downton, J. V. (1973). *Rebel leadership: Commitment and charisma in the revolutionary process.* New York: Free Press.

Eccles, J. (1983). Expectancies, values, and academic behaviors. In J. T. Spence (Ed.), *Achievement and achievement motives* (pp. 75–146). San Francisco: W. H. Freeman and Company.

Egan, G. (2010). *The skilled helper: A problem-management and opportunity-development approach to helping* (9th ed.). Belmont, CA: Brooks/Cole Cengage Learning.

Eisenbach, R., Watson, K., & Pillai, R. (1999). Transformational leadership in the context of organizational change. *Journal of Organizational Change Management,* 12 (2), 80–90.

Farber, B. A., & Doolin, E. M. (2011). Positive regard. In J. C. Norcross (Ed.), *Psychotherapy relationships that work: Evidence-based responsiveness* (2nd ed.). New York: Oxford University Press.

Farber, B. A., & Lane, J. S. (2001). Positive regard. *Psychotherapy: Theory, Research, Practice, Training,* 38 (4), 390–395.

Fishbein, M., & Ajzen, I. (1975). *Belief, attitude, intention, and behavior: An introduction to theory and research.* Reading, MA: Addison-Wesley.

Fisher, E., McClellan, M., McKethan, A. J., Lewis, J., Roski, J., & Fisher, E. (2010). A national strategy to put accountable care into practice. *Health Affairs,* 29 (5), 982–990.

Fisher, R., & Ury, W. (1991). *Getting to yes: Negotiating agreement without giving in* (2nd ed.). New York: Penguin Books.

Ford, J. D., & Ford, L. W. (1994). Logistics of identity, contradiction and attraction in change. *Academy of Management Review,* 19 (4), 756–785.

Foulds, L. R. (1983). The heuristic problem-solving approach. *Journal of the Operational Research Society,* 34 (10), 927–934.

French, J. R. P., & Raven, B. (1959). The bases of social power. In D. Cartwright and A. Zander. *Group dynamics.* New York: Harper & Row.

Garfield, E. (1990). Fast Science vs. Slow Science, Or Slow and Steady Wins the Race. *The Scientist,* 4 (18), 14.

Gawande, A. (2011). *Cowboys and pit crews, 2011 Harvard Medical School commencement address.* Retrieved from http://www.newyorker.com/online/blogs/newsdesk/2011/05/atul-gawande-harvard-medical-school-commencement-address.html

Glasser, M. (1984). *Control theory: A new explanation of how we control our lives.* New York: Harper & Row.

Goleman, D. (1995). *Emotional intelligence: Why it can matter more than IQ.* New York: Bantam Books.

Goleman, D. (1998). *Working with emotional intelligence.* New York: Bantam Books.

Greenberg, L. S., Elliott, R., Watson, J. C., & Bohart, A. C. (2001). Empathy. *Psychotherapy: Theory, Research, Practice, Training,* 38 (4), 380–384.

Harvard Mentoring Project. (2003, January 5). Step-by-step guide to mentoring. *The New York Times,* p. 30.

Hettema, J., Steele, J., & Miller, W.R. (2005). Motivational interviewing. *Annual Review of Clinical Psychology,* (1), 91–111.

Hicks, R., & McCracken, J. (2009). Coaching the abrasive personality. *The Physician Executive: Journal of Medical Management,* 35 (6), 82–84.

Hicks, R., & McCracken, J. (2010a). Coaching from an adult ego state. *The Physician Executive: Journal of Medical Management,* 35 (5), 60–62.

Hicks, R., & McCracken, J. (2010b). Three hats of a leader: Coaching, mentoring, and teaching. *The Physician Executive: Journal of Medical Management,* 36 (6), 68–70.

Hicks, R., & McCracken, J. (2011). How to give difficult feedback. *The Physician Executive: Journal of Medical Management,* 37 (3), 84–87.

Hirsh, W., Jackson, C., & Kidd, J. (2001). *Straight talking: Effective career discussions at work.* Retrieved from the National Institute for Careers Education and Counselling (NICEC): http://www.vitae.ac.uk/CMS/files/upload/nicec_straight_talking_effectivecareerdiscussions_report.pdf

Hoag, D. (2012). *NLP Meta Programs.* Retrieved from http://www.nlpls.com/articles/metaPrograms.php

House, R. J., & Podsakoff, P.M. (1994). Leadership effectiveness and future research direction. In G. Greenberg (ed.), *Organizational behavior: The state of the science.* Hillsdale, NJ: Lawrence Erlbaum.

Hutt B. (2009). Points of Interest. *Beingpoint*.com. Retrieved November 5, 2012 from http://www.beingpoint.com/trust-only-movement-life-happens-at-the-level-of-events-not-of-words-trust-movement-alfred-adler/.

Ilgen, D. R., Fisher, C. D., & Taylor, M. S. (1979). Consequences of individual feedback on behavior in organizations. *Journal of Applied Psychology, 64* (4), 349–371.

Iveson, C., George, E., & Ratner, H. (2012). *Brief coaching: A solution focused approach.* New York: Routledge.

Jacob, S. (2012). *Health Care in 2020: Where uncertain reform, bad habits, too few doctors and skyrocketing costs are taking us.* New York: Dorsam Publishing.

King, A. (1993). From sage on the stage to guide on the side. *College Teaching, 31* (1), 30–35.

Kline, N. (2008). *Time to think: Listening to ignite the human mind.* London: Ward Lock, Cassell illustrated, A member of Octopus Publishing Group Ltd.

Korzybski, A. (1994). *Science and sanity: An introduction to non-Aristotelian systems and general semantics* (5th ed.). Brooklyn: New York Institute of General Semantics.

Kotter, J. P. (2008). *A sense of urgency.* Boston, MA: Harvard Business School Press.

Kouzes, J. M., & Posner, B. Z. (1990). *The leadership challenge: How to get extraordinary things done in organizations.* San Francisco, CA: Jossey-Bass.

Kremers, S. (2006). *Communicating through listening.* Retrieved July 16, 2012, from http://www.afcp.org/TLI-Archive/Effective Listening Student's Module-TLI105.pdfKyle, N. (1993). Staying with the flow of change. *Journal for Quality and Participation, 16* (4), 34–42.

Lazarus, R., & Folkman, S. (1984). *Stress, appraisal, and coping.* New York: Springer Publishing Company.

Lefcourt, H. M. (1982). *Locus of control: Current trends in theory and research.* Hillsdale, H. J: Lawrence Erlbaum Associates Publishing.

Lord, R. G. (1976). Group performance as a function of leadership behavior and task structure: Toward an explanatory theory. *Organizational Behavior and Human Performance, 17*, 76–96.

Lundberg, G. G. (2004). *Medicine must remain a learned profession.* Retrieved from http://www.ncbi.nlm.nih.gov/pmc/articles/PMC1480546/

Maier, S. F., & Seligman, M. E. (1976). Learned helplessness: Theory and evidence. *Journal of Experimental Psychology: General, 105* (1), 3–46.

Manning, B. H. (1991). *Cognitive self-instruction for classroom processes* (1st ed.). Albany: State University of New York Press.

Marquardt, M. J. (2004). *Optimizing the power of action learning.* Palo Alto, CA: Davies-Black.

Martin, G. (1988). *Behavior modification: What it is and how to do it.* Englewood Cliffs, NJ: Prentice-Hall.

Maslow, A. H. (1943). A theory of human motivation. *Psychological Review 50* (4), 370–96.

McClelland, D. C. (1976). *The achievement motive.* New York: Irvington.

McShane, S., & Von Glinow, M. A. (2005). *Organizational behavior* (3rd ed.). New York: McGraw-Hill /Irwin.

Medow, A., & Zander, A. (1965). Aspirations for the group chosen by central and peripheral members. *Journal of Personality and Social Psychology,* 1, 224–228.

Mehrabian, A. (2007). *Nonverbal communication* (1st ed.). Piscataway, NJ: Transaction Publishers.

Miller, H. (2009). *How to create accountable care organizations.* Retrieved from http//www.chqpr.org

Miller, G. A. (1956). The magical number seven, plus or minus two: Some limits on our capacity for processing information. *Psychological Review,* 63 (2), 81–97.

Miller, W. R., & Rollnick, S. (1991). *Motivational interviewing: Preparing people to change addictive behavior.* New York: Guilford Press.

Miller, W. R., & Rollnick, S. (2002). *Motivational interviewing: Preparing people for change* (2nd ed.). New York: Guilford Press.

Neenan, M., & Palmer, P. (2012). *Cognitive behavioural coaching in practice: An evidence based approach.* New York: Routledge.

Pandey, S. K., & Wright, B. E. (2006). Connecting the dots in public management: Political environment, organizational goal ambiguity and the public manager's role ambiguity. *Journal of Public Administration Research and Theory,* 16, 511–32.

Peck, M. S. (2003). *The road less traveled, 25th anniversary edition: A new psychology of love, traditional values and spiritual growth.* New York: Touchstone.

Pemberton, C. (2006). *Coaching to solutions: A managers toolkit for performance delivery.* Oxford, UK: Elsevier.

Podsakoff, P. M., & Farh, J. (1989). Effects of feedback sign and credibility on goal setting and task performance. *Organizational Behavior and Human Decision Processes,* 44 (1), 45–67.

Porter, L., Bigley, G., & Steers, R. M. (2002). *Motivation and work behavior* (7th ed.). New York: McGraw-Hill.

Prochaska, J. Q., & DiClemente, C. C. (1983). Stages and processes of self-change of smoking: Toward an integrative model of change. *Journal of Consulting and Clinical Psychology,* 51, 390–395.

Prochaska, J. O., Norcross, J. C., & DiClemente, C. C. (2005). Stages of change: Prescriptive guidelines. In G. P. Koocher, J. C. Norcross, & S. S. Hill III (Eds.), *Psychologists' desk reference* (2nd ed., pp. 226–231). New York: Oxford University Press.

Prochaska, J. O., Wright, J. A., & Velicer, W. F. (2008). Evaluating theories of health behavior change: A hierarchy of criteria applied to the transtheoretical model. *Applied Psychology,* 57 (4), 561–588.

Reynolds, L. (1997). *The trust effect: Creating the high trust, high performance organization.* London: Nicholas Brealey.

Rogers, C. (1951). *Client-centered therapy: Its current practice, implications, and theory.* Boston: Houghton Mifflin.

Rogers, C. R. (1961). *On becoming a person.* Boston: Houghton Mifflin Company.

Rogers, C. R. (2007). The necessary and sufficient conditions of therapeutic personality change. *Psychotherapy: Theory, Research, Practice, Training,* 44 (3), 240–248.

Rollnick, S., Miller, W. R., & Butler, C. (2008). *Motivational interviewing in health care: Helping patients change behavior.* New York: The Guilford Press.

Rosengren, D. B. (2009). *Building motivational interviewing skills: A practitioner workbook* (1st ed.). New York: Guilford Publications.

Rotter, J. B. (1954). *Social learning and clinical psychology.* Englewood Cliffs: NJ: Prentice Hall.

Saleebey, D. (Ed.). (2007). *The strengths perspective in social work practice* (4th ed.). Boston: Allyn & Bacon.

Sashkin, M. (1988). The visionary leader. In J. A. Conger & R. N. Kanungo (eds.), *Charismatic leadership: The elusive factor in organizational effectiveness.* San Francisco: Jossey-Bass.

Schwartz, J., & Gladding, R. (2011). *You are not your brain.* New York: Penguin Group.

Silvia, P. J. (2005). Deflecting reactance: The role of similarity in increasing compliance and reducing resistance. *Basic and Applied Social Psychology, 27,* 277–284.

Skinner, B. F. (1953). *Science and human behavior.* Oxford, England: Macmillan.

Smith, B. O. (1969). A concept of teaching. In Bandman, B, & Gutchen, R. S. (Ed), *Philosophical essays in teaching* (p. 10). New York: J.P. Lippincott.

Stroh, L. K., Northcraft, G. B., & Neale, M. A. (2002). *Organizational behavior: A management challenge* (3rd ed.). Mahway, NJ: Lawrence Erlbaum Associates.

Szabo, P. & Meier, D. (2008). *Coaching plain and simple: Solution-focused brief coaching essentials.* New York: W.W. Norton & Company.

Thomas, L. (1995). *The youngest science: Notes of a medicine-watcher* (Alfred P. Sloan Foundation Series). Harmondsworth, England: Penguin Books.

Trevino, J. G. (1996). Worldview and change in cross-cultural counseling. *Counseling Psychologist, 24,* 198–215.

Weber. M. (1968). Max Weber on charisma and institution building, The University of Chicago Press: Chicago.

Wicker, A. W. (1985). Getting out of our conceptual ruts. *American Psychologist, 40,* 1094–1103.

Wigfield, A. (2000). Expectancy-value theory of achievement motivation. *Contemporary Educational Psychology, 25,* 68–81.

Windschitl, P. D., Rose, J. P., Stalkfleet, M. T., & Smith, A. R. (2008). Are people excessive or judicious in their egocentrism?: A modeling approach to understanding bias and accuracy in people's optimism. *Journal of Personality and Social Psychology, 95* (2), 253–273.

Yukl, Gary R. (2008). How leaders influence organizational effectiveness. *The Leadership Quarterly, 19,* 708–722.

Index

Folkman, Susan 142
Four-square Coaching Framework: about 23–4,
    29; boundary-setting coaching conversation
    example/commentary 159–62; example
    of process 26–8; as fluid process 158–9;
    overreacting coaching conversation
    example/commentary 162–6; as process
    map 167–8; *see also* Challenge-for-Action;
    Challenge-for-Thought; Support-for-Action;
    Support-for-Thought
frames of reference 90–1, 92
future, designing 72, 78–9, 94; *see also*
    discrepancy, developing; outcomes

Gawande, Atul 7–8, 9
Getting to Yes (Fisher and Ury) 32
Gladding, R. 85
Glasser, William 79
global labels 124
goals 82–3, 93–4

healthcare, changes in 7–9, 154
Hebb's law 85
helpers, behavioral characteristics of 15–16
helping conversations 11–16, 21; *see also*
    helping hats
helping hats: about 16–17; coaching 19–21,
    56; mentoring 17–19, 21, 56, 118, 119–
    20, 122–3, 166–7; teaching 17, 21, 56
Helping Interview, The (Benjamin) 31–2
heroic leadership 115
heuristic approach 96–7
Homer 17–18
"How" questions 64–5, 149
human information processing 75–6

Idealized Influence 2, 51–2, 76, 155, 171
ideas suggested by questions 56
"I" language 47, 48
Importance 118, 138, 141, 144–6, 154
Individualized Consideration: about 170–1;
    Confidence and 155; defined 3; in
    helping conversations 21; interpersonal
    competence and 38; solution talk and 76
inertia, overcoming 106–7
Influence, Idealized 2, 51–2, 76, 155, 171
information processing, human 75–6
inputs, in equity theory 142

inquiry *see* questions
inspirational leadership 115
Inspirational Motivation 2, 76, 94, 171
"instead" questions 85–6, 92
instrumental value 137
integration in healthcare 8–9
Intellectual Stimulation 2–3, 66–7, 76, 171
intelligent listening: about 169; defined 58;
    deletions, recovering 59–63, 100;
    linguistic maps 58, 59, 64; process 58–9;
    rules 64–6; "Why" questions, avoiding
    63–4; *see also* questions
intentions 123–4, 148
internal dialogue 35–6
internal locus of control 87
interpersonal competence 38
interrogation 66
intrinsic motivation 137–40
inviting 36–7

judgmental listening 50

labels, global 124
language: body 33–4; "I" 47, 48; owned
    47–9; speaker's 65; Surface Structure 58,
    59, 60, 61, 63, 124; "You" 47–8
Law of Least Change 106–8
Lazarus, Richard 142
leadership: action-oriented 104–5; charismatic
    115; Elite Professionals, challenges of
    5–7, 9–10; heroic 115; inspirational 115;
    mundane 115–16; transactional 1–2,
    9–10; transformational 2–3, 10, 105;
    visionary 115
Least Change, Law of 106–8
less, doing 102, 103
linguistic maps 58, 59, 64; *see also* intelligent
    listening
listening 49–50, 64; *see also* intelligent listening
locus of control theory 87
logic, private 32

magic questions 102–3, 104
maintenance stage of change 119
map *versus* territory 58
memory, short-term 76
mental attention 34–6
mental habits, bad 85